Three Anglo-Norman Kings

The Lives of William the Conqueror and Sons
by Benoît de Sainte-Maure

Best known as a Medieval French romance writer, Benoît de Sainte-Maure was the author of the pioneering and widely copied *Roman de Troie*, composed, it is thought, around 1165. This consisted of a 30,000-verse reworking, in twelfth-century terms, of Latin narratives purporting to describe the siege of Troy, enlivened by what the poet refers to as "bons dits" (apposite amplifications). All that is known of him, apart from what can be deduced from his two works, is that he was a learned monk from the region of Tours in North-West France. His reputation as a poet must have reached the ears of Henry II who, sometime in the 1170s, commissioned him to compose a verse history of the English king's Norman ancestors. Benoît thus found himself successor to the Norman historiographer Wace whose vernacular French *Roman de Rou*, named after Normandy's founder Rollo, was abandoned in favour of Benoît's *Histoire des ducs de Normandie*.

In their quest to generate an ethnic identity for themselves, the Normans celebrated their expansionist activities in a corpus of historiographic texts in which the multi-authored and chameleon-like *Gesta Normannorum Ducum* claims pride of place. This and other histories, both vernacular and Latin, were what Benoît de Sainte-Maure adapted into his secular poetic narrative. One of the motivations behind Benoît's royal patronage could have been to tie the Anglo-Norman aristocracy of late twelfth-century England into a cultural homeland from which they were growing increasingly remote. The sense of Norman history that Benoît imparts through his French verse was the one that Henry II and his Anglo-Norman contemporaries must have assimilated as part of their courtly entertainment.

Mediaeval Sources in Translation

Series Editor

Mary Carruthers
Remarque Professor of Literature, New York University
Fellow of All Souls College, Oxford

MEDIAEVAL SOURCES IN TRANSLATION 57

Three Anglo-Norman Kings

The Lives of William the Conqueror and Sons
by Benoît de Sainte-Maure

Translated with an introduction and notes by

IAN SHORT

PONTIFICAL INSTITUTE OF MEDIAEVAL STUDIES

Library and Archives Canada Cataloguing in Publication

Benoît, de Sainte-More, active 12th century
[Chronique des ducs de Normandie. Selections. English]
   Three Anglo-Norman kings : the lives of William the Conqueror and sons / by Benoît de Sainte-Maure ; translated with an introduction and notes by Ian Short.

(Mediaeval sources in translation ; 57)
Translated selections from Chronique des ducs de Normandie.
Translated from the Old French.
Includes bibliographical references and index.
Issued in print and electronic formats.
ISBN 978-0-88844-307-6 (softcover). – ISBN 978-1-77110-390-9 (PDF)

   1. Normandy, Dukes of – Early works to 1800. 2. William I, King of England, 1027 or 1028–1087 – Early works to 1800. 3. William II, King of England, 1056?–1100 – Early works to 1800. 4. Robert II, Duke of Normandy, 1054?–1134 – Early works to 1800. 5. Henry I, King of England, 1068–1135 – Early works to 1800. 6. Nobility – France – Normandy – Biography – Early works to 1800. 7. Normans – Great Britain – Biography – Early works to 1800. 8. Normandy (France) – History – To 1515 – Early works to 1800. 9. Normandy (France) – In literature. 10. Civilization, Medieval, in literature. 11. Nobility in literature. I. Short, Ian, 1939–, translator, editor II. Pontifical Institute of Mediaeval Studies, issuing body III. Title. IV. Title: Chronique des ducs de Normandie. Selections. English. V. Series: Mediaeval sources in translation ; 57

PQ1429.A4 2018   841'.1   C2018-902037-7   C2018-902038-5

© 2018
Pontifical Institute of Mediaeval Studies
59 Queen's Park Crescent East
Toronto, Ontario, Canada M5S 2C4
www.pims.ca

MANUFACTURED IN CANADA

Contents

Abbreviations

Fahlin *Chronique des ducs de Normandie par Benoît,* publiée d'après le manuscrit de Tours avec les variantes du manuscrit de Londres. Vols. 1
and 2: *Texte,* ed. Carin Fahlin (Uppsala, 1951–54).

GND *The Gesta Normannorum Ducum of William of Jumièges, Orderic
Vitalis and Robert of Torigni,* ed. Elisabeth M.C. van Houts, 2 vols.
(Oxford, 1992–95).

GRA William of Malmesbury, *Gesta Regum Anglorum / The History of the
English Kings,* ed. and trans. R.A.B. Mynors, completed by Rodney
M. Thomson and Michael Winterbottom, 2 vols. (Oxford, 1998–
99).

Henry of Huntingdon *Historia Anglorum / The History of the English People,*
ed. and trans. Diana Greenway (Oxford, 1996).

Michel *Chronique des ducs de Normandie par Benoît,* trouvère anglo-
normand du XIIe siècle, publiée pour la première fois d'après un
manuscrit du Musée britannique, ed. Francisque Michel, 3 vols.
(Paris, 1836–44).

SATF Société des anciens textes français

Wace, *Rou* *The History of the Norman People: Wace's* Roman de Rou, trans.
Glyn S. Burgess (Woodbridge, 2004), pp. 91–220. [Original French
text in *Le Roman de Rou de Wace,* ed. A.J. Holden (Paris, 1970–73).]

Introduction

The jewel in the crown of the literary culture of twelfth-century Anglo-Norman Britain was without doubt historiography, and such luminaries as Orderic Vitalis, William of Malmesbury, Geoffrey of Monmouth and Henry of Huntingdon are today universally recognised as past masters in the art of composing complex historical narratives in elegant Medieval Latin prose. Among the achievements of the Renaissance of the twelfth century, however, room needs also to be found to celebrate the works of some more modest pioneers in the recording of history.

These are people whose innovation entailed breaking the monopoly that Latin had previously enjoyed over historiography, and offering an alternative to its Church-centred perspective. These are the Francophone writers who preferred to use the everyday vernacular of the Norman conquerors and their descendants to tell the story of their newly adopted homeland or to celebrate the deeds of their ancestors back in their country of origin. They broadened the accessibility of learned culture by translating it into the vernacular. By including those hitherto excluded from the language of the Church, these writers were able to bring whole swathes of society into the world of learning. The vernacular itself became a vehicle for the preservation of culture, and the bilingual clerics who translated and creatively adapted their sources, both written and oral, found themselves fulfilling the role of cultural intermediaries.

This they did in the only literary form available to them at the time, namely narrative poetry, more specifically octosyllabic rhyming couplets. Such narratives provided an alternative, largely secular view of history designed for the instruction, edification and entertainment of the secular aristocracy that patronised them and listened to them being recited. This was a new genre of "history as romance and romance as history."[1] Its exponents were all linked, in one way

---

1 Rosalind Field, "Romance as History, History as Romance," in *Romance in Medieval England*, ed. Maldwyn Mills et al. (Cambridge, 1991), pp. 164–73; cf. Matthew Bennett, "Poetry as History? The *Roman de Rou* of Wace as a Source for the Norman Conquest," *Anglo-Norman Studies* 5 (1983): 19–39.

or another, to post-Conquest Britain and to Anglo-Norman royal and baronial courts.[2]

They include Geffrei Gaimar, who wrote an *Estoire des Engleis*, a national narrative stretching all the way from England's mythical Trojan origins down to 1137 when he finished writing it.[3] He was closely followed by Wace, a Norman by birth but an Anglo-Norman by adoption (he wrote for, and was recompensed by, Henry II), who between the 1150s and the 1170s composed histories of Britain (*Brut*) and of the dukes of Normandy (*Rou*).[4] One Jordan Fantosme began the writing of contemporary events in the vernacular with an account of the 1174 revolt against King Henry.[5] And even though Guernes de Pont-Sainte-Maxence was of Continental origin, he can also be considered an honorary Anglo-Norman in that he crossed the Channel to Canterbury in order to com-

2 Laura Ashe, *Fiction and History in England, 1066–1200* (Cambridge, 2007); Monika Otter, *Inventiones: Fiction and Referentiality in Twelfth-Century English Historical Writing* (Chapel Hill, 1996); Peter Damian-Grint, *The New Historians of the Twelfth-Century Renaissance: Inventing Vernacular Authority* (Woodbridge, 1999); Jean Blacker, *The Faces of Time: Portrayal of the Past in Old French and Latin Historical Narrative of the Anglo-Norman* Regnum (Austin, TX, 1994); Dagmar Tillmann-Bartylla, "Höfische Welt und Geschichtsbedürfnis: Die anglo-normannischen Verschroniken des XII. Jahrhunderts," in *La Littérature historiographique des origines à 1500*, ed. Hans Ulrich Gumbrecht et al., Grundriss der romanischen Literaturen des Mittelalters 11.1 (Heidelberg, 1986), pp. 313–50; cf. also M. Dominica Legge, *Anglo-Norman Literature and Its Background* (Oxford, 1963); Reto R. Bezzola, "La Cour d'Angleterre comme centre littéraire sous les rois angevins," *Les Origines et la formation de la littérature courtoise en Occident, 500–1200* (Paris, 1960–63), 2.2: 418–22, 451–55, 3.1: 149ff.; R.W. Southern, "England in the Twelfth-Century Renaissance," *History* 45 (1960): 201–16.

3 See Geffrei Gaimar, *Estoire des Engleis*, ed. and trans. Ian Short (Oxford, 2009); cf. John Gillingham, "Kinship, Chivalry and Love: Political and Cultural Values in the Earliest History Written in French: Geoffrey Gaimar's *Estoire des Engleis*," in his *The English in the Twelfth Century: Imperialism, National Identity and Political Values* (Woodbridge, 2000), pp. 233–58.

4 See *Le Roman de Brut de Wace*, ed. Ivor Arnold, 2 vols. (Paris, 1938–40); *Le Roman de Rou de Wace*, ed. A.J. Holden, 3 vols. (Paris, 1970–73); *The History of the Norman People: Wace's Roman de Rou*, trans. Glyn S. Burgess (Woodbridge, 2004); Gioia Paradisi, *Le Passioni della storia: Scrittura e memoria nell'opera di Wace* (Rome, 2002); cf. Françoise H.M. Le Saux, *A Companion to Wace* (Cambridge, 2005); Jean Blacker, *Wace: A Critical Bibliography* (St Helier, 2008).

5 See *Jordan Fantosme's Chronicle*, ed. and trans. R.C. Johnston (Oxford, 1981); cf. Philip Bennett, "La Chronique de Jordan Fantosme: Épique et public lettré au XIIe siècle," *Cahiers de civilisation médiévale* 40 (1997): 37–56; Ashe, *Fiction and History*, pp. 81–120; Geoff Rector, "*Faites le mien desir*: Studious Persuasion and Baronial Desire in Jordan Fantosme's *Chronicle*," *Journal of Medieval History* 34 (2008): 311–46.

pose his *Vie de Thomas Becket* between 1171 and 1174, a work that survives today exclusively in Anglo-Norman copies.[6] To this already impressive list of vernacular historiographers can be added a scholarly and remarkably productive poet of unusual versatility from Western France.[7]

The same Benoît who, sometime in the 1160s, it is thought, had written the much-copied Medieval French verse romance *Le Roman de Troie*, was also the author, sometime later, of a verse history of the dukes of Normandy.[8] This is a little known and little read narrative poem of which the outstanding feature, to modern eyes, is its unusual length: 44,544 rhyming octosyllables. According to Wace, whose *Roman de Rou*, written intermittently between 1160 and 1174 under royal patronage,[9] covers much of the same historical material, Benoît was appointed by royal commission to succeed him as court historiographer. At the end of his *Rou*, Wace writes:

> The person who has the responsibility of continuing this history should now go ahead and do so. I am referring here to Master Benoît who, following his

6   Guernes de Pont-Sainte-Maxence. *La Vie de saint Thomas de Canterbury*, ed. and trans. Jacques T.E. Thomas, 2 vols. (Louvain, 2002); *A Life of Thomas Becket in Verse: La Vie de saint Thomas Becket by Guernes de Pont-Sainte-Maxence*, trans. Ian Short (Toronto, 2013).

7   See *Dictionnaire des lettres françaises: Le Moyen Âge*, ed. Geneviève Hasenohr and Michel Zink (Paris, 1992), pp. 139–41. For historical background, see Emily Albu, *The Normans in their Histories: Propaganda, Myth and Subversion* (Woodbridge, 2001); for literary orientation, see Douglas Kelly, *The Art of Medieval French Romance* (Madison, 1992), esp. pp. 214–17; Jean Blacker, *The Faces of Time: Portrayal of the Past in Old French and Latin Historical Narrative in the Anglo-Norman Regnum* (Austin, 1994), pp. 119–34, 185–90; Marc-René Jung, "La *Translatio* chez Benoît de Sainte-Maure: De l'*estoire* au livre," *Perspectives Médiévales* 26 (2001): 155–76; Peter Damian-Grint, *The New Historians of the Twelfth-Century Renaissance*, pp. 58–61, 126–30; Karen Broadhurst, "Henry II of England and Eleanor of Aquitaine: Patrons of Literature in French?" *Viator* 27 (1996): 53–84.

8   The identity of the two Benoîts was convincingly demonstrated by the linguistic analysis of Gustav Beckmann, *Trojaroman und Normannenchronik: Die Identität der beiden Benoît und die Chronologie ihrer Werke* (Munich, 1965). For the *Roman de Troie*, see *Le Roman de Troie par Benoît de Sainte-Maure*, ed. Léopold Constans, 6 vols. (Paris, 1904–12); cf. Marc-René Jung, *La Légende de Troie en France au Moyen Age: Analyse des versions françaises et bibliographie raisonnée des manuscrits* (Basel, 1996). There is a new English translation of *Troie*, *The* Roman de Troie *by Benoît de Sainte-Maure: A Translation*, trans. Glyn S. Burgess and Douglas Kelly (Cambridge, 2017).

9   Wace added a reference to the 1174 siege of Rouen to his *Chronique Ascendante*. The narrative of events in the *Rou* proper ends in 1106, though Wace adds a passage (10165–294) describing the White Ship disaster of 1120.

appointment by the king, has now assumed the task of producing this history. Since the king has requested him to take this on, I must stop writing and give up. In the past the king has been very generous to me: he gave me a great deal and promised me even more. Had he given me everything he promised to give me, it would have been better for me. But this was not possible since the king was not willing. None of this, however, was my doing.[10]

Why Wace apparently fell from favour, and why Benoît was selected to replace him, we shall never know for sure. They were certainly very different writers and historiographers. In contrast to Benoît's theological and providentialist vision of history, Wace offers a more realistic, more critical and more questioning interpretation of the past.[11] The difference between the two in political terms is nowhere easier to see than in their portrayals of Henry I and of Robert Curthose. For Wace, Curthose represents a loyal and generous exemplar of chivalry, whereas for Benoît, he is an inept and irresponsible playboy. In the case of Henry I, whom Benoît promotes (following Robert de Torigni) to champion of a golden age of peace and prosperity, Wace appears to find his military aggressivity and his acquisitiveness more worthy of censure than of praise – a judgement on his grandfather that could hardly have been calculated to warm the heart of Henry II. In comparison to the maverick Wace – some have even called him subversive – Benoît must have been much more in tune with his master's voice. If Wace was awkwardly questioning, then Benoît was comfortably complacent.

From among the endless speculation that has fuelled the debate over Wace's replacement by Benoît, the simplest explanation is one that has most to recommend it: Wace's patron for his *Troie* had presumably been its dedicatee, Queen Eleanor, who from 1173–74 fell into serious disfavour and was detained more or less a prisoner of Henry's for the next ten years. Had he been Eleanor's protégé, Wace, who, we discover, added nothing more to his *Rou* after 1174, might well have shared her disgrace. The same year also happens to mark Henry's reconciliation with the Church as a result of his public penance following Becket's murder. Advice from his bishops to replace the somewhat independent-minded Wace by a much more orthodox Benoît might well have appealed to the king in such circumstances.[12] Strictly literary considerations can probably be discounted in the case of Henry who, in the opinion of his not always reliable contemporary Ger-

10 Wace, *Rou* III: 11419–30 (my translation).
11 Laurence Mathey-Maille, *Écritures du passé: Histoires des ducs de Normandie* (Paris, 2007), p. 258.
12 For an opposing hypothesis see Jean-Guy Gouttebroze, "Pourquoi congédier un historiographe: Henri II Plantagenêt et Wace," *Romania* 112 (1991): 289–311.

ald of Barri (Giraldus Cambrensis), was "much preoccupied with other matters and had little or no interest in literature."[13] There is indeed no convincing evidence, either, to indicate that Henry II might ever have deliberately used literature, vernacular or otherwise, to forward any political or ideological views that he might, or might not, have held.[14]

Unlike Wace, whose Norman French reveals signs of his having spent some considerable time in England, Benoît's language, a Touraine dialect, shows no trace of Anglo-Norman influence, and this could possibly indicate that, as some critics have surmised, he was never actually resident at the Anglo-Norman court and never left his native Touraine or the monastery of Marmoutiers near Tours to which he is thought to have been attached.[15]

Wace was, presumably, a secular cleric, whereas the outlook that informs Benoît's history is unmistakably monastic. His *Troie*, of course, had been decidedly more secular in spirit, but it needs little imagination to visualise this learned cleric, in his maturity, embracing a life of contemplation. The manuscript evidence gives no grounds for thinking that Benoît's history enjoyed any measure of popularity: it survives only in two copies: a more or less contemporary one written in Touraine (Tours, Bibliothèque Municipale, 903),[16] the second an Anglo-Norman copy from early in the following century (British Library, Harley,

13 *Giraldi Cambrensis Opera*, ed. J.S. Brewer, Rolls Series (London, 1861–91), 7: 7 (preface to *Itinerarium Cambriae*).
14 This view, of course, runs counter to prevailing orthodoxy, the most recent manifestations of which are Françoise Laurent, *Pour Dieu et pour le roi: Rhétorique et idéologie dans l'Histoire des ducs de Normandie de Benoît de Sainte-Maure* (Paris, 2010), and Charity Urbanski, *Writing History for the King: Henry II and the Politics of Vernacular Historiography* (Ithaca, NY, 2013); cf. also Elisabeth M. C. van Houts, "Le Roi et son historien: Henri II Plantagenêt et Robert de Torigni," *Cahiers de civilisation médiévale* 37 (1994): 115–18; Gioia Paradisi, "Enrico II Plantageneto, i Capetingi e il 'peso della storia': Sul successo della *Geste des Normanz* di Wace e della *Chronique des ducs de Normandie* di Benoît," *Critica del testo* 7.1 (2004): 127–62. Many critics in the past have failed to differentiate between passive dedication and active patronage, and ignored the fact that kings and queens routinely had literary works dedicated to them. On the question of Henry II's literary patronage, see the more rigorous analysis by Karen Broadhurst, "Henry II of England and Eleanor of Aquitaine," *Viator* 27 (1996): 53–84, and John Gillingham, "The Cultivation of History, Legend and Courtesy at the Court of Henry II," in *Writers of the Reign of Henry II: Twelve Essays*, ed. Ruth Kennedy and Simon Meecham-Jones (New York, 2006), pp. 25–52.
15 The *Gesta Consulum Andegavorum* written by John, abbot of Marmoutier, towards 1164–73 also proves to have been dedicated to Henry II.
16 See Maria Careri, Christine Ruby, and Ian Short, *Livres et écritures en français et en occitan au XIIe siècle: Catalogue illustré* (Rome, 2011), no. 91; Carin Fahlin, *Étude sur le manuscrit de Tours de la* Chronique des ducs de Normandie *par Benoît* (Uppsala, 1937).

1717).[17] The work's exceptional length, of course, hardly made it conducive to recopying.

Benoît's principal source text was the Latin prose *Gesta Normannorum ducum* [*GND*] of William of Jumièges in its final version, the so-called F-redaction, from the pen of Robert de Torigni, who completed it between 1137 and 1139.[18] Other sources include William of Poitiers' *Gesta Guillelmi*, Orderic Vitalis's *Historia Ecclesiastica*, and some unidentified oral sources and vernacular texts, including Wace's *Roman de Rou*.[19]

The date of Benoît's *Histoire* is difficult to ascertain.[20] Calculations of medieval poets' rates of composition allow us to conjecture that the whole work could have needed as many as twelve years of concerted writing to complete. The only internal dating evidence available is a veiled reference to the Becket controversy (37355–65), which could indicate that before the end of 1170 Benoît had already finished more than three-quarters of his poem. The conclusion to be drawn from this is that Benoît did not simply start work when Wace stopped,

---

17   The manuscript has nine historiated initials; see *Catalogue of the Harleian Manuscripts in the British Museum*, 4 vols. (London, 1808–12), 2: no. 1717. Cf. H.L.D. Ward and J.A. Herbert, *Catalogue of Romances in the Department of Manuscripts in the British Museum*, 3 vols. (London, 1883–1910), 1: 312.

18   *The Gesta Normannorum Ducum of William of Jumièges, Orderic Vitalis and Robert of Torigni*, ed. Elisabeth M. C. van Houts, 2 vols. (Oxford, 1992–95). Wace had used earlier redactions ending in 1109–13; see van Houts, "The Adaptation of the *Gesta Normannorum ducum* by Wace and Benoît," in *Non nova, sed nove: Mélanges de civilisation médiévale dédiés à Willem Noomen*, ed. Martin Gosman and Jaap van Os (Groningen,1984), pp. 115–24. Robert de Torigni met Henry II on several occasions between 1147 and 1166; see van Houts, "Le Roi et son historien."

19   For William of Poitiers, see *Guillaume de Poitiers, Histoire de Guillaume le Conquérant*, ed. and trans. Raymonde Foreville (Paris, 1952), English translation in *The* Gesta Guillelmi *of William of Poitiers*, trans. R.H.C. Davis and Marjorie Chibnall (Oxford, 1998). For Orderic, see *The Ecclesiastical History of Orderic Vitalis*, ed. and trans. Marjorie Chibnall, 6 vols. (Oxford, 1969–80); Hugo Andresen, "Über die von Benoît in seiner normannischen Chronik benutzen Quellen, insbesondere über sein Verhältnis zu Dudo, Wilhelm von Jumièges und Wace," *Romanische Forschungen* 1 (1883): 327–412; 2 (1886): 477–538, in particular 2: 500–538, for our text. Benoît appears to have used the first, shorter version of Wace's *Rou* III, represented by MS B (Paris, BnF, fr. 375); see Françoise Vielliard, "Les deux versions de la partie octosyllabique du *Roman de Rou*," *Medioevo Romanzo* 35 (2011): 35–57, esp. 49. For textual parallels between Benoît and Wace, see notes to 35528 and 36128 below.

20   I follow the late lamented Emmanuèle Baumgartner, and after her Françoise Vielliard, Laurence Mathey-Maille, and Françoise Laurent, in modifying the traditional title of Benoît's *Chronique* and re-baptizing it as *Histoire*, since from a literary point of view, it has little or nothing in common with the chronicle genre.

sometime in the early 1170s, but that he had already been composing his own version for a number of years when he took on the royal commission. The fact that Benoît proves to have used the older, first version of the *Rou*, written after 1170, which Wace subsequently enlarged, is a further argument in favour of their activities having overlapped.[21] There is no firm date of composition, either, for his *Roman de Troie*; it is generally ascribed to around 1165, so perhaps Benoît started his history immediately after completing his romance.[22]

"Master" Benoît is above all a scholarly author, and the 352-line cosmographical proemium that opens his history can only be intended to establish this fact in the minds of his listeners from the outset. Introducing a vernacular poem with mentions of Pliny, Isidore and St Augustine sets an unmistakable tone.[23] The constant truth assertions that recur throughout his narrative, his repeated references to his authentic Latin source and to his reliability as a translator, as well as his liberal use of the *industria* and modesty topoi, leave us in no doubt that these are essential elements of his self-image, and that he is deliberately presenting himself as a learned intermediary between the clerical and lay cultures.[24] This, combined with the moral and moralising subtext that underpins his history from beginning to end, points to an essentially monastic ideology. Having earlier in his career engaged with the profane, albeit classical, he is now in his maturity embracing orthodoxy by placing his literary gifts at the disposal of his secular lord, one who is presumably only too happy to use some of his leisure time, when not out hunting, listening to his ancestral heritage being simultaneously celebrated and legitimised. The wider function that Benoît's poem could have fulfilled is that of reminding Henry's aristocratic French-speaking contemporaries of their heritage, and of refreshing their sense of connection and cultural continuity with the Continent, which must, at the time, have been felt as progressively alien. By the 1170s the process of assimilation, which saw the Norman incomers identify more and more with the English and their culture, was already well

21   Vielliard, "Les deux versions" and "De la première Rédaction de la partie octosyllabique longue du *Roman de Rou* à la seconde: Étude des procédés d'amplification," in *Le Texte dans le texte: l'interpolation médiévale*, ed. Annie Combes and Michelle Skilnik (Paris, 2013), pp. 41–61; Paradisi, *Le Passioni della storia*, pp. 306–7. See note to 37355–65 below. Cf. also note to 32054 for a reference that could not have been written before March 1162.

22   See note to 37355 below.

23   Peter Damian-Grint, "Learning and Authority in Benoît de Sainte-Maure's Cosmography," *Reading Medieval Studies* 24 (1998): 25–52.

24   Peter Damian-Grint, "*En nul leu nel truis escrit*: Research and Invention in Benoît de Sainte-Maure's *Chronique des ducs de Normandie*," *Anglo-Norman Studies* 21 (1999): 11–30.

advanced, and as a result any residual sense of *Normanitas* must have been in imminent danger of being lost.[25] It could, at the same time, be argued that the work of Wace and Benoît is the Normano-Angevin counterpart of the Anglo-centric historical tradition popularised by Geoffrey of Monmouth and Wace's *Brut*. In this perspective, Benoît's poem could be seen as the product of a bicultural Anglo-Norman community still searching for self-definition and whose sense of ethnicity and cultural identity remains in a state of flux. Norman history had, in any event, the additional advantage of having inherent entertainment value. It was, as Hugh Thomas reminds us, a history of winners, "an exciting historical tradition, filled with adventures, feuds and, above all, warfare."[26]

How did Benoît set about his task? He reveals himself, first and foremost, to be a dutiful interpreter of his sources. Medieval *translatio* being a literary rather than a linguistic exercise, his objective was to provide an interpretative vernacular adaptation of his Latin material which would permit its wider accessibility, and this he achieves with considerable skill and success.[27] He is careful always to respect the integrity of his sources, though the selection of episodes he takes from them often seems to privilege successions of military encounters. In the interests of his narrative dynamic he can deliberately omit whole chapters of his original, or even alter the order in which events are presented.[28] Only occasionally does he allow fictionality to impinge on historiography. Interpolations in which the romance mode, so well developed in his *Roman de Troie*, intervenes to enliven an otherwise bland, sometimes monotonous, narrative, are few and far between. Exceptional, for example, in its liveliness and dynamism, is the elaborate story of Herleva/Arlette and the circumstances surrounding the conception of King William (33445–33796).[29] History is momentarily eclipsed in the interests of literature. Among examples of Benoît's most successful writing, in literary terms, are also the episodes featuring Golés and Hubert de Ryes (35021–35318), the battle of Mortemer (37517–37784), the dragon-slaying Tostain (38409–38492) and the bear-slaughtering Rodulph (40331–40345), and the Conquest narrative (39219–39910). All bear the hallmarks, in varying degrees, of romance discourse. Benoît's extended account

---

25 Gillingham, "Henry of Huntingdon and the Twelfth-Century Revival of the English Nation," in *The English in the Twelfth Century*, pp. 123–44; Ian Short, "Tam Angli quam Franci: Self-Definition in Anglo-Norman England," *Anglo-Norman Studies* 18 (1995): 153–75; Hugh M. Thomas, *The English and the Normans: Ethnic Hostility, Assimilation, and Identity 1066–c. 1220* (Oxford, 2003), pp. 74–79; Ashe, *Fiction and History*, pp. 55–80.

26 Thomas, *The English and the Normans*, p. 350.

27 Damian-Grint, *The New Historians of the Twelfth-Century Renaissance*, pp. 22–31.

28 For detail see note to 38550 below.

29 See notes to 33469 and 33545 below.

of Rufus's nightmare, to take another example, and its interpretation (42773–42988) forms an impressive piece of imaginative poetic narrative.

Amplification is one of Benoît's most conspicuous skills. Passages of direct speech and imaginary dialogue designed to dramatise particularly climactic encounters are frequently inserted.[30] He takes particular pleasure in the detail of battle scenes, and manipulates with ease the stereotyped expressions that are specific to such descriptions. He also occasionally embroiders the text he is translating by adding explanations, clarifications and realistic detail. He is also capable of sometimes omitting critical or conflicting material in order to maintain the positive tone of his narrative and the promotion of the interests of his patron. More conventional rhetorical flourishes include the over-use of superlatives and diverse sorts of exaggeration.

Benoît's principal narrative mode is also rhetorical in so far as it has panegyric at its centre. His ideological aim is a propagandistic one: to glorify the dukes and then kings that successively people his pages. In a narrative overburdened with the repetition of such routine epithets as *preux*, *vaillant* and *sage*, and of ever more matchless superlatives, little room is left for descriptions, for the niceties of characterisation or psychological analysis. His history, a dynastic one, organised around the individual lives of consecutive dukes, has a linear, chronological structure but in which precise dates are kept to an absolute minimum. It is peppered instead with insistent truth claims which are both self-authorising and designed to remind his audience of the unimpeachable authority of his Latin sources. It has, however, a narrative dynamic of its own, a tempo capable of sustaining its audience's interest by presenting figures, both semi-heroic and villainous, emblematic of the chivalric ethos of his day.

As for the value of Benoît's text as a repository of new and original documentation, it naturally falls far below that of Robert de Torigni's continuation of William of Jumièges' *Gesta*, itself described as deliberately setting out to present a selective version of familiar events in order to praise the achievements of the Norman rulers. While naturally adhering to the providentialist view of history adopted by his Latin predecessors, Benoît is not averse to occasionally flirting with the profane and enlivening his narrative with a discourse more appropriate to the epic and hagiographic literature of his day. Where he succeeds as a historiographer is in improving the accessibility of his sources to a wider, secular audience by exploiting his considerable skill as a vernacular poet. He adapts the culture of the past to suit the tastes of his present by means of a sophisticated literary language that excites and stimulates parts of society that Latin cannot reach.

---

30 Laurent, *Pour Dieu et pour le roi*, pp. 253–88.

Unlike Wace, Benoît never writes from personal experience, never pauses to question his source texts or their reliability, nor does he ever draw attention to his own ignorance or inadequacy as a historian, as Wace so notoriously did. Such an umproblematic and orthodox approach to historiography does not, of course, exclude partialities or tendentious views on individuals or events. All of these, however, prove, on closer inspection, not to be of Benoît's own devising but to originate in his Latin source. What looks to be Benoît's critical attitude to Curthose, in contrast to Wace's decidedly more positive, chivalric portrayal, is in fact Robert de Torigni's, as is his lavish and unreserved praise of the empress Matilda. Another view espoused by Benoît is the denigration and condemnation of Rufus, typical of twelfth-century Church historians in general, and far removed from the more tolerant, baronial perspective that had been favoured by, for instance, Geffrei Gaimar. Benoît's most fervent admiration – one might almost say adulation – is reserved for the exemplary Henry I, though had his narrative not come to a premature halt, Henry II, his patron, would almost certainly have eclipsed his predecessor. Benoît's short but vicious diatribe against an unnamed Thomas Becket (37355–37365), independent this time of his source, must have provided an unmistakable echo of his master's voice in the years immediately preceding 1170.

Our knowledge of Benoît, as distinct from the judgements we arrive at about him, is restricted to the texts he has left behind him, and in the case of his *Histoire*, listening to his verse and to the authorial voice that it articulates allows us a means of encountering him, as it were, at first hand and of better understanding the persona which he is projecting. Benoît, we will find, intervenes in his own narrative with regularity, and his intention seems most often to be a self-promotional one. He also interrupts the flow of his narrative to signpost structural divisions and to mark major transitions, to draw attention to his own digressions, to apologise for his slowness in writing, to deplore the vast volume of the material he has to cover and the difficulty of translating it, and to stress his own diligence as well as the accuracy of his rendering and the absence of any extraneous, that is non-historical, material from it. He contrives also to find room to praise his royal patron and to look forward to the time when, in the chronology he is careful to follow, he can finally cover his reign – an ambition that he was never, for whatever reason, to fulfil.

Before embarking on the long doctrinal sermon of Richard I to the Viking chieftains (25853–26506), Benoît enters meta-discourse mode with an interpolation *ex persona poetae*, the intention of which is to impress on his audience the inherent difficulty there is in translating from Latin into vernacular verse:

Se me fiasse tant en mei
E je m'en osasse entremetre,
Ce qu'en truis escrit en la letre

En retraissise cherement.
Mais li latins dit e conprent
Od somme, od glosse, ce m'est vis
Ou ronmanz ne puet estre mis
Choses moutes; por ce m'est gref.
Mais moct me torne a grant meschef
Que sa haute escience tace
Autresi cum fist maistre Wace.
Ce ne porreie j'onques faire,
Quer si dei mostrer e retraire
Quex fu sa feiz, quex sis corages ... (25828–41)

If I had had sufficient confidence in myself and if I had dared apply myself to the task, I would have given a close rendering of what I find written in the Latin text. However, it is my opinion that Latin, as used in treatises and glosses, expresses and connotes many things for which the French vernacular has no equivalent – and this I find regrettable. It would, however, be very much to my discredit if I were to stay silent on the subject of [Duke Richard's] high level of knowledge, as Master Wace did. This is something I could never do, for it is my duty to show and give an account of what sort of religious faith he had and what his thinking was ...

It is Benoît the scholar who bewails his inability to do justice to the complexity of his Latin source with the vernacular he has at his disposal. It is, on the other hand, as a moralist that he discreetly criticises Wace for his omission, a decision, one presumes, intended to spare his audience yet another example of pious panegyric.

At another important narrative juncture towards the end of his poem, Benoît pauses to take his audience into his confidence: he is finding his task onerous and still resisting the temptation of introducing tangential or superfluous material. Nor is there any question of him abandoning his project at this late stage. He is sorry if the volume of his material is leading some listeners to lose patience with him. The end, however, is in sight, and like any good workman, he is ensuring that his preparation is careful and thorough:

I am sorry that it is taking me so long, but in the same way as people apply plaster and colour to the wall on which they are painting, so that the brush strokes are better-formed, more delicate and correctly coloured, so I have taken a long time to prepare the plaster for my painting without being lackadaisical or allowing myself to be distracted. The reason I am so assiduous, determined and persistent is so that the work can be brought to completion this side of Judgement Day. (42062–71)

The arresting simile of the poet as fresco painter (cf. note to 42062–68 below) strikes a rare note of originality in an otherwise routine interruption of the narrative flow designed to revive the flagging attention of any impatient listeners.

The end of the section that he devotes to the Conqueror provides Benoît with another opportunity of emphasising how faithfully and accurately he follows his written sources:

> I can state in all truthfulness that I have translated and recounted this history exactly as I found it written down. I have added nothing false or untruthful. Since the fruits of my labour have cost me a great deal, I pray to our Lord God that the work be pleasing to my lord [Henry II]. This is what I seek and desire more than anything else, for his approval would stand me in good stead. (42034–42)

Though part and parcel of the rhetorical stock-in-trade of narrative poets, Benoît's self-validation seems here to conceal a certain defensiveness. Conscious of how much material he still has to cover, he shows himself to be all too aware of the danger of lapsing into prolixity and of boring his often unattentive listeners:

> I cannot give the names of all those who played a role ... If I wished to list their deeds, it would take far too long to recount, and even after filling three quires of parchment, I would not have reached the end. The reason I should finish writing my history expeditiously is because some people – perhaps many – become restive, inattentive and distracted and quickly get bored with listening; often they turn their minds to anything else at all rather than listen to such fine exploits and learn from them. (39744–56)

He is no less conscious of the danger of digressing from the chronology of his narrative, as he in fact did when he adapted his sources to intercalate a long, all-inclusive chapter (38287–38724) on the Normans in Sicily. His anxiety is not to delay further and not lose control of his material now that he is approaching the crucial turning point in Norman fortunes:

> At this point, I am not willing to say any more on this topic in order not to digress from my subject matter, to which it is now time for me to return. For anyone who might now wish to hear how Duke William conquered the land

and the kingdom of England from Harold who had had himself crowned, I will tell the true story of what happened. (38725–32)

Pausing earlier in his narrative at the transition between the sections he devotes to the Viking Hasting and to Rollo, Benoît gave an early indication of the constant preoccupation he has with the overall structure of his work. He was clearly concerned about the narrative architecture of his poem – what his contemporary Chrétien de Troyes would refer to as its *conjointure* – since this was directly dependent on what material he decided to select from the wide chronological span covered by his Latin sources, and the level of detail he attributed to specific sections or episodes. The compositional decisions he had to take cannot always have been easy ones:

> Des or m'est vis que je demor:
> Ne vuil de cestui plus traitier
> Qu'autre chose ai a commencier,
> Bele, sainte, doce a oïr ...
> Granz est l'estuide e li labors,
> Granz esmais sereit as plusurs
> De sifaite ovre translater,
> Mais ne m'i puis desconforter:
> Se mi senz est humle e petiz,
> Je crei que li Sainz Esperiz
> I overra ensemble od mei ... (2112–15, 2123–29)

It seems to me now that I am taking for too long over this. I have no intention of saying anything more [about Hasting], for I have other material to start on – attractive subject matter, this time, uplifting and music to your ears ... There is a tremendous amount of concentrated thought and hard grind necessary here, and for many people it would be an extremely daunting task to translate a work such as this. But that is no reason for me to be disconsolate. In the event of my intelligence being found limited or inadequate, I believe I will have the Holy Spirit as my collaborator.

A mere ten thousand verses into his history, on reaching the end of his account of the life of Rollo, Benoît interrupted himself to express his happiness at reaching this narrative milestone:

> Ce m'esjoïst e ce me haite
> Dum s'ovre est acomplie e faite

E dum j'en sui venuz a fin. (10535–37)

I rejoice and am happy to have finished and completed this part of my work and to have brought it to a conclusion.

Such first-person authorial interjections have the dual purpose of signalling successive stages in the development of the narrative, and of reinforcing the bond between narrator and audience by using the narratorial voice as a means of "authorising" the text.[31] At the end of the subsequent section that he devoted to William Longsword, Benoît again allowed himself a self-conscious, and perhaps self-congratulatory, aside designed to draw his listeners' attention to the progress he was making:

Ci me repos e ci fenis,
Mes n'achieve pas mis travaiz.
Or vient l'estoire des granz faiz
A translater e a escrivre,
U mervilles avra a dire
E a oïr e a retraire. (14778–83)

This is where I reach the end and can mark a pause. My work is not, however, finished, for I still have to translate and write up the story of the great deeds, where there will be some extraordinary things to tell and recount, and for you to hear.

Exceptionally, he can be found in one passage turning his attention to the wider implications of the task he is engaged in. Whereas historiography is traditionally regarded, in the medieval vernacular perspective, as a vehicle for the transmission of knowledge as it rescues the past from oblivion, Benoît fails even to pay lip service to this topos.[32] Instead he adopts the alternative, moral and didactic, topos: the purpose of history, he tells us, is to place instruction and

---

31 On authorial interventions, see Damian-Grint, *The New Historians of the Twelfth-Century Renaissance*, pp. 143–71.

32 As Wace memorably put it: "In order to commemorate the deeds, words and ways of life of our ancestors, both the crimes of the criminal and the noble deeds of the noble, books, histories and heroic tales should be read out at festivals. If things were not written down and then read out and recounted by clerics, much of what happened in olden days would be forgotten" (*Rou* III, 1–10). For Henry of Huntingdon, knowledge of the past is a more fundamental necessity: "It is the knowledge of past events ... which best distinguishes rational creatures from irrational ones. For irrational creatures, whether they

enlightenment at the disposal of its audience. Listeners should, ideally, be gleaners:

> Autresi sunt cum mirëors
> Les estoires des anceisors:
> Maintes choses i ot l'om dire
> U l'om mult cler se veit e mire.
> Ausi cum cil, ceo m'est avis,
> Qui vait coillant les bons espis
> E ce laisse qui n'a valor,
> Deivent faire li oëor:
> Le bien retiengent des escriz
> Quant il lor ert contez e diz,
> E si·n vivront plus sagement
> E mieuz e plus honestement.
> Par bons essamples, par bons faiz,
> Ceus qui orribles sunt e laiz
> En eschive l'om mainte feiz. (14837–51)

The histories of our ancestors are just like mirrors: people hear many things said that enable them to look at and see themselves with clarity. My view is that the hearers of history should be like people who go out to gather the good ears of corn and who discard what is not worth keeping. Let them keep what is good in the writings when they hear it recounted and recited to them, and they will accordingly lead better, wiser and more virtuous lives. Good examples and good deeds allow people, time and time again, to avoid what is wicked and objectionable.

Discerning the lessons of history involves, we are told, listening and acquiring knowledge:

> Quer ne connois ne je ne vei
> Qu'en l'estoire ait rien si bien non

---

be humans or animals, know nothing of their origins, their race, or the exploits or events that have taken place in their native land – nor indeed do they have any desire to know" (*Historia Anglorum*, p. 4). William of Malmesbury, on the other hand, famously defined historiography as adding spice to moral instruction by providing entertaining accounts of the past: "historiam ... quae iocunda quadam gestorum notitia mores condiens, ad bona sequenda vel mala cavenda legentes exemplis irritat" (*GRA*, p. 150).

E doctrine e cognicion
A ceus qui i voudront entendre;
Maint buen essample i porront prendre.
Les diz, les faiz des anceisors
Unt mestier eü as plusors;
Nus ne set rien perfietement
S'il n'ot ou ne veit e n'aprent. (2130–38)

For to my way of thinking history has nothing but positive lessons in it, moral instruction and knowledge, for those who are ready to take notice of them. Such individuals can find exemplary models of behaviour in them. The deeds and opinions of their ancestors have proved to be of benefit to a large number of people. No one can have a complete understanding of anything unless they are willing to listen, look and learn.

Understanding is not, however, innate, the poet's listeners are warned, but needs careful cultivation:

Sen ne naist pas es cuers humains –
De ce vos faz je bien certains –
Com fait un arbre en un verjer.
Tot autre chose i a mestier:
Oïr, veer, aprendre e faire,
Retenir, ovrer e retraire.
Sanz ce ne puet de nul aage
Nus estre proz, vaillant ne sage. (2139–46)

One thing I can tell you for certain is that intelligence does not spring up naturally in the human mind like a tree growing in a garden. It requires something altogether different: listening, seeing, learning, doing, working, remembering and recalling. Without all of these, no one, of whatever age, can claim to be valiant, worthy and wise.

Cultivating the mind by learning moral lessons is in fact what distinguishes a truly learned person from the hoi-polloi, continues Benoît, drumming his homiletic message into his captive audience:

Tex sunt afaitié e corteis
E maistre des arz e des leis

Si ne fust buen enseignemenz
Doctrine, oïrs, retenemenz,
Qui fussent sanz discrecion,
Vilain, sanz sen e sanz raison. (2147–52)

There are people who are refined and courtly, university graduates in arts and the law, who would have remained unenlightened and irrational peasants lacking any discernment if there had not been good moral lessons to be learned, teaching, listening, and retention.

Switching from the moral into the panegyric mode, Benoît moves seamlessly from his virtual to his ideal listener with the traditional praise-of-patron trope. What better and more appreciative audience could he hope to have than Henry II?

Avantaige ai en cest labor
Qu'au soverain e au meillor
Escrif, translat, truis e rimei
Qui au munt seit de nule lei,
Qui meuz connoist ovre bien dite
E bien seant e bien escrite.
Dex m'i dont faire son plaisir,
Quer c'est la riens que plus desir. (2157–64)

Where I am at an advantage in this laborious task of mine is in having the best and most highly placed of all possible patrons in the world, of whatever persuasion. The person for whom I write, translate, compose and find my rhymes is the one best able to recognise a well-rhymed, appropriate and well written work. May God grant that I can carry out his wishes, for that is my greatest desire.

Later in his history Benoît seizes on a reference to Henry II's re-interment of the bodies of Dukes Richard I and II at Fécamp to salute his patron once again:

... le buen rei Henri segunt,
Flors des princes de tot le munt
Cui faiz sunt digne de memoire,
A cui Dex dunt force e victoire
Longue vie, prosperité,

Sanz ainsse e sanz aversité.
Saintisme e buenne seit sa fins! (32061–67)

... good King Henry II, flower of all the world's rulers whose deeds are worthy of commemoration. May God grant him strength and victory, long life and prosperity free from anxiety and adversity. May his end be a good and highly pious one!

He had also, while still at an early stage in his narrative, anticipated all the work he would need to do before he was able to reach his main goal, that of recounting the deeds of Henry II ("ainz que vienge al buen rei," 14785). He had, nevertheless, made a start, and this encouraged him:

Auques est ma pense esjoïe,
Kar des or est l'ovre envaïe.
S'il ne pleüst a mun seignor,
Trop i eüst aspre labor
E esmaiable e demoranz,
Mais sis voleirs e sis talenz
M'est jois, douçors a acomplir,
Kar rien sus ciel tant ne desir.
Deus m'i dunt tant terme e espace
Que l'ovre li achef e face
E que, si davant lui la lise,
K'il ne la blasme ne despise! (14793–804)

This gladdens my heart to some extent, for I have by now made a definite start on the work. Were it not to be to my lord's liking, it would be an extremely painful undertaking, daunting and long-drawn-out. However, it is a joy and delight for me to fulfil my lord's wishes and desires, for there is nothing in this world that I want so much. May God grant me a space of time sufficient to work on and complete this history for him, in such a way that if I were to read it out in his presence, he would not criticise or deride it.

He was henceforth ready and able, under divine guidance, to persevere and to take up the next challenge awaiting him, the life of Duke Richard I, with renewed vigour and optimism. His metaphor is a nautical one:

I am henceforth racing full sail ahead, for the bright star shining resplendent in the high heaven is guiding me surely on my way. (14883–86)

At the beginning of the following section Benoît once again saw fit to work in a eulogistic mention of his patron, this time with the addition of a personal variation on the modesty and *industria* topoi:

> Or donge Dex par sa douçor
> Qu'au plaisir seit de mun seignor,
> Deu buen rei Henri, fiz Maheut,
> Que si benigne cum il seuct
> Seit a l'oïr e a l'entendre!
> N'est pas de mes poors la mendre
> Que de mesdire e de mesfaire
> Chose qui ne li deie plaire ...
> E ge qui jor ne nuit ne fin,
> Qui si truis encombros latin,
> Se g'i mesfaz n'est pas merveille,
> Quer riens fors Deu ne m'i conseille. (28711–18, 28723–26)

May God in his clemency grant that my lord, good King Henry, son of the Empress Matilda, is pleased with my writing, and that when he listens to it and hears it, he is as kind-hearted as he usually is. It is not the least of my fears that my saying the wrong thing or being offensive should incur his displeasure ... It is little wonder that I, being someone who never stops working day or night, and who finds Latin so burdensome, should make mistakes, for the only advice I receive is what God gives me.

Similar sentiments reappear some fifteen thousand lines later, by which time Benoît had succeeded, by the grace of God, in bringing his narrative up to the reign of Henry I:

Now that, by the gift and by the leave of the almighty King of Heaven, who makes little children into rational, skilful and intelligent beings, and gives the deaf and dumb eloquence, hearing and understanding, I have been translating the history of the dukes of Normandy – a very voluminous history in which I have found a great deal of material to treat, much learning and many different subjects – and have now come right up to Henry I who is to be the eighth duke and one of the most important, it would not be right for me to stop at this point and give up writing. My task is to keep going straight ahead in an orderly and uninterrupted fashion until I come to good King Henry II, the place on which my heart is set. May God be willing to grant me the opportunity of recounting his illustrious deeds! (42043–60)

Exactly why Benoît was refused the opportunity of fulfilling his ambition of crowning his marathon enterprise with the deeds of Henry II is another of the unanswered questions which his surviving text poses. What is noticeable is that the final thousand lines of his poem cover the closing years of Henry I's reign at what can only be described as a breathless pace. It has been suggested that Benoît stops his narrative in the place he does simply because that is where his Latin source came to an end, and no alternative Latin history was readily available to enable him to continue his narrative through Stephen and Matilda on to Henry II. The same argument is made in the case of Wace's *Rou* which fails to pursue its principal narrative beyond Tinchebray. An alternative interpretation, advanced by Laura Ashe,[33] is that there was resistance to the shift in cultural focus onto England, and an unwillingness among Continental historians to engage with the history of England's Anglo-Angevin kings. Be that as it may, Benoît's ending as it stands certainly does not give the impression of any reluctance to continue, and the extant text argues, if anything, in favour of an unanticipated rather than a pre-meditated explanation.[34] The simplest would be intimations of mortality.

Benoît's literary legacy as a historiographer was extremely modest given the length and wide coverage of his history, let alone its patronage, and its influence does not extend far beyond the prose *Bruts* of the fourteenth century. In terms of literary history, Benoît represents a tradition in decline: apart from the Norman Ambroise's eye-witness account of the Third Crusade from the 1190s, the rhymed chronicle has few significant exponents after Philippe Mouskés' *Chronique rimée* from the middle of the thirteenth century and *Le Règne d'Edouard Ier* by Peter Langtoft (1280–1307). Narrative prose history in French, whose rise is heralded by the earliest *Pseudo-Turpin Chronicle* translations (1195–1205), opens with the texts associated with the Anonyme de Béthune, and these in turn are the precursors of the accounts of the Fourth Crusade from the secular pens of Villehardoin, Robert de Clari and Henri de Valenciennes. Thereafter the *Chronique de l'Anonyme de Chantilly-Vatican* (1217–30) prepares the way for the emergence of the *Grandes Chroniques de France* in 1274.[35]

The history-as-romance tradition is a productive offshoot of this vernacular preoccupation with historiographic literature. Fictionalised versions of the Insular past are composed for the consumption of a by now bilingual Anglo-Norman audience who are presented with English heroes in Francophone dress, such as

---

33   Ashe, *Fiction and History*, pp. 57–59.
34   See note to 44409 below.
35   Gillette Labory, "Essai d'une histoire nationale au XIIIe siècle," *Bibliothèque de l'Ecole des Chartes* 148 (1990): 301–54; Gabrielle M. Spiegel, *Romancing the Past: The Rise of Vernacular Prose History in Thirteenth-Century France* (Berkeley, 1993).

Horn, Waldef, Gui de Warewic, Boeve de Haumtone and Fouque le fiz Waryn. Set in a fantasy world of formulaic romance and adventure, these capacious narratives from the late twelfth and early thirteenth centuries are destined also to swell the ranks of a resurgent Middle English literature.[36]

Benoît worked, as we have seen, from the final (F) redaction of the GND, whose text he in his turn recast to accommodate it to the requirements of vernacular narrative poetry and to the literary tastes of his intended listeners. Into his version he occasionally inserted material from other works such as William of Poitiers' *Gesta Guillelmi*, Orderic Vitalis's *Historia Ecclesiastica* and Wace's *Roman de Rou*, as well as more popular sources, some of which might have been oral.

After an introductory geographical proemium (1–352), Benoît opens his narrative with an account of the earliest Viking incursions into France and the arrival of the first Northmen at Rouen (985–996). This is followed by a long section celebrating the exploits of the Danish invader Hasting (1173–2164). It is only several thousand lines later that we reach the pivotal moment when Rouen and Upper Normandy are ceded to the incomers by Charles the Simple in 911 and Normandy comes into existence (8777–8983). A section of over 8000 lines (2355–10540) is devoted to the Normans' founding father Rollo, including the long and curious episode of a knight who walks on water (9839–10122). Rollo is endowed with all the power, all the chivalric qualities, all the nobility needed to justify the patriarchal role that history attributes to him, and to legitimise the dynasty he inaugurates.

Within the overall architecture of Benoît's history, Rollo's coverage compares closely to the space reserved later for William the Conqueror, though both are far outstripped by the attention that Benoît lavishes on Duke Richard I the Fearless. Richard claims over 13,000 of the poet's octosyllables (14805–28710),[37] into some of which the supernatural, conscientiously avoided elsewhere in Benoît's narrative, is permitted to intrude. If his father William Longsword

36 Ashe, *Fiction and History*, pp. 121–58; Judith Weiss, "'History' in Anglo-Norman Romance," in *The Long Twelfth-Century View of the Anglo-Saxon Past*, ed. Martin Brett and David Woodman (Farnham, 2015), pp. 275–87.
37 Before line 14805 the Tours manuscript has the following chapter heading in alexandrine couplets:
L'estoire de Guillaume fenist ci, Long' espee,
Sicum Benëeit l'a escrite e translatee.
Iceo est le prologe, puis comence la vie
Del premerain Richart, le duc de Normendie.

(10541–14777) had lived an exemplary life and died a martyr's death, Richard I achieves, under Benoît's pen, a semi-legendary, semi-regal status. He does so not only by virtue of his outstanding piety but also thanks to a long series of "marvellous" adventures, including exemplary anecdotes, which culminate in the construction of a figure which, in literary terms, belongs as much to hagiography as it does to historiography.

Richard II (28793–32070) follows the model set by his father and presides over an increasingly courtly society, while the brief reign of the ever-generous Richard III (32081–32220), is one of humanity, peace and justice. The life of Robert I the Magnificent (32225–34008), whom William of Malmesbury suspects of having poisoned his brother Richard, is another in a by now predictable line of praiseworthy and exemplary Norman dukes. It leads us into the section of Benoît's history devoted to William the Conqueror and his sons, and which is the object of our translation.[38]

It opens with duke Robert's courtship of Herleva and the birth of William the Conqueror with accompanying presages (33445–33824). The duke then insists, despite protests from his vassals, on making the pilgrimage to Jerusalem, and leaves the infant William to govern Normandy. Robert dies at Nicaea on his return in 1035 (34008). A climate of anarchy creates severe difficulties for William in his early years as duke (34009–34086). War breaks out between Vauquelin de Ferrières and Hugh of Montfort, culminating in their mutual slaughter (34118). The murders of Gilbert, count of Brionne (34114) and of William's steward Osbern (34172) follow, as does, thereafter, the death in battle of Roger de Beaumont at the hands of Roger de Tosny (34173–34312).

William's trials continue as the king of France tricks him with false promises into handing over the castle of Tillières. Henri then attacks and razes it to the ground, only to rebuild it soon afterwards and occupy it himself (34548). Thurstan Goz then defies William by taking over Falaise castle, but William retaliates and succeeds in defeating him (34549–34656). William's uncle, William, count of Arques, in cahoots with the king of France, now revolts. William besieges him and, against all the odds, emerges victorious (34854).

Betrayal continues to dog the adult William as, thanks to the active intervention of some loyal vassals, he thwarts the faithless Guy of Burgundy's conspiracy to usurp power by assassinating him (34855–35332). With the country fast falling into lawlessness, William turns to his overlord the king of France for help. Joining forces with Henri, he routs his enemies at Val-ès-Dunes in 1047

---

38   The heading announcing this section follows line 31778: "Ici comence l'estoire del rei Guillaume sicum Beneeit l'a translatee."

thanks to the timely intervention of a loyal Ralph Taisson. Guy returns igno-
miniously to Burgundy, while Grimoult du Plessis, the evil influence behind so
much of Normandy's misfortunes, perishes in prison (36148).

The scene shifts to England where we find Edward and Alfred disinherited
following the death of King Cnut. Earl Godwine, having treacherously contrived
Alfred's death (36336), attempts to ingratiate himself with the newly crowned
King Edward. Edward declares his intention of making William his successor to
the English throne (36461).

Back in Normandy, Geoffrey Martel, count of Anjou, has taken possession
of the strongholds of Alençon and Domfront, leading William to besiege them.
He deals harshly with the defenders of Alençon who impudently mock his parent-
age (36744). At Domfront Geoffrey's advisers convince him to leave and cede
victory to the Normans (37036). William Werlenc, count of Mortain, is exiled
when his plot to overthrow Duke William is exposed (37180). The same fate
befalls William, count of Eu, a kinsman of the duke, who is forced to seek refuge
with the king of France (37200).

Duke William marries Matilda, daughter of the count of Flanders, and
together they produce three sons and a number of daughters (37219–37288).
Encouraged to invade Normandy, the king of France launches a massive attack
in 1054 and, encountering little opposition, presses on as far as Mortemer in the
Pays de Caux. Here the Normans launch a surprise attack while the French are
still sleeping. They set fire to the town, and slaughter ensues (37457–37784).

Following the death of Count Herbert II of Maine, William had been expecting to become lord of Le Mans, but finds, in 1063, that he has to assert his right
to it by force of arms, which he does with great success (37859–38062). In 1057
the king of France, joining forces with Geoffrey Martel, invades Normandy.
Reaching the river Dives, the invaders are taken by surprise by the turning tide,
on seeing which the Normans pounce and thoroughly defeat them (38063–
38212).

There follows a long digression (38287–38725) on the Norman presence
in Italy and Sicily, and a celebration of the exploits of the Drengots, Tancred,
Bohemond and Robert Guiscard. The scene then reverts to English matters and
to Harold Godwinson's embassy to Normandy where he swears homage to
William as King Edward's designated successor to the crown of England (38856).
On Edward's death in 1066, however, Harold seizes the crown for himself,
thereby provoking William's astonishment and fury. The Normans' ultimatum is
contemptuously dismissed (38992). Arrangements are immediately put in hand
for a Norman invasion. A comet appears in the sky, and the pope seals his
approval of William's decision by the gift of the Standard of St Peter (39042).

The Norman fleet lands at Pevensey at the same time as Harold returns to London from defeating the Danes in the north. Both Harold's mother and brother attempt to dissuade him from attacking the Normans (39424), but he angrily spurns their advice. Battle is joined, with the English occupying the higher ground. At one point the Normans find themselves retreating in confusion, but God comes to their assistance, and William urges his troops on to victory. The perjurer Harold falls, and the English are defeated (39836). Agamemnon had not been able to take the city of Troy in ten years, but William conquered a whole kingdom in the space of a single day (39873–39884).

Brushing aside some token resistance, William is crowned king of England (40060). Having founded Battle Abbey, fortified Winchester and entrusted Dover to his half-brother Odo, the king returns to Normandy (40222). Meanwhile Eustace, Count of Boulogne is enlisted by the English to storm Dover castle but is repulsed (40449–40558). The next English conspiracy, under Edgar Ætheling, ends in the destruction of Durham (40674), while an attack mounted by Harold's sons is brutally punished (40712). William's mistrust of Edwin and Morcar proves to be well-founded, and the rebellion initiated by Mærle-Sveinn and Gospatric fails (40864). When York is attacked, William responds ruthlessly (41025). The threat posed by Swein Estrithson is contained (41338). As from 1069 William's mastery of his new kingdom is complete, and he reigns henceforth in peace, prosperity and tranquillity. (41454)

Back in Normandy, William demands that King Philippe hand over the French Vexin to him, but following a Norman attack on Mantes William falls seriously ill (41572). After a long and edifying death-bed speech (41595–41712) during which his son Rufus is allotted the kingdom of England, and Robert Curthose succeeds to the duchy of Normandy, William expires (41901).

Robert grants the Cotentin to his brother Henry but then takes it back again by what can only be described as extortion (42252). Rufus meanwhile crosses the Channel with the supposed aim of seizing Normandy for himself, but comes to an agreement with Robert to the detriment of Henry, who nevertheless begins to consolidate his position (42436). The people of Maine, taking advantage of Robert's increasing weakness, negotiate with Hélie de La Flèche to be their new overlord (42476).

Robert, having decided to leave for the Holy Land, arranges with Rufus what amounts to a mortgage of Normandy (42512). In England Rufus successfully pursues his military campaigns against the Welsh and the Scots, then comes to the relief of Le Mans (42658). His hostility to St Anselm and to the Church, however, is to lead to his premature end. After the most gruesome of nightmares (42780–42846), he arrogantly ignores all warnings and goes hunting in the New Forest where he is the victim of an accident that costs him his life (43060).

His brother Henry is crowned king of England four days later. He marries Matilda, daughter of the king of Scots, and their daughter, likewise named Matilda and destined for greatness, makes a superlative marriage to the emperor Henry V (43273). Henry's only son, William Ætheling, is drowned in 1120 in the White Ship tragedy (43386).

Returning from the East, Robert Curthose fails in his attempt to challenge Henry for the crown. He is a failure also in governing Normandy, and is defeated and captured by his brother in 1106 at the battle of Tinchebray (43642). He dies, still a prisoner, in 1134 (43754). Henry restores peace and harmony in Normandy by imprisoning the troublesome Waleran of Meulan (43898), and deals decisively with problems of counterfeit coinage (43944).

On her return as a widow from Germany, Matilda is married to Count Geoffrey of Anjou, with whom she has Henry, the eldest of her three sons (44070). A genealogical excursus on the house of Anjou (44071–44188) demonstrates its suitability for a marriage alliance with that of Normandy. There follows a list of the castles which Henry I constructed, and the abbeys he founded and patronised, including Marmoutier (44328). An account of the various daughters of William the Conqueror brings Benoît's history up to Stephen, "made king under false pretences," and Matilda, "Henry's true heir" (44480). The narrative ends, unexpectedly and somewhat abruptly, in 1135 with the death of Henry I (44544).

The standard edition of Benoît's history is that of Carin Fahlin (1951–54), who edited the Tours manuscript, and this is the text I follow for my translation. Very occasionally, however, when Fahlin's text has unsatisfactory or inferior readings, I adopt variants from the London manuscript as edited by Michel in 1836–44 (e.g. 42759). I have even ventured to correct Fahlin's text on a couple of occasions (42085, 42250, 43004). Square brackets indicate editorial additions to the text, and the sign "=" is used on occasion to rectify errors. All line references, unless otherwise specified, are to the text of Fahlin's edition. An asterisk draws attention to the existence of a note to the text. These notes are intended not only to elucidate certain textual references and allusions, but also to offer observations of a more literary nature on Benoît's skill as a writer as outlined in our Introduction.[39]

The eleven thousand lines I have chosen to translate (lines 33445–44544) constitute the last quarter of the poem. It begins with the conception of William the Conqueror in 1027, and goes on to cover the reigns of his two sons, William II (Rufus), who died in 1100, and Henry I. The death of Henry in 1135 marks the

39 My grateful thanks go to John Gillingham who kindly read the first draft of this work and with his expertise and customary insight helped improve it significantly.

end of the Anglo-Norman dynasty, at which point Benoît's narrative also comes to a close.

I have opted to translate the post-Conquest section of Benoît's inordinately long poem primarily because it is the part most likely to be of interest to today's medieval historians. But it also contains a number of episodes whose poetic qualities will not fail to impress literary scholars as outstanding specimens of early romance discourse. Issues of practicality have dictated my decision not to translate the text in its entirety, and I can only apologise to readers for depriving them of an English version of the remaining 33,444 lines of Benoît's poem.[40]

It will be immediately apparent to the reader that I have deliberately avoided giving a literal translation of Benoît's verses. What greater disservice can a translator do to a medieval poet than to give a prosaic, word-for-word rendering of their work? Benoît's text is not only literature but, more importantly even, poetry, and to reduce it, in translation, to neutral, everyday prose is to betray the very quality that gives the work its distinction. The need to salvage something of the author's tone and style is self-evident. In the quest for the maximum equivalence between source and target language, literality, both lexical and syntactic, has to be expendable in the interests of transparency and fluency. The functional, in other words, has precedence over the formal.[41] Whilst I see no inherent virtue in attempting, for example, to preserve or reflect the sentence structure of twelfth-century French poetic syntax in a twenty-first-century English prose translation, I do take particular care to respect what I understand to be Benoît's exceptional powers of poetic expression. A translation is, moreover, not a substitute for the original; it is simply a second-best means of access to it. Its role is not to replace but to represent the language in which it was originally composed. This, of course, is a highly subjective endeavour which some conservatives and some purists will inevitably deplore. I can only plead in mitigation that accuracy both of meaning and of tone has always been my primary concern. Unfortunately, my long experience of translating Medieval French has taught me only that I am still a long way from having mastered the art.

---

40 Readers eager to get some idea of the earlier, pre-Conquest part of Benoît's poem are directed to pp. 7–122 of Glyn Burgess's translation of Wace's *Roman de Rou*, and to the first volume of Elizabeth van Houts' translation of the *Gesta Normannorum Ducum*.

41 For translation methodologies, see Susan Bassnett, *Translation Studies*, 4th ed. (London and New York, 2014), pp. 33–39. Cf., for a wider perspective, *The Oxford Handbook of Translation Studies*, ed. Kirsten Malmkjær and Kevin Windle (Oxford, 2011), and the annual volumes in *The Medieval Translator* series, published by Brepols.

BENOÎT DE SAINTE-MAURE

The Lives of William the Conqueror and Sons

Histoire des ducs de Normandie, 33445–44544

Parenthetical references following each paragraph refer to line numbers of *Chronique des ducs de Normandie par Benoît,* ed. Carin Fahlin (Uppsala, 1951–54). See the Introduction above, page 25, for further details.

The notes following the translation are also keyed to line numbers; in the translation, the presence of a note is indicated by an asterisk.

[1] *How King William [the Conqueror] was conceived at Falaise.*

Good Duke Robert [I] of Normandy was staying at Falaise [in 1026–27]. It was somewhere he found most agreeable, a delightful spot, beautifully situated and with a healthy climate. One of his great pleasures, so I am informed, was to spend time with the young women there. He was returning from hunting one day when, along a river bank, his eye fell on a girl standing in the stream from a small spring washing some fine linen. She was accompanied by three or more other townswomen, and, as girls usually endeavour to do in such circumstances when they are on their own and feeling light-hearted and playful, she had hitched up her skirts. It was a fine, hot day, and what was not covered by her tunic lay open to view: her legs and feet were so beautiful and white that it very much seemed to the duke that snow and lilies were pale in comparison with the extreme whiteness of her skin. He fell madly in love with her. (33468)

The young lady was a townsman's daughter, intelligent, well-mannered and honourable, as well as beautiful.* She was fair-haired with a fine forehead and beautiful eyes full of goodness and openness without any hint of pride. No woman was more refined than she was. Her complexion was more delicate than rose or hawthorn in full bloom, her nose, mouth and chin were finely delineated. No one had more attractive features, a finer neck or more beautiful arms. I give you my word that she was comely, pale-skinned and buxom to the extent that she outshone in beauty all the other women in the country. I'll have you know that what I have told you so far of her beauty amounts to very little indeed compared to what it actually was. The duke desired her more than anything else in the world. He had the girl's father informed of this through a very discreet knight of his and one of his household chamberlains. He requested a date be set for a meeting, and made such offers and promises that she would have no alternative but to consent to grant him her love wholeheartedly. Thereafter he would find a wealthy and powerful husband for her. (33494)

Her father, however, at a loss to know exactly what to do, flatly turned down the request. He was amongst the most prominent families of Falaise, and for this reason he was very unhappy at not being able to decide for himself, in consultation with his kinsmen, whom to marry his daughter to. He had received several different requests for her hand, and the last thing he would have wanted in his life was for his daughter to be a kept woman or the mistress of some man or other. Had it not been for a brother of his, he would certainly have spirited his daughter away to a place of safety. The brother was a man of religion, a very devout person who lived as a hermit in Gouffern,* and it was he who, in his wisdom, dissuaded the girl's father from carrying out his plan. Whether it was a wise or a foolish move, the hermit succeeded in making his brother settle the matter by agreeing to give his consent. (33512)

The young woman in her turn was quite prepared to speak to her father along the same lines, wisely pointing out to him the advantages that they could both derive from the arrangement. In this way they reached agreement. The night and the hour were designated: it was to happen almost immediately, before the end of the week and without the usual fortnight's notice. The young lady is in a state of great excitement and takes considerable care over her appearance so that the duke should find nothing disagreeable or unpleasant in her behaviour or her bearing now that the future has been settled. As far as her resources and her situation permit, she has a brand new dress made for her in order to be able to show off her figure – a beautiful, well cut and extremely elegant dress that shows her body to its best advantage. (33530)

On the agreed night the duke sent to her the two men who had organised the affair. Their intention was to bring her to the castle surreptitiously and in secret. This arrangement, however, did not meet with her approval. "Fair lady," they said, "so that no one should see you and in order to prevent you from becoming the object of gossip and of mockery among the low-born, put on this woollen cloak to avoid your neighbours catching sight of you, since before day dawns bright and the crested lark starts singing, we will have brought you back home here." (33544)

To this the intelligent young lady replies*: "It never entered my mind that, with the duke calling me to him and seeking to enjoy this fine body of mine, I should go to him like a hireling or like some lowly chambermaid. The long and short of it is that I shall go instead as a young lady, the daughter of a reputable citizen, to enhance my honour and for my own advantage. I have no cause to feel ashamed. And let anyone know who cares to that my honour will in fact be all the greater, since no one will ever be able to reproach me with being wicked, irresponsible or wanton. This is why I am absolutely not willing to go on foot to sleep with the duke. I humbly beg and request you to have your saddle-horses fetched, and we will then be able to go to the duke's in a more dignified fashion." (33564)

The men understand how wise her words are; they know that she is right and what she says is true. They grant her request unreservedly and do everything she asks for. She had taken great pains to dress attractively in a magnificent shift over which she had put a dress lined with squirrel fur, new and shining white, free-flowing and strapless, which showed her figure, and, better still, her arms to good advantage. Over this she had placed a short mantle that became her beautifully. On her head, over her rich mane of very fair hair, she had a loosely fitting head-band with delicate silver braiding. This is how she was when she mounted her horse, her clothing still uncovered for all to see. I do not know if such a beautiful creature had ever been born. She bade farewell to her father and mother, but before she had gone out of the door, she could not help tears coming to her eyes and running down onto her breast at the emotion she felt in attempting to comfort and bring them solace. If at that moment she had been able to see into the future, her heart would have been filled with joy, for since the time of Hector, the brave Trojan, son of King Priam, I cannot recall or think of a greater leader being born than the one who was conceived that night in her.* Arthur performed great deeds, as did Charlemagne who conquered Spain by force of arms, but once you have heard the history of the ruler about whom we have written here, you will not, in my opinion, be able to say that any ruler could possibly have been more highly prized than he was. (33600)

This shows that God frequently allows things to happen that are generally considered to be transgressions but from which great good is seen to result, as you can understand for yourselves in the present case.* If there obviously was sin in the pleasure that the duke had with her that night in taking the virginity of someone he had not made his lawful wife, it was abundantly clear and universally recognised that God loved and sustained the heir that came into the world as a result of what they did together. (33612)

This young lady, far from being naïve, was intelligent, honourable, clever, and resourceful. Just hear what she did next! The two men who had brought her there and were looking after her came to the castle gate, and as it was a bright, clear night, they had her dismount outside. The door-keeper was waiting ready and the wicket-gate unlocked. The men went in first, but she made no move and was unwilling to put even a foot inside. This surprised the men who said: "Come on in, fair lady, have no fear! There's no one who knows you're here. Look! The whole place is deserted." "That's not what's worrying me," she replied. "But it's not right or proper that, when the duke has me come to him, I am forbidden from going through the main gate. Either you have it opened for me, or I'll simply not be doing what I want to. Given that the duke wants me as he does, it is disrespectful for me to be forced to go through such a narrow side-gate. God forbid that I should do so! For the duke to ask me to come to him under such conditions would be to show little respect for me. Open up the main gate, fair friends!" (33639)

When they heard her speak so intelligently and with such good sense and decorum, they gave a good-humoured laugh. The gate was quickly unlocked, and they led her up to the vaulted chamber with its many painted wall pictures in crimson, gold and various other colours. No welcome was so joyful and no consideration so attentive as those the duke showed her. He told her the whole story of his love for her, how much he desired her and how much he wanted to possess her. He has many favours in store for her, he promises, and with a sweet bow she tells him how truly grateful she is. "My lord," she says, "my heart and my mind are now amply provided for and both are filled with great joy, for now, sire, that I have your heart, I cannot possibly think that any greater goodness or any greater honour or happiness could come to me from any other source. Henceforth I place myself at your disposal as slave, lover, mistress and concubine. May God now grant me renewed happiness, the sort I long for and pray for!" (33667)

They stayed up until late into the night talking to each other on many different topics. And when the duke had gone to bed and the chamber had been emptied, the beautiful young girl began to undress. She gracefully removed her fur-trimmed dress, but when it came to her shift, she ripped it open, tearing it from top to bottom – much to the puzzlement of the duke. The candles were burning brightly in the room and she quickly freed her arms, revealing such a beautifully formed body that it made all the others that the duke had ever seen in his life, clothed or naked, look ugly in comparison. He spent a long time gazing at her great beauty. Then he asked her why she had ripped her shift. Her reply was perceptive: "My lord," she said, "to my way of thinking it was something I very much needed to do. I'm not the daughter of a king or a queen, and felt that I should not place before your eyes something that I have dragged at my feet over the ground and through the dust. Although it was new and freshly sewn, once I had worn it and once it had touched the ground, it was not something I should have placed before your face. That would have been an insulting and rude thing to do. You are a lord and the duke of Normandy, and this is a fact that I need to bear in mind, so as not to put myself in a position where I might be imprudent and offend you." (33700)

At this the duke gave an understanding smile. He finds such refinement in her, such amusing conversation and such maturity that he feels great affection for her. He had never in his life known such perfect happiness or met anyone who was more to his liking. He embraces her and kisses her with great tenderness; she submits entirely and consents. It was almost daybreak before they felt like going to sleep; in a word, they fully satisfied their desires. The young woman had fallen asleep before dawn, and dreamt a harrowing dream that she found exceedingly frightening. When she could no longer bear it, she uttered a sigh then gave a piercing cry. She woke up terrified and was shaking so violently that the duke was concerned and asked: "What is it that has startled you, fair one? Tell me." "My lord," she replied, "I don't know. But one thing I should not hide from you is that, in my dream, it seemed as if a tree was growing out of me – so huge, tall, upright, so wondrous that it reached up to the sky directly above us both. It cast a shadow that filled me full of fear, for it covered the whole of Normandy, the sea and the great land of England. I'm very upset that I don't have the knowledge of a soothsayer to interpret the dream and what it foretells."* (33734)

After listening to her the duke said: "Fair, sweet love, what you can be quite certain of is that it is a portent of great good fortune." And it is true that it was indeed a sign of great good fortune, for already, in this young woman Herleva, William, who one day was to take possession of the kingdom of England, had been conceived. She had had this vision very shortly after the moment of his conception, a vision of high significance, as you will hear in what follows, as I compose it. The wise and honourable Herleva put her virginity to extremely good use, since I believe, indeed I know for certain, that she is to be the mother of a king. This happened just as God wished, thereby indicating that it was pleasing to him. (33752)

Of their moments of joy and of passion and their frequent love-making I will not seek to give you any account, for there are many other topics that will need to be covered. But as time passed, month by month, as was only right and customary, the beautiful Herleva grew plump with child. At the end of her pregnancy she had the child [in 1027–28], and after delivery she regained her health before the end of forty days. The child had been conceived at an auspicious moment, but his birth was even more auspicious still. Hear how an incontrovertible revelation at the child's birth showed this to be true! The midwife present when he was born – I do not know who she is supposed to have been – placed him on a beautifully decorated cushion of fresh straw that had been brought for the occasion. The infant kicked out so much that he became entangled in the cushion. In less than no time he had pulled the straw all over him, with the result that his hands and feet disappeared and he seemed no longer to be lying there. When the woman came running to pick him up – hear this! It's beyond belief – despite the straw being painfully sharp, he had lifted armfuls of it up into the air. Immediately the woman said: "Ah, my fine young man, what a conqueror you will be, with so many more valuable fiefs than any of your ancestors ever had! What joy your birth brings! You will have so much honour in this world, and your exploits will be so great, that none of your ancestors will ever have had such tales told of them. May God grant you, in his holy name, joy, good health, long life, understanding and salvation, and his special blessing!" The prophecy that this woman made, and expected to be fulfilled, was a true one. This is in fact how things subsequently turned out, and the prophecy was seen to come true.* (33796)

When Duke Robert was told and learnt that the beautiful Herleva had had a son, he was wonderfully happy. He had the child brought up in opulence and no less attentively than if he had been born, beyond dispute, to the king of France's daughter. In a very short time the child had become good-looking and good-natured, so full of understanding and intelligence that he was marvellously adept at all manner of things. His face and complexion were glowing, fresh and rosy. Everyone absolutely loved him, and all those who looked on him predicted a future for him full of honour and success. Nor was this slow in coming about, and we are in a very good position to tell you exactly how. The child was still young when the duke was not only minded to visit the Holy Sepulchre, but conceived a heartfelt desire to do so. Without more ado he took the cross, a decision that displeased many of his dignitaries who were extremely afraid that they might lose him or that any other similar mishap might occur, for any land that is without a lord for any length of time often has good reason to lament the fact. (33824)

The duke, being anxious to set out, called together his bishops, abbots, and barons, and all other such notables. He set about explaining to them that his intention was to go to Jerusalem barefoot, in a plain woollen cloak and incognito, just like other holy pilgrims. His wish was to expiate his sins, if God were to so allow him. You would not have heard people more dismayed, grief-stricken and distressed as they replied with one voice: "Dearest lord, noble baron, what dreadful news this is! Who will you leave your great, valuable, and beautiful land to, and how will you go about it? You know full well what sort of friends the Bretons, Flemings, French, and Burgundians are to us. You are well aware of the sort of games they get up to. They never miss an opportunity, anywhere or at any time, of showing their hostility and their jealousy of Normandy. Who do you think will defend it or stand up to so many different peoples? The Bretons, whose lineage is the same as ours, claim part of our territory as their heritage. It is the same with the Burgundians, since they are related to you. These two will lose no time in ravaging our land should ever any accident befall you. There is not a single person who is not apprehensive and does not fear this happening." (33858)

"My lords," the duke replies, "your protests are to no avail. It is impossible for me to give up this journey. But the best advice I can find to give you, and the solution that I myself want and desire, and that carries with it my authority, is that you make the young son I have, an intelligent, good-natured, and honourable young man, your new lord. I can tell you all for certain that he is, beyond any doubt at all, my son. It is my opinion and I know that never in the past has Normandy had hopes of finding a wiser and better lord than it will have in him. It is of no importance that he is not the son of a legitimate wife of mine. This will not make him any the less effective in battle, or in a noble court or in a palace as far as dispensing justice and maintaining peace are concerned. If I had not recognised the advantage of such an arrangement, I would not have been willing for it to go ahead. It is the best alternative that I can see in the circumstances. I tell you this in regard to God and the journey that I have to, and will, make. And I will return home, so please God, without delay and without staying away too long." (33885)

The most powerful and wisest of his dignitaries agreed to do as Duke Robert wished. Without any argument they unconditionally recognised the young boy as their liege lord, swearing such fealty and service as should properly be given to a lord, and to which a lord is entitled and which he duly accepts. You would never have heard an oath sworn so willingly or in such harmony. It was with great affection that they acknowledged William as their duke and as their lord. He was then taken before the king of France, and Robert also went in order to take leave of his overlord, who on that occasion showed him particular favour. The king was very pleased to accept the young man's homage for the whole of Normandy and for all its dependent estates. After which, under the circumstances that I have outlined, they returned home. Count Alan [III of Brittany], the duke's first cousin, was then summoned, and all the land was made over to him, and Robert's son and inheritor was placed in his care. Alan happily accepted responsibility for him, did homage and swore an oath of fealty to him, undertaking to act with loyalty in his dealings with him. (33914)

Then without any delay and before the month was out, the wise and valiant duke set out joyfully on his pilgrimage. When he left his country, there were no celebrations, smiles or joking: never were as many tears shed as on that first day. The duke embraces his people, embraces his son; he leaves them with a heavy heart. Now he starts out with a reduced retinue, but a fine one, none the less, splendid and well equipped, and off they ride leaving their country behind. Good Duke Robert persists in mortifying his noble flesh, and no one is more resolute in bringing relief to the poor. No pilgrim, I find, no palmer was a more generous alms-giver. The more bereft he found them, the more needy and wretched, the more solicitous he was in providing them with food and clothing. He made splendid offerings to both churches and chapels. I have no means of knowing or ascertaining whether he travelled by land or by sea, for I can find no such information in my written source, and so it is no part of my task to tell you anything about this.* The fact is that he duly arrived in Jerusalem which he was so determined to see; this much is certain. He gave alms at the Holy Sepulchre in the spot where God was buried. Since that time, I believe, no one who went there shed as many contrite tears as he did. Barefoot, with a hair-shirt next to his skin, he went everywhere there was to go, to all the places that Jesus Christ had most often frequented. At that time, people who went on this pilgrimage did not treat the matter lightly. It is well known, I think, that they behaved in a different fashion from those who go nowadays and who turn out to be worse sinners when they get back than they were before they left. The whole of the land of Syria was still in those days in pagan hands. (33962)

When he had completed his prayers and holy devotions, the duke began his journey home. Without mishap, trouble or any obstacle, he reached Nicaea, according to our source. But a foul and evil demon, a renegade from among his retinue who had repudiated the son of the Virgin Mary, gave him some noxious drink that had the effect of separating his soul from his body.* His death was a grievous loss and caused great sorrow since he was still in the prime of life. On the day of the duke's death, it was the year of our Lord 1035 precisely, so I read. He died a holy and glorious death, and so his soul rests among the blessed in celestial Jerusalem. No man was ever wept over and mourned more than he once the news reached Normandy, and the grief of his son, still a child, was immeasurable. The duke was laid to rest and buried in a magnificent church dedicated to the glorious mother of God. It was a bishop's cathedral, and his tomb can still be seen there today, splendidly and richly decorated. All have passed away, the great and the mighty, the valiant and the powerful. One thing that is certain, as we all know, is that death spares no living creature. Everything dies, expires, passes away, [everything is annihilated, obliterated] except serving and loving God, for this is something that can never come to an end. Just like our ancestors, we do not know the day or the hour when it is time for us to go. Our days are numbered. So may God grant and accord us a good and true end, and may he be pleased and willing and deign to admit us into his holy kingdom. (34008)

[2] *Here begins the history of Duke William as Benoît has adapted it into the vernacular.*

I have told you the story of Duke Robert according to my written source which gives a clear and straightforward account of his deeds, his achievements, and his death. Now, in turn, we come to his noble young son, Duke William. There is no one who will not marvel at how things could possibly have turned out as they did, once they have heard tell the story of the hardships and the struggles which his corrupt and treacherous vassals deviously inflicted on him time and time again, of all the misfortunes they brought on him – from which God delivered him – of how he subsequently constrained and overcame them, and made the most arrogant amongst them grovel at his feet, browbeaten, cowed and fearful, and of how he became, as a result, mighty and glorious and more feared than anyone else by virtue of his military power. (34028)

We find recorded in several places how, because of the horrendous crimes committed by their fathers during their lifetime, sons are then driven from their lands, fiefs and castles, killed, ruined or exiled, and how these sons afterwards atoned for the sins of their parents and family. But such things should not have happened to the fine, valiant and intelligent young duke, for we can be sure beyond a shadow of a doubt that his father never committed any illegal act that would have caused him any harm, vexation, hurt or injury. But as we frequently see happen, one good turn ends up getting you a broken neck. We have already told you for certain that some people to whom the father had shown great affection, whom he had promoted, enriched and exalted, afterwards did everything in their power to humiliate and harm the son. Even if his father had shown them particular favours, the son saw little sign of this, finding that they behaved with great cruelty towards him, that they were disloyal, mendacious, and deceitful. (34054)

They showed their respect for his authority as overlord by inflicting suffering on the whole of Normandy. In two hundred different places they erected a large number of fortresses, spiked stockades, tall motte-and-bailey castles and keeps, from which the land and the country were pitilessly laid waste. No request to the duke for justice would ever have been made, since he had neither the power nor sufficient forces to allow him to redress the wrongs that were being committed. His presence did not stop people from inflicting damage and shame on each other. There were few who, even if he had insisted, would ever have held back because of him. Most people rightly said that the land had no lord. It was the duke's own people who suffered the most hardship and humiliation. The young duke himself, noble and peace-loving as he was, suffered also from a situation which would cause him heartfelt anguish but which he could find no means of remedying – a situation for which he could find few people capable of advising him or in whom he could possibly place his trust. Someone he considers one day to be a dear and trustworthy friend turns out the following day to have abandoned him, intent now on doing him harm and driving him out of the land. There is nothing to be done about it: the individual with most power does exactly what he wants to. No one ever heard of such a woefully distressing state of affairs lasting for so long; simply no one was capable of living in peace with his neighbour. (34086)

[3] *How Vauquelin de Ferrières and Hugh of Monfort killed each other.*

Hear now the story of two mighty barons and the culmination of the hostilities and the fierce and merciless wars that those deadly enemies, Vauquelin de Ferrières and Hugh of Monfort, waged against each other. Never was it possible, at that time, for any man alive, any bishop or abbot, to bring about an agreement or any sort of love between them. Both their lands and their armies were finally destroyed. Their disagreements had lasted so long that everyone else, high or low, had no alternative but to seek a place of safety for themselves. The two had repeatedly hurled insults at each another, then pursued each other, defeated each other and reached a point of mutual destruction. (34102)

One fine day the Devil, regardless of the consequences, brought the two sides together in combat. Full of rage and rancour, they duly charged at each other, vicious and beside themselves with mad fury. Many of them were killed there and then. So violently did they strike out at each other with javelins, swords and feathered arrows that the two sides did not separate before both Hugh of Monfort and Vauquelin de Ferrières – so I read in my Latin source – fell dead and bleeding on the battlefield together with most of their fighting men. And this is how, as you can hear for yourselves, these wicked renegades met their end. (34118)

A trustworthy and true friend of the duke, Gilbert, count of [Eu],* also died a particularly callous death. We can tell you exactly how it happened. This Gilbert, so I understand, was the son of Count Geoffrey [of Eu]. He was a forceful, valiant and wise knight, mature in years but not old. By virtue of his good nature and his outstanding loyalty, he was made guardian to young Duke William whom he served most efficiently, seeing to his education as well as to his general upbringing. No one looked after him better than Geoffrey, who became an extremely well-trusted friend of his. He had a close associate in the region, Vauquelin de Pont-Herchenfret, who asked Gilbert to come and see him. What a fine piece of iniquitous behaviour you are about to hear! Gilbert duly went along with a very small retinue, as he had no misgivings or anything to fear. But Vauquelin's intention had been a treacherous one, and he killed Gilbert along with Fulk fitz Giroie, a friend of Gilbert's who had accompanied him. The country was, as you can see, in the grip of depravity, unrestrained lawlessness and injustice. (34144)

Very shortly thereafter the closest of William's chamberlains – Turold he was called, I believe – a wise and courtly person of great refinement, was treacherously killed in similar circumstances, and the duke never discovered why. (34150)

Listen now what happened to William's steward Osbern, a noble, valiant, and loyal knight, who was the nephew of the most noble, worthy and wise Countess Gunnor [wife of Duke Richard I].* Courtly, urbane, and honourable, Osbern was a person of unrivalled authority. The duke was, I believe, at Vaudreuil, and here he shared a bed with Osbern. Just listen to the extraordinary plot that the Devil hatches! Osbern was, then, sleeping next to his lord who had a particularly strong affection for him, and it was here that he was strangled to death as he slept. So dismayed was the duke at this, so distressed and so furious that he was all but inconsolable. He did not know who to turn to. He had no friend more intimate than Osbern had been, no one to whom he could better confide his secrets. There was no one at all who dared venture out to travel to wherever it might be.* (34172)

[4] *How [Roger de Beaumont, son of Honfroi de Vieilles,] killed Roger de Tosny in battle.*

My Latin source here records and preserves the memory of an exceptionally criminal and base knight whose deeds brought him hostility and infamy. His name was Roger de Tosny, and he was descended from an aristocratic family of Danish extraction founded by someone who was known as Malehuche and who had come over with Rollo. Such was the ancestry of Roger, an effectively combative knight. With a large company of his relatives he went to Spain in pursuit of wealth. He acquired, I find, considerable renown as well as a great deal of gold and money. Once he was quite certain that Duke Robert had died, he came back to Normandy, full of arrogance and bent on mischief. His greed and his deluded ambition are such that he believes he can simply take whatsoever he wants without anyone offering any resistance or putting up any defence. His intention is to fish in troubled waters, but he is going to find that he has a high price to pay for that. (34196)

Once he was back in Normandy, heavily loaded down with riches, hostile and implacable, he launched into his criminal activities, behaving with great arrogance towards the young duke, his lord. His view was that the present state of affairs was wrong and disreputable, and that things could not go on like this. It was unseemly and not right for the son of a concubine to be duke. "It is shameful and humiliating for us in Normandy," he said, "to have as lord someone born to this Herleva, the small-town daughter of Fulbert, the small-town tanner from Falaise.* This is something I will not put up with. There are other members in the ducal family, worthy and distinguished sons and nephews. Let one of these be taken on and made duke, for it will be shameful and humiliating for us to be in any way the subjects of some non-entity, some puny little bastard!" (34218)

This is how he spoke, like the uncouth lout he was, bent only on inflicting harm on people of every description. So malicious was he that he paid allegiance to no one. With the people he had made his allies and with the armed men he enlisted from his family, he frequently caused trouble for the duke, and would let nothing deter him. He had no relationships with his neighbours and showed them no loyalty, kindness or affection. In particular he hated Honfroi de Vieilles: he would plunder, lay waste, and burn his land almost every day and frequently hurled abuse at him. Though Honfroi was an old man, advanced in years, he was nonetheless a high-born and intelligent knight. (34234)

One day Roger, as was his habit, had taken a large number of armed men and forced his way into Honfroi's land in search of booty. Being unable to tolerate such behaviour any longer, Honfroi singled out his second son Roger, who at that time was lord of Beaumont, and said to him: "However it turns out for you, go, fight and take our revenge on them. What I want is for you to put an end, once and for all, to this outrageous behaviour. How is it possible for anyone to tolerate so much?" Roger de Tosny, having seen his men duly armed, believed that in no time at all they would go and collect their plunder. As for Roger de Beaumont, he was extremely happy when he saw them riding towards him, convinced as he was that things would go his way and that they would all soon be his prisoners. Without another thought, both sides charged at full tilt. The fighting was so intense that many of those in the first clash found their sides covered in blood, and such violent blows were exchanged that, before long, the battlefield was flowing with the blood from their chests and their sides. I can tell you that, with their trusty sharp steel spears and their glinting swords, they struck down dead first of all Roger de Tosny and then, immediately afterwards, his two sons, Herbert, the elder, and Elinant. None of the three emerged alive from the attack; all died on the same day. Such was the joy that nothing similar had ever been seen, since as long as they were alive, no one could live in peace. These arrogant and base criminals met their doom, and it was no great loss or cause for grief, since this is what they inevitably deserved. Robert de Grentemesnil was mortally wounded in this battle and greatly mourned by his sons. He did not survive for very long but died within three weeks, leaving his land to his sons, Hugh, the elder of the two, and Robert. (34281)

Life has always been like this: people struggle and resist, some die and others live on, one comes out on top while the other ends up underneath. But it is always the bravest who are at an advantage, and people go out of their way to pay them respect, just as long as loyalty is their guiding light and shows them the way, as was the case with Roger de Beaumont. Our source explains how, after God had allowed him to enjoy the glory of having killed his enemies, he remained, for the rest of his days, a loyal, sincere and truthful person. Roger was the founder of the monastery of Préaux,* where God's service is celebrated with great devotion, much to the benefit of his soul. He showed great fidelity to Duke William, who loved him as much as he loved himself, and to this he owed an eminence and the sort of honour that none of his ancestors ever enjoyed. He married a noble young lady named, I discover, Adeline, the eldest daughter of Count Waleran of Meulan. I believe they had two sons, Robert and Henry. The former was later count and lord of Meulan for a full twenty-seven years – no one would deny this – while Henry, according to my source, was made earl of Warwick, as will be described later. (34312)

[5] *How [Duke] William arranged the marriage of his mother to Lord Herluin [de Conteville].*

After the death of Duke Robert, as my written source informs me, the duke most fittingly gave his mother Herleva to be the wife of a knight of noble descent called Herluin [de Conteville]. Within a short time, she had two sons with him, who were brought up with great care and at considerable expense; they were called Robert and Odo, the first a knight and the second a cleric. The duke was very fond of both, making one a count [of Mortain] and the other a bishop [of Bayeux], as my source records. (34326)

[6] *How the king of France had Tillières destroyed and taken away from Duke William.*

The young duke was much wiser than was usual for someone of his age. It upset him a great deal to see such great outrages happening before his eyes, and so much diabolic violence throughout Normandy, ever-rising and continually on the increase. This displeased and irked him enormously, but the rebellion nevertheless grew day by day in boldness, power and strength. The wisest, those with most influence, the most loyal-hearted, all those with the most substantial estates and to whom his father had shown the greatest affection, these were the sort of people that William drew around him, whom he rewarded with honours and gave expensive presents to. He went to great lengths to solicit them and then to treat them with affection and love. Those who loved and believed in God were more than willing to serve the duke and help maintain his authority. Acting on their advice, he agreed to appoint one particular baron, called Ralph de Gacé, a fine, loyal, brave and upright knight, to be principal master of his household, his own personal guardian, and leader and commander-in-chief of his armed forces. These were the people who strove to uphold the duke's rights which had been forcibly denied him on so many occasions. There was much opposition to this, giving rise to serious disputes, disgraceful and irksome behaviour, much high-handedness and lawlessness. These disloyal criminals and law-breakers, in order to carry out their plan to disinherit Duke William without restraint – something they were unable to do for themselves – went off to the king of France. Both in private and in public they told him that, unless God intervened, the writing was now on the wall as far as the young duke was concerned. (34368)

The king at that time was, as I told you earlier, Henri [I]. He had no objection, indeed he was quite willing, to give orders to a large number of men to go and destroy Normandy. They duly invaded the country, robbing and dealing death and destruction. The poor were absolutely distraught. Acting on the advice of several of the invaders, King Henri, in a spirit of enmity, brutality and sedition, came to Evreux with the intention of capturing it. The people, however, proved unwilling to surrender, so he laid waste the whole land and took and carried off its wealth. All the requests, all the kindnesses and all the great favours which Duke Robert had granted the king, many of which I have already told you about, were forgotten, lost sight of, and never even brought to mind. What the king did do was to say quite openly, and make clear to everyone, that never would Duke William find peace in the kingdom of France at his hands, or indeed at anyone else's, for whatever reason, right or wrong, unless he handed Tillières over to him or razed it completely to the ground in such a way that no trace of any sort of fortress was left standing.* Were he to do so immediately, he would be assured of the king's goodwill. Henri promises and swears that he will maintain peace with Normandy for four years, as long as, within this time, William refrains from fortifying or rebuilding Tillières, and as long as, during these four years, no wall or moat would be built up or repaired, and no keep or palisade reconstructed. William took advice on this, but the advice he was given was extremely bad, namely that he should do exactly what the king required of him and to refuse the king nothing for fear that he might take Normandy away from him. The people who urged this concession on him subsequently came to regret it bitterly. (34414)

There was no means of concealing this arrangement, and news quickly spread far and wide that Tillières was to be knocked down, demolished and levelled. To put it in a nutshell, this distressed a large number of people. The duke had appointed Gilbert Crispin commander of the castle and he had held the post for a number of years. When he got to hear of this, he was extremely annoyed and unhappy. He swore that he would never hand Tillières over to William. He immediately took possession of it along with the best of his fighters and, determined never to abandon it or to surrender, they set about preparing the best defence they could. (34428)

When the king of France got to know of this, he lost no time in coming with a large army to attack and besiege Tillières. He summoned the Normans to come, together with the young duke, whether he wanted to or not. They erected their siege engines, declaring that they would not leave until they had taken the castle, if it was at all possible. In this way the siege of the castle began, and it would not have been taken as quickly as it was had Gilbert not known that his lord would not have acted to his detriment. The duke had joined the king at the siege and repeatedly asked Gilbert to hand the castle over to him without the need for any fighting. He told him that it would be beyond his control if he or the king's men destroyed it. Bitter tears come streaming down from both his eyes, but in present circumstances that is what fate decrees. (34448)

Gilbert addresses William angrily: "My fair lord," he says, "I can tell you that you look like a pretty poor sort of conqueror coming here and forcibly expropriating what is in fact your own land. I shall live to see the day when you will bitterly regret this. The people who advised you to do this are tricksters, liars, perjurers and traitors. Had I not feared being accused of acting wrongfully, there would never have been any question of my handing over the castle keep. I would rather have been burned alive or hanged. But you are indisputably my lord, and it is not right for me to go against your wishes and occupy a castle that belongs to you." With great sadness and sorrow he and his men left the castle. The king swore on holy relics that he would abide strictly by the agreement they would reach, whereupon, without further ado, they made the castle over to him. Like it or not, it was set on fire, demolished and razed to the ground. They pulled it down in full view of the Normans and before their very eyes in order to shame, thwart and insult them. The king very much wanted to see their arrogance brought low. This was to be his tactic for the future, and he starts by seizing the opportunity to do so now. He will ruffle their feathers just as his ancestors before him used to do; he will follow suit even at the cost of creating thousands of enemies. You could often have heard him laughing and joking to those around him on seeing the Normans shedding tears and lamenting over the castle. The Normans were extremely distressed at what they saw as a humiliation, but this sort of suffering is inevitable in a country where traitors and ill-intentioned people find opportunities for inflicting damage on their lord. (34490)

Off the king rides, happy and rejoicing at having demolished the castle. Duke William hopes that Henri will deliver a durable, stable and unbroken peace without any detriment to him or any loss of status. His hopes are, however, very naïvely misplaced, and within the space of two months, the king showed him precisely why. There was never any more talk of trust or of oaths, and the terms of the agreement between them were not even mentioned. The king simply ignored it and dropped everything. Then, together with his knights and the army that he had raised, he came back into Normandy. He advanced as far as the Hiémois which they stripped bare, pillaging and capturing everything, and taking all the possessions they could back to France. (34508)

The king had Argentan burned to the ground and left nothing standing. The inhabitants had, to some extent, moved off elsewhere. You never heard of a town so utterly and completely destroyed. The king went back home by way of Tillières, and he gave orders for it to be rebuilt, strengthened and refortified, and for its huge moats to be renovated. The walls were raised and built high, walls that were thick, strong and provided with battlements, while the keep and defensive scaffolding were tall, well designed and impregnable. He has the castle garrisoned and has men stationed in it. Henceforth he is in a very good position, and he can prosper now that he has succeeded in doing what he set out to do. He may well be right as far as other situations are concerned, but in this particular case he has completely overstepped the limits in matters of pledged word, trustworthiness and truth. There was much discussion about this in Normandy, and much advice sought and given. They say that the whole business of rebuilding the castle is extremely unsatisfactory: they have reached the point where they are being deprived of what is rightfully theirs. This is their undoing, the end. They bitterly curse those who had approved of the castle being handed over and then pulled down and demolished. "Alas," they say, "how painful it is when a land loses its rightful lord! As soon as there is no one to defend it, anyone can come along and buy, sell or destroy it. That's all there is to it. From now on the French have got the upper hand. From now on they're going to despoil us even more than before. Ah! William, noble young lord, what a tragedy, what a calamity that you are not yet a knight! This seems to be far too long in coming, for they are already in the process of depriving you of your inheritance."* (34548)

[7] *How Thurstan [Goz], viscount of the Hiémois, fortified Falaise in defiance of his liege lord [ca. 1043].*

According to my written source, there was a viscount in the Hiémois by the name of Thurstan, a powerful man of noble lineage. Just hear how badly he behaved towards his legitimate lord! He saw William as a little boy with no power to raise a significant number of fighting men. He sees him under pressure from the king of France and is afraid more than anything else that Henri might declare war on him, take his land away from him, capture his castles, his men and his property without his being able to put up any defence. Just hear what sort of criminal act he devises: however painful it might be for his lord, he will take over Falaise castle from him. He intends to make it his personal property, and this is the end to which he will devote all his efforts and energy. Who would have thought that he, the guardian of the castle, would have dreamt up such a crime? When he knew for certain that the castle was well equipped and provisioned, and that he had henceforth nothing to fear, he had a challenge issued to his lord. He treacherously reneged on his homage and his oath of fidelity. He had some knights brought from France in whom he placed great trust, together with some tough aspiring knights, archers, men-at-arms and crossbowmen. His plan was to hold out against his legitimate Norman overlord for as long as he lived, but his great crime and arrogance are such that the end result will soon turn out to be entirely different. (34584)

When the duke learned what was going on and how serious this act of opposition was, how Thurstan had acted so shamelessly before God, and had so wickedly turned his back on his lord, William summoned and brought together as many fighting men as he could and, furious and incensed, went immediately and laid siege to Falaise. He begs his men to do their utmost in the name of God to ensure that the castle is brought back into his hands. With their helmets strapped on, and spurred on by their courage and fury, the duke's troops begin the assault. It was an extremely savage exchange, because there was a great deal of hand-to-hand fighting. Arrows were shot, spears were hurled, there was so much shouting and uproar, so many wounded people, many dead bodies, such unbelievable forays, such scaling of the ramparts by foot soldiers, so much shooting of crossbow bolts into the castle, be it out of fear or self-assurance, so much shattering, knocking down and demolishing of the wall with pickaxes, and so much fighting with those defending inside that it will never be said or recounted that any army fought so fiercely or so defied death to take such a strongly defended castle as these people did. And no one will ever have succeeded, as these men did, in piercing, knocking down and completely demolishing most of the walls where they were at their thickest and strongest. The result was that, had not night fallen, and had not the defenders shown such resilience, the duke's men would have managed to take the fight right into the castle. But the fighting came to an end because nightfall was upon them so soon. The attacking army was extremely confident because they believed it was certain that they would take the castle the following day. (34622)

Those on the inside defending were terrified, with each man going in fear of his life. Neither did Thurstan have any reason to feel at ease. He cannot help being highly anxious at seeing the walls collapse around him, and so many casualties among his men. He could have had no idea that he would see himself attacked in this way so quickly – he thought he would be safe for at least seven months. What he sees now are the huge armies, the unspeakable slaughter, the ground running red with his men's blood, he sees the duke rousing his troops, and he dares not wait for a second attack. Before day dawns, he sends word to the duke of Normandy asking him to be kind enough to let him and his men go free:

he will hand the castle over to him as well as all the land in his possession. Most unwillingly the duke granted his request. What William would have wanted was to have got his hands on Thurstan. People had difficulty in convincing him to act as he did, for what he really wanted was to forcibly take Thurstan prisoner to have him hanged on the scaffold or mutilated or drawn and quartered like a common criminal. But in short they persuaded him to agree to Thurstan's request. It was still early morning when the defenders vacated the castle. Most of then make off on foot in disgrace, reviled and the object now of a storm of catcalls and insults. Thurstan's irresponsibility cost him all of his inheritance in Normandy, and I find no record – and little do I care – of his ever being reinstated thereafter. (34656)

Robert, archbishop of Rouen, a fine cleric and an upstanding man held in great respect in the secular world, died and passed over at this time [1037]. Malger was elected in his place, but before he could take up his crozier, numerous disputes broke out. He was hated by a large number of people: he was overweeningly arrogant, untrustworthy, envious and deceitful. He was Duke Robert's brother, but they did not have the same mother. Duke Richard [II] had had children with two wives, the first of whom was called Judith who gave birth to only two siblings: the youngest being Richard, the one who died when still a young knight, and Duke Robert. Richard's second wife was called Papia, and with her he had two sons: one was Malger, according to my written source, the other – and the fairer of the two – was William. These were the uncles of the young duke, and they ought to have cherished him and sought to increase and enhance his honour. But they were always incapable of loving him, and he could never place his trust in them, for both were most deceitful liars. The duke granted Malger's brother William the whole of the county of Talou about as far as Eu, and he made him a rich and powerful man by creating him master of the Pays de Caux as far as Ponthieu. He had a tower and keep constructed, palisaded and walled, at the very top of the hill at Arques,* providing him with a strong and safe castle. Just hear now the story of this cursed and execrated renegade of an uncle! His nephew, the young duke, had granted him such fiefs as these in order that he serve him and remain faithful, but the count conceived a ruthless plan: he enlists the assistance of the king of France and, having thoroughly fortified his castle, revolts against his lord in a base act of treachery. The duke summoned him to his presence with the aim of punishing so great a crime and curtailing his criminal, irresponsible and depraved behaviour. But the count had grown so emboldened and so entrenched in his lawless animosity against him that he openly declared that, as long as he lived, he would never miss an opportunity of doing him harm. And if the duke wanted to make peace with him, he had only to give him more land, for he was so closely related to the ducal family that he had a claim on a share of the inheritance. He concentrates on making careful and thorough preparations and on holding himself in readiness, for he knows that the duke will come and attack him. And this is what happens without delay. William sends for and summons his fighting men from all over, and with as many Norman troops as he can muster, he marches against his uncle. If he can get his hands on him, his aim is to give him such a hard time that his pain, his anguish, his unhappiness and his grief will last for a whole seven years – and not a single day less. The duke did not, however, find sufficient strength or any opportunity to storm and take the tower. But they did find time to have a huge ditch dug out and a securely enclosed siege-work constructed right there at the foot of the hill, in such a way that the people at the top would not dare to venture down unless it were to capitulate and surrender. (34734)

Once his siege castle had been provided with supplies and with a garrison of brave and competent knights and men-at-arms, the young duke rode off home. My guess is that the men up in the tower are in an extremely uncomfortable position: none of them can come down, and no one can go up to support them or maintain their morale. There is no possibility of them fetching provisions despite the fact that their food is beginning to run out and they do not even have enough to last the month. This is a cause of great distress to them, and they send word to King Henri to make him aware of their plight, begging him, for pity's sake, to come to their assistance and not to let them down, so short of supplies are they. They tell him how much the siege has cut them off, shut and hemmed them in: he should come without delay and bring help, just as he had promised. This is what the king did immediately, and there was no competent knight in France that he did not bring with him there to Saint-Aubin in Normandy. The foot soldiers and the mounted knights made camp close to Arques. Never were there anywhere cheerier or more merry troops or people who would have liked to have enjoyed themselves so much. Those of the duke's men whom he had left in the lower castle bravely and courageously selected the best fighters among themselves, and these were sent off, in their shining white chain-mail hauberks, to lie in ambush. The others, meanwhile, came close up to the king's army to see whether they might possibly goad anyone into engaging with them. They were putting more effort into doing this than into luring them into the ambush they had prepared. This was their tactic on this occasion, for when the French caught sight of them, they immediately seized their shields and rode their horses straight at them. You can be sure that in the clash that ensued there was many a lance shattered and many a saddle left empty. The Normans withstood the attack until they found themselves outnumbered seven to one. At this point, the French forced them to retreat and pursued them so closely that they would have had the worst of it and been taken prisoner before they could have reached the lower castle, had it not been for their comrades waiting in ambush who lost no time in coming to their rescue. They came bounding out of their hiding place, shouting their battle-cry in unison, and without hesitation ferociously set about splitting their enemies' hauberks, ripping open their midriffs and hurling them dead off their horses onto the ground, as out came their naked steel blades. Why spin out further my account of the battle? No one will ever hear tell of this number of knights performing such feats. They stunned the French and inflicted such damage and devastation on them that one hundred corpses were left lying on their backs, bleeding, deathly pale and black and blue. Among the first to be killed was Count Enguerrand of [Ponthieu],* a noble knight of high repute, together with many other important knights, all fine, powerful, brave and experienced men whose loss caused much grief. Another name I find recorded was Hugh Bardolf, who was made prisoner along with the closest of his kinsmen. Before the king duly arrived, the Normans had time to celebrate their victory. They left the battlefield strewn with dead bodies, having taken many valuable prisoners and fine war-horses. Unhurried, they had taken refuge in their strongly palisaded fort well before the king was able to get back. And even when he did attack them, they did not let him have his own way without putting up such a stout defence that they ended up incurring no losses. (34822).

The king of France was extremely annoyed to see how badly his men had fared. So displeased was he at the opposition he encountered that he was unwilling to stay around any longer. His men supplied those who were besieged in the castle, and who had almost reached the point of starvation, with reinforcements and provisions. But their fear is that their food will run out again before the king, in due course, comes back in time to help them. They begin to realise the folly of their ways; no one amongst them is foolish enough to make a joke of it. Shame-faced, unhappy and ill-humoured, the king of France returned home. (34836)

William, [count of Arques] acknowledged and knew what he had to do. He could neither seize the castle from his nephew nor defend it against his attack. This lying and despicable traitor, painfully, unhappily and very much under duress, surrendered the tower and the fortress without coming away with anything but his own life and those of his men. Count William was subsequently exiled from the whole of the country. He had got his just deserts. It is quite right for anyone who does what he did to have to pay the price. May the same fate befall all those dishonest liars and traitors, malevolent and ill-intentioned enough to act disloyally towards their lords! (34854)

[8] *How Duke William was almost betrayed and murdered at Valognes.*

This strife and discord, all this warring and these unheard-of events had lasted for a very long time, but there was something even worse in store. Up until now everything had been child's play compared to what you are now about to hear. As you know, it often happens, in times of strife and terrible suffering, that people will not see peace come about until some really grave misfortunes have occurred. When some great building that cannot survive any longer collapses, a new one is made, a better decorated and more beautiful one. A kingdom can remain a long time in a sorry state, torn apart, ruined and at the point of death, until the point is reached when certain people turn out to be losers and others to come out on top. It is these latter, as God disposes, who bring about joy and lasting peace. This is precisely what happened in Normandy. There was so much war and devilry that the worst sorts of lawlessness seemed, all of a sudden, universal. Then they ceased, and it was all over, with the result that the fatherless kingdom grew in power over many years. I will tell you the story of this just as I find it in my written source, without my deliberately adding anything that is untrue. (34884)

Duke William, having governed the country now for twelve years, had grown up and left childhood far behind him. Such a handsome man as he could not be seen: he was so well-built, had such a striking appearance and such a noble bearing, that other handsome men were ugly in comparison. No one rode with such skill, no one was so brave-hearted. In all the hardships he had to bear, no one would have ventured to behave as he did in knowing how to wait for the favourable opportunity or the right moment. He was intelligent and clear-sighted. He loved and served God and was God-fearing, and never remiss in such matters. He often had the deeds and the sayings of the most illustrious and greatest of his ancestors read out in his presence, for these provided him with both the material and the pattern on which to base his own behaviour and actions. These taught him many of the things that turned out to be of most use to him. He sought just and lawful advice where he knew he would find it, and this was the basis on which he very much wished to act. He knew exactly how a knight should behave, and showed such competence in bearing arms that everyone thought it remarkable to see such skill and courage in a person of his age. It was during this time, as the Latin history records, that a horrendously difficult situation arose, one of such wicked deception and life-threatening treachery that it was a wonder – and always will be – that William managed to extricate himself safely from it. (34920)

In the Cotentin and the Bessin there were two noblemen, one called Nigel, the other Rannulf. They were both viscounts, powerful and well-endowed with land, forceful and well connected, yet at the same time cunning scoundrels and law-breakers. They embarked on an undertaking that, before they could with-draw from it, had caused a thousand men to drop lifeless to the ground, their souls separated from their bodies. (34930)

Just hear the violent conflict they caused!* Guy, a nobleman from Burgundy, was the son of Count Rainald who had married Adeliza, daughter of good Duke Richard II. According to our Latin source, this lady was the sister of Duke Robert, as closely related to him as that. This Guy, her son, was taken to his cousin Duke William in Normandy as a small child, a young boy. He was brought up in luxury at William's court, for they were of approximately the same age. William very much loved and cherished Guy, and when he had dubbed him a knight, he granted him an estate of which he and his heirs were owners in their own right – a magnificent estate with a fine, rich and well-fortified castle at Brionne. He was also granted Vernon in addition to many other fiefs. Guy concentrated day and night on consolidating his position as much as he was able. He grew more arro-gant than anyone else and then betrayed his lord. Knowing him to be a bastard, Guy despised William and talked of him in highly derogatory terms. He was the one who should have been duke, Guy said; he had more right to the title than William. It was demeaning for him and unreasonable to consider him as his lord. No one spoke of William in such vicious and unbecoming terms, or so disre-spectfully. Guy wished to claim Normandy for himself and started to wage war on William. In doing so, he acted just like those reprobates who, because they desire everything, end up losing everything. May God for ever deny that sort of specimen any good fortune! It was on the advice of the renegades Rannulf from the Bessin, Nigel from the Cotentin, Haimo [Dentatus], an antichrist, and one Grimoult du Plessis, that Guy set out on this venture that was subsequently to turn out so disastrously for them and all their families. (34978)

But this Guy was a very crafty customer as well as a faithless and base scoundrel, and, thanks to his unrivalled deceitfulness, he inveigled many of the duke's vassals into deserting him. He promised that he would share out the land amongst them. He was just like Absalom who forsook his father King David: if Absalom was in the wrong, as he was, so Guy acted disloyally by waging war on his cousin the duke and by alienating the duke's men from his affection and turning them thereby into forsworn traitors. Guy gets them to support him in everything he does, to attack William head-on, and to swear to kill him. The duke is the victim of numerous hostilities, and the situation takes a turn for the worse. (34996)

Before the duke had any inkling of the conspiracy of those men who has sworn to kill him, he went, together with the members of his personal household, to Valognes to relax, hunting and shooting, and to deal with his affairs that were weighty, complicated and forever piling up. One evening, when the knights and his attendants had gone and the court was deserted, the duke was left on his own. When everyone had departed and, since it was bed time, gone to bed, all in different places, the malevolent four struck: Nigel, Haimo, Rannulf and Grimoult, those dastardly, forsworn traitors to God and to their lord, together with their closest accomplices and without anyone seeing, slip their shining white hauberks on over their under-shirts and under their tunics. Something drastic is going to happen here. Unless he is under the protection of the Holy Spirit, William is about to be murdered: he is a dead man. (35020)

Hear the reason why he was saved from death! A fool, a deranged lunatic, insane and the frequent victim of stone-throwing, was at that time resident at court. He was called Golés.* That particular night he had gone to bed in the same house where the authors of this dastardly plot had put on their armour. He had fallen asleep but then woken up again, much alarmed and frightened at finding himself surrounded by armed men. He immediately got up, crept away and fled. With a heavy staff flung over his shoulder, he came running straight to the great hall, shouting, calling out, knocking and making a commotion. He is rushing around in great distress. Coming up to the chamber door, he shouts loud enough for everyone to hear: "Run for it!," he began, "They're coming to kill you all. Get up, you poor wretches, get up and run for it! You're going to be slaughtered. Hey, William, what are you to do? They're going to kill you. You're going to die. Unless you get out of here in some way or other and make a run for it, you're going to be butchered. Watch out, don't be complacent, because I've seen them putting their armour on. Get up, my fair friend, be quick and escape so as not to get caught right here!" (35052)

When the duke heard this commotion, it was little wonder that he feared for his life. He has no desire to get further information or to enquire what is going on. He leaps out of bed, crosses himself, and without pausing to find his socks and shoes, runs to put on his short riding cape and grab his steel sword. One of his stewards, who was thoroughly frightened, had brought him a strong, swift and frisky horse, which the duke lost no time in mounting. He had not yet ridden out of the hall when he heard the men arrive who had come to murder him. This is how our Lord God protects those it pleases him to love. The fool, far from calming down, keeps shouting, so uncontrollably mad is he. When he catches sight of the plotters, he berates them: "You've got here too late, it seems to me. You've been cheated, and your plot has failed. The duke is off and away. He'll make life difficult for you from now on: he will retaliate and put you to shame. If you've given him a bad night, he's sure to give you a bad day. May the traitor come to a bad end!" (35082)

When they heard that the duke was making off and escaping from them, they were seized with despondency, mental, emotional and physical. They all cried out: "To horse! Let's see who will be brave and courageous enough now to catch up with him! We must not lose heart, for if he gets away from us, never again, as long as he lives, will he have confidence in us or show us any affection, nor will he even let us remain anywhere in Normandy. Let's pool all of our energy and strength, all of us together, young and old, before he manages to find his way into some hiding-place or castle!" That night the duke was pursued for over fifteen leagues. If they can find the opportunity, their stratagem will turn out to be life-threatening for him. Our Lord God forbid! (35104)

The duke rides on, forsaken, avoiding death as best he can. It was a fine, moon-lit night with no wind. He came to the ford to find that the tide was out, which made him very happy. God is keeping watch over him and showing him the way so that he comes to no harm that night; otherwise he would have been in for a nasty surprise. Rather than waiting for his pursuers to catch up with him, he rode around here and there, sometimes wading in water, sometimes following roads, trying to find his way – in great trepidation, all alone and without a guide. Before dawn broke, he had crossed the fords on the river Vire. Dejected and bitterly angry, he sighs at having all the time, and unremittingly, the same bad luck: always horrible, always harsh, always brutal in the same way, always painful with no remedy in sight, and it gets worse and worse the whole time. Before he had eliminated one misfortune – having already dealt with a large number of others

– and before being able to get over it properly, a half dozen others have sprung up, more agonising and more distressing and a hundred times more dispiriting. He has no idea at present what road to take, where to go or where he is going to end up, since Bayeux would not provide him with any security, any possibility of finding somewhere to stay or people he could trust. He is minded to go across country, without knowing exactly where, to lower down towards the sea, somewhere where he would not be recognised. It was already mid-morning when he turned off in that direction and passed through a small country town,* taking great care to keep his identity hidden. (35144)

The lord of the town, so my Latin source informs me, was a wise knight called Hubert [de Ryes], a minor noble who attached great importance to reputation and honour.* He had got up early to go to mass, and William, whether he liked it or not, could not avoid him when he suddenly crossed his path. Hubert examined him, then recognised him, and began speaking to him. On recognising him, however, he had never been so astounded, and his heart gave a leap: there William stood, alone and with no attendant, without socks or shoes, his sweating horse exhausted and drained, with blood streaming down its flanks. He was in great difficulty, of this Hubert had no doubt. He lifted his hands in consternation: "My lord," he says, "do tell me what is happening. Why are you travelling like this? Is anyone pursuing you? What trouble are you in? Your horse is sweating profusely. Hide nothing from me; tell me frankly what's on your mind. What's happening? This is something quite extraordinary, and I've never seen anything like it before, a prince behaving in this way. Something terrible and violent is going on. Tell me the whole story, and have no fear on my account." (35176)

To this the duke replies: "Noble knight, see to it that you remain truthful, honest and loyal to me. There is no question of my hiding anything from you. Will you swear fealty to me, just like you would to God? I'll reveal the whole business to you, but I'll need to cut a long story short. Yesterday evening I was in bed asleep when I was suddenly woken up. Circumstances were such that, had I taken the trouble to get dressed, I would have been in imminent danger of losing my life. I had no time even to put my shoes on, or wait for any attendant or companion." He goes on to tell him the gist of what happened next. "Nigel and the others," he says, naming them, "those traitors and Judas-like renegades would have killed me on the spot if I hadn't got away. But I will still not be free of them until I can reach somewhere where I could do my best to defend myself. They are after me, of that I am sure, and this fills me full of sorrow and dread. If they catch up with me or get in front of me, I can be quite sure I'll lose my life. I'm in urgent need of your help." (35203)

"Oh my God," says Hubert, "holy Mary! Whoever heard of such disloyalty, such a crime, such unheard-of betrayal? How could they ever have dreamt up something like this? Who can you trust anymore? Place yourself in my hands, fair lord, and I'll see to it that you are rescued and kept safe." "My friend, endless thanks be to God!" Hubert helps him dismount. His horse was no longer of any use to him, and there was no alternative but to leave it behind. Hubert hands his own horse over to William by placing the bridle squarely in his hands, and telling him that he need not fear it will let him down. (35218)

This gentleman had three sons, first-class knights, brave and bold. He has them make ready immediately and strap on their trusty steel swords. "Here is your lord," he says. "He is being pursued by traitors and forsworn renegades who want to see him dead. See to it that he remains safe and that nothing bad happens to him through your fault. And if things turn out really badly, change places with him. Ensure that you get the worst of it rather than that harm comes to him or he dies. Make certain for as long as you live that he is never killed while he is under your protection. Someone who dies for his lord earns for himself glory and honour. If there is no other alternative, you will die yourselves in his place. I insist on your giving up your lives for his." "My lord," they say, "we will be delighted to do whatever you want. He will have nothing to fear as long as there is strength left in our bodies." Whereupon they each mount their horse. Hubert says: "Take him straight to Falaise; straight there, mind you, however much it might irk those traitors!" He told them exactly the way to go, all the secret byways and the villages to cross to get them there in the most direct way. They set off instantly, crossed the Foupendant* ford and, after meeting and speaking to no one, much to their delight reached Falaise. The news spread rapidly and was known throughout the town: countless faces streamed with tears of grief, anxiety and suffering. No case of treason gave rise to so many conversations, to such uproar, such hostile gossip or so much dismay among a large number of people. (35262)

Hear what was happening meanwhile to worthy Hubert! He was anxious about how things were going and fearful of getting news. There he was, nervously standing on the drawbridge to his house, when up galloped the men who had been pursuing the duke all night. Hubert recognised them from afar. It was urgent for them not to lose a minute, for they were not very far behind William. (35274)

They shouted out to him in an intimidating fashion: "On your word and by everything you hold dear, tell us if you saw William pass by here. Hide nothing, and be careful not to lie to us!" "Which William are you talking about?" "We mean that evil, arrogant bastard." "Oh yes," Hubert replied, "just a moment ago. Why do you ask, and what's happening?" "Come with us and we'll tell you. Join forces with us!" "Gladly. I want nothing more than to see his huge arrogance cut down to size. One thing I'll tell you and that's for sure: he'll get no truce or fealty from me. If I can possibly do anything about it, we'll have a different lord from him before I come back here. It was a shameful day for Normandy when he became its lord." He mounts his horse and sets off in front of the others, doing everything in his power to misdirect and deceive them. He leads and steers them far away from the path and the direction which the duke and his sons had taken. He continued doing this right up to midday until his behaviour could no longer come under suspicion, and at this point he returned home. That was the start of a spate of extraordinary false rumours resulting in everyone in the country saying that Duke William had been treacherously murdered that night and killed. This is the reason why the whole of the Bessin and the territory of the Cotentin lapsed into lawlessness. Whoever had the power and the brute force could simply take and keep other people's property. The peasants put up little resistance, since they could not be sure of acquiring any means of self-defence. In this way there was a sense of free-for-all in the area. (35318)

Those who were supporters of the duke, grieving, disconsolate and now reduced to tears, do not know where on earth to go to look for their lord's body, so great is their distress at believing him to have been killed that night. Ah! How they shed tears as they set off to fly across the country, grieving and weeping, to seek news of their lord! They curse and fulminate against the traitors, and against Grimoult in particular, the lawless renegade who planned and carried out the entire coup. (35332)

[9] *How the duke went to ask for aid and succour from the king of France.*

In this way the country fell into a state of complete turmoil, becoming a land of pillage, destruction and death. For more than sixty years, the common people and the good folk had not been in such a wretched state, and so much violence had been unheard-of. Normandy had few viscounts or people in positions of authority who recognised the duke as their overlord, or who responded by paying him a single penny of the rent they owed him, and he was not able to impose his justice on such people. Barons, counts and minor nobles as well as those forsworn traitors had taken over control of the whole country, and had destroyed it all. The duke would not venture out and cross his own country, and the general opinion was that he should be disinherited. (35350)

Seeing what the situation was and how people had forsaken him, Duke William felt heartbroken. So he went off to France to King Henri and told him his tale of woe. "Sire," he said, "I have no one I can trust anymore to come to my rescue except God and yourself. All my vassals are waging war on me, and they have so withdrawn their loyalty from me that they no longer keep their promises or agreements or observe their oaths, and they refuse me homage and allegiance. They seize, steal and burn my land with the result that I have nothing left. Sire, I say to you and remind you that it is your duty not to let me down. My father had me pay homage to you when he went off and left me the land. You are my liege lord for Normandy, and I owe you military service and aid, and this is something that you cannot, in your turn, refuse me. And may I remind you that, when your mother Constance tried to expel, disinherit and exile you, it was thanks to my father that France was restored to you.* You came to him in Normandy with a much reduced retinue, and he acknowledged you as his overlord and received you with honours. He came to your assistance in your time of need, whether near or far, and brought about such peace for you in France that you have never since had any trouble there. Now, I pray and beg you, reward me for this and pay me back in kind. Come back with me to Normandy and avenge the wrongs and injustice I have suffered at the hands of those traitors against the country who had sworn to kill me. If you do so, it will be an act of great magnanimity and, for the rest of my life, above everything else I will be your liege vassal. This I ask, pray and request of you." (35396)

What could King Henri possibly have replied were he to have refused to come to William's aid? William is his vassal and is formally requesting to have and to be granted his aid, and he is reminding him of what great honour, aid and succour his father [Duke Robert] had given him in the past. All I can tell you at this point is that, benevolently and unhesitatingly, Henri is going to summon the great armies of France, to search out those who are in revolt against William wherever they find refuge, and he will either make them grovel at his feet or have them exiled from the land. (35410)

Confident, then, of having Henri's aid, Duke William returned home, happy, content and feeling more secure. By proclamation throughout his kingdom Henri summons huge forces: knights, foot-soldiers, men-at-arms in many battalions. The duke, for his part, had done all he could to procure and assemble his fighting men. His lordship did not extend very far within Normandy, but he nevertheless secured men from Evreux, the Pays d'Auge, Liévin, Caux, Rouen, Sées, Falaise and the Hiémois. He takes great pains and concentrates on making the best possible preparations that he can. King Henri had advanced so far with his enormous army that they were able to dismount at the river Laison, in the grassy meadows near to Argences. This is where the huge army made camp, in shelters and in bowers. (35434)

Straightaway the duke, who was by now well prepared, came up to the edge of the river Muance with such companies as he had been able to muster. His treacherous enemies had made ready for battle earlier, and their forces were numerous, extraordinarily fierce, hostile and arrogant. The rebels were well aware that the king, who was furious with them, had arrived with such strength in numbers that, unless they were spared in battle, they were sure to die. If they are found to have tired, broken ranks or scattered, all their lands will be seized, ravaged and destroyed. They themselves will be banished or, if handed over, mutilated, hanged or burnt alive. The decision they came to was not to shirk or give up, but to courageously and zealously go forth into battle. This they would do so as to get peace and quiet from the king of France and his men by means of their shining white steel blades, and avoid the risk of losing the fine Spanish steeds they had brought along, and also "so that we no longer have to put up with that misbegotten, arrogant bastard." (35464)

It was under this misapprehension, in the way I have just described, that they each goad on and urge the other to march against their lord. They are oblivious to William's honour and his rights, make no effort to moderate their behaviour towards him, but wrong-headedly and bloodthirstily – because the battlefield will soon be stained red with their congealed and stone-cold blood – they charge straight into battle against him. They had no intention of losing heart and were more than willing to stay and fight. They had been summoned by proclamation and brought together from all over the country: barons, castellans, minor nobles, viscounts and peasants, brothers, nephews, cousins, family relations and others, indiscriminately. The army together with their commoners crossed the river Orne and came directly to Val-ès-Dunes. There they drew up their battalions in serried ranks, assigned their companies and stood there ready for the clash of lances and for whatever fortune might throw at them. (35488)

Val-ès-Dunes is a series of plains surrounded by hillocks. Situated between

Argences and the Cinglais, it is not too wild a place, having neither rocks nor woods, and the ground there is firm without any marshes. It has a southern exposure and is encircled by a river. (35496)

When the battle was imminent [in August 1047],* the king of France heard mass at Valmeray. Then you would have seen the French taking up arms, donning their hauberks, lacing on their helmets, barding their horses. Many a pennon, many a banner, many a fine, richly decorated standard is attached to smooth wooden shafts tipped with good steel lance-heads. They seized their trusty swords, mounted their steeds, deployed their fighting men and, without further ado, rode off straight to Val-ès-Dunes. (35510)

Brooking no delay and with his helmet ready strapped on, Duke William rode out of Argences on his warhorse. He passed over Béranger ford with those of his fighting men that he had hand-picked and selected, all poised ready to shoot, hurl their spears and strike with their steel blades. They followed the river far upstream until they made contact with the French. Off towards the west, facing them they saw the gold and silver of their enemies' armour glinting brightly. I do not know what more to tell you except that the two armies drew closer and closer, ready and prepared to engage combat. (35526)

In the insurgents' camp, there was a powerful and rich baron by the name of Ralph Taisson,* from the Cinglais. On seeing the French, the Normans and Duke William his lord with such powerful forces, he withdrew some distance away. He understood only too well that the situation was very different from what he had thought the previous morning. His head lowered in sorrow, he strapped on his helmet in the company of a hundred of his own élite knights, but they all stood there waiting. They held their lances erect and had attached streamers to them, unfurled to catch the wind, so as to make them clearly recognisable. They made a splendid company of men, with equipment that was both lavish and eye-catching. (35544)

The king, the duke, the counts, the most senior and experienced figures, drew up and deployed their troops to engage the defiant enemy they saw before them. In the distance the king caught sight of the company with the white banners in front of him, stationed to one side by themselves. It was Ralph Taisson's men, but the king was unsure whether they were on his side or the rebels'. He asked Duke William: "Are these our enemies? They look magnificently equipped and intent on putting up a good fight. They are well disciplined and accomplished. I'm not at all sure if they're going to attack. But what I do know for certain is that any side they support and fight for with their shining sharp steel swords will come out on top and win the day. I'm firmly convinced that they won't be amongst the losers today. Have you any idea of what their intentions are?" The duke's reply was a shrewd one: "Never in my life have I ever done them any wrong or harm, or insulted or acted basely towards them, and my instinct tells me that they will not fight against me, for to do so would be an act of gross disloyalty. Their lord is a fine upstanding man called Ralph Taisson. His support will be extremely valuable, and that's what I want to ensure. But even if he himself were to double the opposition's strength by putting at their disposal as many troops as he has, I still know that they will not defeat us. This is what my instinct tells me and what it predicts, and what everything shows us to be predestined for." (35582)

Ralph Taisson, meanwhile, was weighing up and deciding which of the two alternatives he should adopt: either go, here and now, to the assistance of his lord, or go over to the insurgents. He cannot for all the world see himself failing William and going into battle against him. The traitors had made him many promises, and he had joined their cause, swearing that he would go into battle with them, and that he would be the first – without question and without fail – to go and strike the duke down if ever he were in a position to do so. This was a vow made on oath that he had to fulfil, and this caused him to have serious misgivings. He was on the point of taking the wrong decision, but his men, who were both intelligent and discerning, dissuaded him and made him abandon it. Just hear how each of them beseeches him: "My lord," they say, "we are your faithful vassals, and our advice is that you should not, on this of all days, fail to support your legitimate lord. For the rest of your life you would be considered dishonourable and a spent force – you, your heirs and your family. See what needs to be done and what must be done! Give the duke the service which it is your duty to give, and which it is his right to expect you to give him. You are his sworn vassal for the entire fief you hold of him. Were you not to go to his aid against his deadly enemies, you would today forfeit your estates and be condemned for acting unlawfully towards him. Your duty is to keep him safe, life and limb, with your sword of burnished steel. If you do otherwise, it will be wrong of you, and you will rue the day and pay dearly for it." (35620)

Ralph replied: "I welcome this advice; I am very much in favour of it and am willing for us to do as you propose in order that the land over which Duke William rules is free of opposition and is truly his. I know and can say for certain that he will encounter no hostility in Normandy. Wait for me here and don't move! I will go on my own and speak with him." This is what he did without any more ado, putting on his helmet and mounting his horse. Before addressing the duke and before even saying a word to him, he struck him twice with his gloves, and this was witnessed by a large number of people. "My lord," he says, "I know perfectly well, and let no one be in any doubt, that people who strike their lord with evil intent are law-breakers and traitors. But I am not in the wrong here, because I can assure you that I did not strike you maliciously. What I am doing is fulfilling a vow I made under oath to your enemies. I had sworn to them that I would be the first to strike you if ever I found the opportunity or was in a position to do so. And now I find myself in that position, and I have indeed been the first to strike you. I have, in my view, fulfilled the oath I made to them, but if I have offended you, please excuse my lapse. While I might have struck you with my gloves, it is with our drawn blades, sharp and shining white, that we today will spatter a hundred of your enemies with blood. You can rely on me and on my men." The duke thanks him profusely, and Ralph rides back to his men. What happened here was a huge setback for the insurgents. They can henceforth have no confidence in him or rely very much at all on his coming to their assistance. (35662)

It was a very fine morning, and long past six o'clock when the two sides joined battle. The ground shakes all over and rocks, startling and frightening the horses. Countless brightly coloured banners are lowered to eye level, and will not be raised again until, having passed right through men's midriffs, they have emerged again covered in blood. No one could possibly describe to you how much shouting there was as the two sides clashed, lances shattered against lacquered and decorated shields, how often men went tumbling onto the grass where many a one stayed still and lifeless, and, once the lines had been breached, the clang of swords against burnished steel helmets, spattering many a double-meshed hauberk with blood. So violent is the fighting that it ensures that no one will ever hear tell of such a lethal battle or of anything remotely like it. (35686)

The duke is not alone in the middle of the battlefield mêlée, having some three hundred armed companions at his side. They have their shining white helmets on their heads and strive zealously to offer him assistance. William, in a loud voice that can be heard all around him, rides round seeking out the traitors: unless they leave the battlefield, he declares, or steal away or flee, before evening falls they will feel the full weight of his resentment towards them. He gallops straight at them; he has nothing else on his mind. Sword in hand, furiously and viciously he strikes and hits out. Never did a young man of his age show such daring. (35702)

His enemies, strong, brave and confident knights, are fanatical and full of arrogance, but such is the plight they have rashly brought upon themselves that a hundred of their men are already left lying in the battlefield on their backs, wan and deadly pale. The battle lines draw ever closer, but now under their helmets the men are silent and subdued. There is a tremendous clashing of lances; never were there hostilities of such violence. (35712)

King Henri saw how violent the fighting was and how deadly. He understood the situation and took it into account, because he drew up his companies cleverly and with great skill. He has his standard, with its resplendent gold eagle, raised in the middle of his well-equipped battalions boasting a large number of knights of high repute. Many of them will be drenched in blood before the time comes for him to withdraw today. This is how, exactly as you can hear, each side attacked the other, with the result that, within a short space of time, the ground was stained red with blood. Never did you hear of people fighting with such extraordinary ferocity, exchanging so many death-dealing blows, soaking and staining so many sharp steel blades with people's blood, leaving the brightly embroidered silk banners drab and discoloured. Before the fighting came to a close, you would have seen so many stray and wounded horses bolting, and their riders lying prone in the fray. Varnished shields, gleaming, shining and burnished helmets shattered by swords, littered the ground. With armies in such a sorry state as this, I do not think that anyone will ever again hear tell of a more crushing disaster. (35744)

The French, shouting their battle-cry "Montjoie!,"* are performing splendidly. They are experienced and expert in the arts of war, and exceedingly good knights. They attack with great skill and inflict significant losses on the Norman rebels. The noble and valiant Duke William outstrips everyone else in his determination, for he sees and is fully aware of the fact that this is the one and only chance he has of asserting his power and gaining honour; otherwise he will live deprived of his inheritance for the rest of his days. Confidently and in a loud voice he shouts "Deus aïe!," the battle-cry of the lands his ancestors before him had ruled over. Nigel and his men shout "Saint Sauveur!" to the rank and file as they launch their fierce attacks. They crossed lances with our men repeatedly, I can tell you, and unhorsed a good number of them. Rannulf kept shouting "Saint Sever!" The men he had with him – he was certainly not fighting alone – were brave, strong and war-like knights and men-at-arms. They are paying a high price for the company they keep and for their shameful acts of disloyalty. As for that scoundrel Haimo Dentatus, he kept shouting out his battle-cry "Saint Amant!" and striking our men down close to death. He had a huge body of knights with him, fierce, courageous and daring. So violent, so distressing, so perilous and deadly was the combat that no one could know or even guess which side fate would favour, for in both camps there was extremely strenuous fighting, leading to a very high number of fallen. (35784)

The people from the Cotentin and their forces joined battle with the French – a distressing, merciless, harsh and ruthless battle fraught with danger. They strike and hack at each other. Their blood-soaked under-shirts stick out from between the broken links of their shattered hauberks. Some of the bravest fighters are knocked to the ground, shields are pierced, the grass on the fields runs wet with blood. Savage are the sword-thrusts, and the wrenching ferocious. But the people from the Cotentin are on the losing side. The French gave them something to remember by knocking their brains out! There is no joust or jousting here, but when someone draws his sword, there is no need for him to stand there gaping: he has got to smash, hit, strike and kill, and this is what they are all intent on doing. The struggle is as ferocious as those two wild boars you have seen exchanging blows – fearless, untamed and vicious, merciless with no quarter given until one of them has overcome the other, forced it to concede defeat, chased it off without any reprieve and put it either to flight or to death. This is how it is with the French and Normans, this is exactly how they attack each other, straining every sinew for fear of failing. But before evening falls, it will be necessary for one side to lose their nerve, to turn their backs and flee in insulting and shameful defeat. Before the fighting came to an end, King Henri was knocked from his horse. A brave knight, a Norman and native of the Cotentin – his name is not given in my source book – saw that the king was fighting with such bravery, attacking the Normans so aggressively, striking out so speedily with his sword and so reinvigorating the French that there were few knights in the field inflicting so much damage on them.* Despite all this he had been unhorsed in the fray and, according to this knight, this gave the opportunity of shaming the king and harming his cause. So, taking up his shield and lowering his lance, he hits the king sideways on and sends him tumbling from his horse onto his back. Had it not been for the thickness of the king's double-meshed chain-mail, the steel lance-head would have gone right through him. This is how the king was knocked to the ground, and because of this he became the butt of jokes. This became proverbial and still today people say:

"His name is lost by great mischance,
But a Cotentin knight gave us the lance
That overthrew the king of France."

This knight would have performed a courageous and daring deed in front of a large number of people had he been able to make off there and then, but as chance would have it, he ran into someone from the other side who, in front of a hundred or more knights, struck him down onto the ground. He might easily have got up again, mounted his horse and prepared to make good his escape, but he was not given this possibility. He was hurled to the ground in his turn, crushed and smashed to pieces by countless horses trampling over him until his soul was driven from his body. (35858)

Immediately and without losing a moment, the king of France remounted. He was surrounded by a mass of people, and the fighting around him was intense, but his fellow countrymen acted very bravely, and he was back on his horse again straightaway. Emboldened and fuming with anger, Henri hurls himself into the thick of the enemy, smashing their helmets down onto their heads. The Normans came off worst in the battle. My Latin source informs me that Haimo Dentatus, the strong, rich and powerful lord of Creully, Evrecy and Torigny – fiefs that were his rightful heritage – was killed together with the most prominent members of his family. What else can I say but that there was a great massacre of knights, and their corpses littered the ground, and the Normans suffered such huge losses that they were greatly disheartened. (35879)

Duke William then charged yet again with three hundred of his own knights, valiant, courageous and great fighters. The object of their attack was Viscount Rannulf and his men who were fighting against William. They struck them with such force that the air was thick with fragments and splinters of burnished spearheads. People imagining they were secure in the saddle found themselves taking a spill. Hardré, a brave and expert knight of high repute, and a native of Bayeux, rides up on his high stepping horse and strikes Duke William so violently on his golden-coloured shield with the lion motif that his lance splits and shatters. The good duke of Normandy strikes back, directing his blow over the top of his assailant's shield with such force that he plunges his ash-wood lance shaft deep in between Hardré's neck and his chest, smiting him down dead in the fray before the very eyes of his beloved lord Rannulf.* (35904)

Rannulf, seeing that his own life is now in danger, does little or nothing to avenge Hardré's death. He has lost the will to resist and to keep fighting, and he is minded to flee, so deeply despondent is he. He can see the slaughter and the carnage, so many fine knights killed, he can hear people howling and screaming out in pain, he can see the battlefield running bright red with blood. He is aghast and distraught. He now realises what a hopeless predicament he has landed himself in. If the duke can get his hands on him, there will be no question of him being ransomed; William will be merciless and have him strung up on the gallows. His whole face, his chin and the back of his neck start to quiver. Even for a thousand gold marks he would not have dared make as much as a single charge, and when his men set off to join battle and attack the enemy, it was without him. Rannulf had resolved not to go anywhere near the enemy, so violent and cruel he considered them to be. He no longer wanted anything to do with their conflict, and for him the most urgent thing to do was to put some distance between himself and them and to flee to prevent them catching him. He had to abandon his weapons, for he was hardly in a position to carry them. As he makes off, he says to himself that getting involved in a venture that led to the maiming of so many knights was the stupidest thing he had ever done in the whole of his life. It was foolhardy and rash of him to have undertaken it. He runs away from the battlefield with only some faint-hearted followers as company. (35942)

Nigel and Guy the Burgundian kept on fighting. They tore into the throng wielding their sharp-edged swords. Nigel, an exceedingly brave and fearless fighter, stands out head and shoulders above everyone else. It is my belief that, had he had a few equally brave companions around him, it would have been difficult to remove him from the battlefield, but he had been severely wounded himself and was seriously hurt. He sees the ground littered with the corpses of his men, while others are repeatedly wavering and attempting to slip away. This makes the French, who are fighting extremely well, redouble their efforts, and increases their daring and their strength. Nigel realised how desperate and perilous his position was and what a thoroughly sorry state he now found himself in. When he heard that Rannulf had fled, he knew he no longer had anyone he could rely on or who could help him regain the initiative against the enemy. He understood that there was no point in waiting any longer, and that he simply had to quit the battlefield. He makes off, defeated and vanquished. (35967)

Many a knight was unhorsed, captured and killed there. No one ever heard tell of any army being in such a sorry state or having been so hardened by suffering. Everyone cares only for his own safety and no one seeks to help others, for each one makes off as fast as he possibly can, their bodies streaming with blood. Little wonder that they are terrified, for they still have one deadly obstacle to

cross – the river Orne over which they have to swim. They continued to be captured or slaughtered as martyrs right up until they reached the river. Between
their entering the water from the steep river bank and climbing up out on the
other side, they suffered agony, great losses and terrible drownings. As far as
Caen, people could see the water stained red from this calamity, and so great was
the number of those drowned that the water mills ground to a halt. (35988)

In this way animosity lives on for a long time before finally decreasing and
dwindling. However long it may have lasted, in the end it ceases and disappears,
and the arrogance that had engendered so much evil comes to an end. Thus the
Devil pays his debts to those who solicit and seek his favour and his approval.
And if the Devil has put to shame those foul perjurers and traitors who failed to
trust their lord and were disloyal to him, then they have fully deserved it. The
Devil seduces many of their sort. Their power is henceforth lost, since they have
been taken prisoner, destroyed or killed. As the Latin source puts it, blessed was
the morning, holy and exalted was the day, when such great arrogance was
brought low, and glorious was the battle – this is undeniable – in which so much
criminal behaviour was defeated. Such wrong-doing was bringing about the
destruction of Normandy: so many of her crenelated towers, so many mighty
fortifications, so many strongholds and palisades and so many mutinous castles
were demolished and came tumbling down, and this restored peace to the realm.
(36018)

Covered in shame, Guy the Burgundian escapes from this great slaughter.
Recognising the vast harm this has done him almost drove him mad, and if the
good duke should live a long life, Guy will have many other losses to endure.
When the river Orne had sent to the bottom those miserable wretches who failed
to swim across it and had drowned, and once this terrible and cruel carnage was
over and the martyrdom had finished, William's army turned to home. Both the
duke and the king were overjoyed, and the French displayed great gaiety. The
dead and the wounded are searched out, and everyone carries off their own men.
Unhurriedly and in places they considered appropriate they buried those of their
vassals, relatives and friends who had been killed. No one could know or even
estimate the value of a fraction of the inordinately vast amount of valuables found
on the battlefield that day. The king and his men took as much as they wanted to
satisfy them. The duke having thanked and expressed his gratitude to the king as
best he knew how, Henri immediately left to return home to France with his huge
army. (36048)

The duke for his part did not remain idle: until his whole country is pacified, he will not be able to live in peace. He has already made a good start, but now his ambition is to break and subdue resistance wherever it is, to exert his lordship everywhere and administer justice far and near. His attitude to Guy the Burgundian was very hostile and ill-intentioned. The count had fled to Brionne, a well-fortified stronghold. He intended to mount his defence from there, as well as from Vernon. Both of these castles had been granted to him by the duke, and Guy had fortified both in defiance of him. His plan was to harry him from there and to drive him out of that part of the country. It is a very bad use of presents if you get this sort of treatment in return. (36066)

The duke led his extremely belligerent troops to Brionne in order to capture the castle and its keep. There is absolutely no way for the traitor to remain there. He is so closely surrounded that he will soon be forced to come out. And this is only right, for had the duke been able to do so, he would have killed Guy with his own hands. The keep, however, proved exceedingly difficult to take. They are able to use it to continue their defence for as long as their provisions hold out, since the river Risle runs right round the castle earthworks and its moat, thus surrounding it on all sides. This is how the castle was defended and what the lie of the land was on this particular day [in 1048]. The Norman army, surrounding it on all sides, kept up its ferocious attacks right up to the walls and earthworks, inflicting repeated reversals on the defenders. The duke then has two sturdy wooden structures erected to guard the entrance to the castle to prevent those inside from receiving any help in the shape of reinforcements or provisions. It was only a matter of time before their food would run out, and before too long this is what happened. Guy then became quite terrified, fearing that the duke, if he could catch him, would have him put to death in an ignominious fashion. When he could hold out no longer, he sent word to the duke begging for pity, and as soon as the castles were handed over, William did in fact forgive him. The only action that the duke took was to find a place for him in his household in order to ensure he received food and lodging, since Guy was not allowed any land or estates of his own. This was Guy's situation for a period of time, but the members of the court as well as the general public showed such hatred towards him, and Guy himself found them to be so hostile, that he was forced to go off back to Burgundy, taking the full weight of his ignominy along with him. (36108)

As far as Nigel from the Cotentin was concerned, the duke had no desire to come to any agreement with him, and he was forced to flee to Brittany with some of the most prominent of his followers. Fearful of losing his life, he accepted being exiled from Normandy. Grimoult du Plessis, the prime mover of all these woes, was captured and imprisoned at Rouen. He found no pity, no forgiveness, and this was right, for had he been able, he would have foully assassinated the duke at Valognes during the night. It is too late if he now repents. He had denied the charge of murder and had accused a particular knight of having planned this despicable crime, forcing him to have to defend himself and clear his name. This person was called Serlo and he came from Lingèvres.* On the day designated for the trial by combat to take place – and no postponement of it was possible – Serlo, to his most pleasant surprise, found Grimoult dead in his prison cell. I have no idea what all this meant or what the circumstances were, but it was the subject of a great deal of discussion with people wanting to know how it happened and whether or not he had strangled himself. Still in his shackles and chains, Grimoult was interred and buried. And as my written source records, his land was not distributed among his relatives, but the duke endowed his own church with it by donating it in its entirety to our Lady Saint Mary's of Rouen.* I do not know whether the land still belongs to the church to this day. This is how things go in the world and how things turn out. What a wretched and miserable way for someone to reach the end of his life and die! (36148)

[10] *How Godwine betrayed Alfred, brother of King Edward.*

According to what I see in my written source, Cnut, king of England, met his end and died, not a youngster or even a young man. He was the father of Harthacnut, a brave and celebrated knight whose mother was Emma,* who had been married to Æthelred and who was also the mother of Edward and Alfred. On the orders of King Cnut, Harthacnut had gone to Denmark where he was made king. A most noble and illustrious king, he ruled over his kingdom in peace. During this time, however, his father died. Being so far away Harthacnut did not learn of this early enough and realise how quickly he would have needed to act. Cnut had an illegitimate son, an untrustworthy, belligerent and ill-natured individual called Harold [I Harefoot], and he had himself crowned king of England and of the English. He had it all, he took it all, he kept it all. This is how things were at the time, and this is what happened. (36170)

In this way Edward and his brother Alfred came to be disinherited. When they learned of the death of Cnut, they were convinced that their time had come.

This was something they had been expecting for a considerable time. As best they knew how and as their resources permitted, they assembled a great fleet and filled it with a huge body of knights. They will do everything in their power to seize the kingdom, for no one has as much legitimacy as heirs as they have. Edward alone, for his part, had forty well-provisioned boats. They set out from Barfleur at the end of the afternoon as evening fell, and headed directly for Southampton where they landed. Their hope was to seize and take possession of the kingdom, but the English had been forewarned, having long since learnt that the two brothers were due to mount a violent and criminal attack against them, and this had caused them to be exceptionally fearful. As soon as they saw the sails appear, they issued a public proclamation for the troops and the local population to assemble. The local people were unwilling to recognise Edward as their overlord, and for this reason a battle broke out on the fine sandy shore. Five hundred people had their heads bloodied there, and the flow of blood was not staunched until they were dead. The English suffered tremendous slaughter, and a large amount of booty was seized from them. Piling up valuables to their hearts' content, the victors loaded themselves down with priceless and precious objects. The English were not capable of stopping them. They would have done better – as they should have done – to accept Edward as their lord, but because of Harold they did not dare do so. This did them harm, and they suffered as a result. A mighty struggle ensued, and from all over the region people came running to join the battle. Edward then understood that by staying any longer his army could rapidly come to a sticky end. He could not easily win the kingdom with such a small number of troops. He sees the strength of the English increasing with the arrival of reinforcements, and there is no point in his waiting any longer. Taking with them their vast quantities of spoils, the likes of which had never been seen, they retreated to their boats, and without having suffered any losses or damage, set sail from the shore. Harold's arrogant defiance had led to the English being put to the sharp steel sword and to a massacre about which tales were told for years to come. Now prosperous and loaded with huge wealth, Edward's troops landed back in Normandy. (36230)

They had acted with great bravery, but hear now how things turned out quite differently for Alfred. He had assembled his fleet – a huge one and magnificently equipped, and they crossed over from Wissant to Dover. From here, fully armed on horseback, they proceeded to cross Kent and advance far beyond. They would never have been driven out had it not been for a traitor, a Judas, a foul, horrible and devilish swine worse than a Saracen woman's son:* the hateful Earl Godwine. In a perfectly friendly fashion he approached Alfred and his army, offering them peace, reinforcements and aid, acting in a subservient manner and putting on a welcoming demeanour as if he were extremely pleased to see Alfred. He immediately placed himself at their disposal, taking great pains to find them somewhere to stay and personally accompanying them there. But what he was really working hard to bring about was a shameful and deadly deed, a horrendous atrocity. He had married a Danish woman [Gytha] with whom he had had three sons: Gyrth, Harold [Godwineson] and, thirdly, Tostig, for whom he had a particular affection. Because of his wife and their children he detested the Normans. His wife came from an illustrious family of Danes, and her three sons shared her Danish origin, hence Godewine's overriding love for King [Æthelred]. This explains why he committed the act he did, as a result of which his soul is sunk in the pit of Hell. Without allowing any time to elapse, this perfidious wretch took on the role of Judas by night by horrendously betraying the son of his liege lord. He had greeted and kissed Alfred, found lodging for him in an agreeably peaceful setting, given his word to assure everyone that they need not be suspicious of him, eaten and drunk with them, only to then deceive Alfred and afterwards kill him. (36276)

Everyone had gone to lie down to rest and sleep when, around midnight, Godwine seized Alfred in his bed. When Alfred realised that he had been taken prisoner, he humbly begged for mercy, asking to be allowed to leave on his own unharmed. He swore to entirely renounce his right to the kingdom, and undertook never, for the rest of his life, to lay claim to his inheritance or his share of it. He entreated Godwine not to carry on with such a criminal act. He had provided him with hospitality; now let him go on the understanding that he will not come back! Alfred is the son of a king who had also been Godwine's overlord; let him not subject him to a painful death! He joins his hands in supplication, but it is to no avail. Far from sparing him, this foul swine of a Judas had his hands tied behind his back before sending him off to King Harold, who was well aware of the treacherous plot: it had all been carefully planned. Alas, what a cruel destiny! Harold treated Alfred in a most shameful fashion: he humiliated, insulted and threatened him. Alfred's knights and companions could not arrange ransom for themselves or obtain clemency or their release, so with much sadness and grief they were taken to Guildford. What a great sin, and what a criminal thing to do! There they were beheaded, and not a single one of them was spared, except for every tenth person who was excluded on the orders of King Harold. The king instructed that all the prisoners were to be placed in a row from which every tenth man was selected, and it was this person's task to then cut off the heads of the nine other people closest to him. It was a most deplorable thing to do, since they were all men of great courage.* (36318)

Having humiliated Alfred in this way, Harold sent him off to Ely with orders for him to be mutilated by having his eyes put out. He was so shamefully humiliated, so terribly mutilated and subjected to so much mortal suffering that inevitably, two days later, he died. Never was there so much grief or such a loss, for he was a good, valiant and wise man. Thereafter, as we read in our source text, because of this horrendous act of treason, the Lord on high was not willing for Harold to continue governing the country. He suffered, I believe, a most painful death without having repented in any way. If the kingdom had been the object of his desire, his enjoyment of it was extremely brief. (36336)

Immediately following Alfred's death, the English met together in order to determine whom they would pay allegiance to and whom they would crown king. There was a great deal of discussion in many different places; many opinions were sought and there was much deliberation. Everyone said that, as far as they were concerned, they dared not ask Edward on account of their having killed his brother so wrongfully and so sinfully, and also because of the Norman knights. These were the reasons why they were afraid of Edward and were unwilling to ask him to come over to England and to receive him. (36350)

They sent word to Harthacnut and were unanimous in agreeing that they wanted him to be king.* They brought him over [from Denmark] and did homage to him. They gave him the crown, withholding none of the rights that went with the office, and considering him to be their one and only king. He was noble, loyal and honest, and much committed to maintaining peace. Only one thing caused him anxiety, namely that he frequently fell ill. And because Emma was not only his mother but also the mother of Edward, his [half-]brother, he loved Edward with particular tenderness. Within a matter of days he had contrived to send for him, inviting him to come to England as his beloved brother. Harthacnut had never welcomed anyone as lovingly as he did Edward, and he showered him with honours. He could not possibly have cherished him more; he let him do anything he wanted and did everything he could to please him. So close was the understanding between them that only the title of king separated Harthacnut from Edward. Everything the king did subsequently, he did only after consulting Edward and seeking his brother's approval. This understanding between them lasted until Harthacnut died. He had not reigned for more than three years, and his life had been extremely short. Thereafter, as reason and justice demanded,

Edward was given the crown. He encountered not the slightest opposition either from the lords or the commoners. (36386)

Godwine, that inveterate criminal and traitor, was one of the country's most powerful earls and had at his disposal a considerable military force. His lordship was extensive as he had taken control of a large part of the kingdom. His relatives, friends and allies were influential also, and he had a large personal household of knights. He was the only person whom Edward was wary of, for he knew that he was wicked by nature – deceitful, disloyal and treacherous. On the advice of the king's Norman barons, worthy and wise knights, the king and the earl entered into an agreement that involved a marriage. Godwine had a daughter, a beautiful woman called Gunnhild [= Edith],* and the good-natured, wise and courtly Edward took her as his wife, thus indicating forgiveness, in accordance with the wishes of his mother Emma, for his brother's death. Thus it came about that the king married, but it is public knowledge, as well as the truth, that he and his wife did not have a sexual relationship. They never even slept together, and not once in their lives did they have intercourse or any sort of intimacy. The life they lived was a chaste one, but without bad feeling or resentment. This caused no disagreement between them and no ill-will. The king was an extremely good-natured person, unpretentious, cheerful, sincere, compassionate, charitable, noble-hearted and wise – a man of true nobility. He loved God and Holy Church. His good works were many and varied, and he was particularly caring in his attitude towards the poor. He revived and gave a new lease of life to the laws and ancient traditions from the customaries of old. God openly revealed to him many sacred mysteries that had been long cherished. He made many a prophecy that was subsequently fulfilled, as everyone could verify.* Trustworthy and an even-handed dispenser of justice, he reigned for all of thirty-three years. How to tell you of the consideration he had for the good duke of Normandy and the favourable attitude he maintained towards him all the days of his life by serving him, showing him affection and reciprocating so warmly the great favours that the duke had done him? He frequently gave him presents of gold and silver, and no one made more effort than he to ensure that William became king of England. He concentrated all his energies on finding how best he could show him his gratitude, namely by making him his heir and enabling him to have the kingdom. What he set his mind on and what he strove for was that William be crowned as his successor. On the advice and with the consent of all of his magnates, Edward sent a certain lord, one [Robert of Jumièges] archbishop of Canterbury, [over to Normandy] to announce that he was granting William his kingdom in succession to him. And in order to avoid any contention, impediment or trickery, he sent him unimpeachable sureties, members and descendants of prominent families, one of Godwine's own sons as well as a close kinsman of his, all rich tenants and fief-holders. This is how William was granted the kingdom of England as a gift. But before he finally came to take possession of it, there was a whole other story to be heard. (36464)

[11] *How the lord of Anjou conquered Tours and Touraine, and how the lord of Normandy conquered Domfront.*

During this time I am telling you about, there was complete peace within all the frontiers of Normandy. The land was fertile and bountiful, and no one had suf-ficient power to dare to move against the duke, to rebel or start a war – none, that is, except Geoffrey [II] Martel,* the powerful, strong and brave count of Anjou, one of the best of all knights. The people of Poitou, Saintonge, Angoumois, Bordeaux and Toulouse all obeyed him as if he were actually their lord. It was because of his intelligence and his bravery that everyone joined his military campaigns. He embarked on a foolhardy course of action that he subse-quently came to regret for the rest of his days: he began to invade the territory of William, duke of Normandy, to occupy and to seize his lands. And just listen to what he had done previously! In the course of a battle between some knights, he had captured the count of Poitiers [William VI], and imprisoned him in shack-les until he was ransomed. He then extracted a lot of gold and money from him, and afterwards made him swear an oath requiring him to live in peace with him. Then, as you will hear, something truly astonishing happened, a misfortune that caused great grief. On the third day after the count of Poitiers had been freed from prison, he met his end, passed away and died. The count of Anjou seized everything, including the count of Poitiers' stepmother [Agnes], a highly esteemed lady, worthy, rich, beautiful and cultivated, of noble family and line-age, distinguished, kind-hearted and wise. Without encountering the least resist-ance, he took her to his bed as his wife. He took the count's brothers prisoner and detained them under guard. All the count's property, the gold and silver and everything that fell under the count's jurisdiction he appropriated without meet-ing any opposition, as no one dared raise their voice against him. His one and only desire was to extend his sovereignty. He undertook many ambitious ven-tures to this end, and made a success of many lucrative ones. Very courageous and

combative, he grew very rich and prosperous. From Count Thibaud he conquered Tours and the valuable territory of Touraine. With a full-scale army he
had besieged Tours for a whole month until he was obliged, by Thibaud de Blois
and large companies of French troops, to lift the siege and leave the region. Count
Geoffrey Martel marched against him, and after a great deal of fighting and jousting Count Thibaud was captured together with several of his wealthy friends and
allies, nobles and barons. What happened to them was that they were taken prisoner, placed in heavy, well-riveted shackles and flung into tall towers with battlements. Before they could regain their freedom, Geoffrey had had Tours and
Touraine handed over to him. My source, as I have read it, does not say whether
he or any of the heirs who came after him were ever divested of these acquisitions.* (36538)

This Geoffrey was such an extraordinary figure that he caused turmoil
throughout the whole of France. His behaviour towards the king was high-
handed, extremely defiant and rapacious. His arrogance and contempt came from
the battles he had become accustomed to winning, and from the acquisitions and
the remarkable wealth that he had been accumulating. This resulted in him making frequent and large-scale incursions into Normandy from which, more often
than not, he would carry off quantities of gold, silver and other valuables. Such
acquisitive behaviour, as well as his sweet talking and scheming, meant that he
had gained control over Alençon, which was the property of the duke of Normandy. The people to blame here were those untrustworthy perjurers and traitors who were garrisoned in the town and who had been just looking for the
chance to loot and ransack the surrounding country. Previously they had not
dared to break the law by stealing and committing other crimes, but Count Geoffrey provided them with ample opportunity of doing so, by day or by night.
(36562)

This Geoffrey Martel had installed in the fine stronghold of Domfront a garrison of his troops consisting of first-class knights, men-at-arms and archers with
the task of extending the fighting across the whole country as far as the Bessin.
This was something that Duke William was not willing to permit. He summoned
all his troops, knights, foot-soldiers and men-at-arms – as many of the fiercest
fighters as he had. He was rightly annoyed that Count Geoffrey had taken
Alençon from him in the way he had, but he had no fear or anxiety that he would
not rapidly win it back. His decision was to go first to Domfront, and this is where
he led all of his troops. But he was almost betrayed there, captured, maltreated or
even killed, and I will tell you how this came about. One of his knights, a disloyal

individual, intended to betray him to the people inside defending the town. God, however, was unwilling to countenance this, even though the traitor had already come to an arrangement with the enemy ... (36585)

He had told and convinced the duke that he could get his hands on a vast amount of wealth – a truly phenomenal quantity of booty. This was a highly tempting prospect. The Normans set out with no more than fifty knights and seventy archers, all with shields, but they were almost immediately followed. The people defending the town opened up a postern gate that they had succeeded in camouflaging, and three hundred proven knights came charging out together with seven hundred well- armed soldiers riding in pursuit of the duke's men. In this way, or so they thought, they would cut off any means of retreat for them. They had almost come within striking distance of them, but no sooner did the duke and the men with him catch sight of them than the Normans wheeled round on the spot as fast as their horses could carry them. If the men from Domfront had dared wait for the Normans to attack them, I am in no doubt that the grass would have been flowing with blood. I find that it did not, however, come to that, since they sought safety in flight. The duke immediately set off in pursuit of them, and was extremely annoyed when he was unable to catch up with them. They piled back in through the gate in a crush a thousand times bigger than when they had originally come out. And the duke was so close behind them that he managed to seize the bridle of a knight's horse with his hand and drag him back, thus capturing him in the most unlikely of places. Even if the whole venture was not a very wise move,* there were, as you can hear and see for yourselves, plenty of brave and courageous exploits displayed there. Duke William and his companions, taking with them the knight they had captured, came back to join the rest of their army. Inside Domfront there was a great deal of discussion, with people saying that never in their lives had they seen a more intrepid, a more courageous, a more fearsome knight than the duke of Normandy. The Norman army took up its quarters and was camped all around Domfront, but access to the castle was extremely difficult. Even getting near it posed problems, which made it very hard to attack, especially as there was no place in the area where a siege engine could be brought up close enough to the keep. (36636)

Duke William examines the country around and sees how the castle itself is sited in wild terrain on a jagged outcrop surrounded by deep valleys with narrow passes and gorges. He understands that mounting an assault against the castle will not enable him to inflict any lasting damage on the enemy; it would be a long-drawn-out business and a protracted waste of time. He therefore constructed three wooden towers in the immediate vicinity, moated, stockaded and equipped with brattice platforms; they were elaborately palisaded with long, thick oak stakes, and in them he placed his bravest fighters. Their task was to put his mind at rest by preventing any external help reaching the people besieged inside the castle. Let them realise that, from now on, there is no possibility of anything more either getting in or coming out! They can finish what provisions they have, but they will get no help thereafter from anywhere else. They are dismayed and extremely afraid, believing that no aid can possibly reach them now. All this time Duke William keeps up the siege, day and night patrolling the access roads and paths without ever tiring. This ruler hardly looks like someone who is about to lose some of his inheritance! (36666)

During this time I am telling you of, when William was besieging Domfront, a messenger from Alençon came spurring up into his camp, informing him and letting him know that he should, without waiting and without any delay, return and take back control of the castle of Alençon from Geoffrey Martel. If he goes, so the messenger asserts, surely he cannot fail to get the castle back. (36676)

The brave young duke, anxious to have what was his by right, declared that he would indeed go and take part of his army with him, despite what anyone else might say. He immediately had the horses fed and then, once he had chosen, summoned by name and designated those who were to accompany him – certainly not the least good fighters by a long chalk – and everybody being ready to set off, there was no reason for further delay. He gave orders for the army to mobilise and instructions on how they were to proceed. He leaves behind some commanders and leaders and rides off with his companies. The most direct route was taken, with the result that, before sunrise, they were able to unfurl, before the startled eyes of the enemy, five hundred silk-embroidered standards and as many brightly burnished arms. (36696)

The people inside Alençon run to the city gates carrying loads of stones and stakes. There is suddenly considerable commotion, but nowhere are people anxious or afraid, for their castle is – they think – a sturdy one, well-fortified, easy to defend and impregnable. But they will have to change their tune before evening falls. With his well-armed troops William rides up, not drawing rein until he reaches the ditch in front of the moat. (36708)

Alençon is situated in the marches between two provinces, and the river Sarthe flows through the town. On one side it is Norman territory, and on the other the land belongs to Le Mans. The people from Le Mans had built a well-fortified castle surrounded by wide, deep trenches, properly maintained and steeply banked, and by palisades and spiked stockades. On the inside there was a highly secure fortress with brattice platforms on every side. You never heard of such a secure stronghold. It was filled with knights, crossbowmen and other armed fighters, all arrogance and insolence. On this particular day the peasants had also gathered inside the castle. Good Duke William directed his troops towards this newly constructed fortress, drawing their attention to how presumptuous and arrogant those defending it were. The people inside hurled abuse at the duke. To show their disdain for him they shouted out: "Here comes the skinner! Get out the needle and thread! Chalk it up!" I fail to understand how they could be so impertinent. They beat [the skin on] their own backs and backsides in imitation of tanners in order to insult him. When he comes within earshot, they keep on shouting out: "My lord Pelterer, lord Pelterer!* Is this trade up your street? Your ancestor, Fulbert of Falaise, certainly knew how to brew a good ale! You're a gentleman, no doubt about it, and just the sort we should surrender to. But first, unless you do something to prevent it, a lot of your men are going to take a tumble into the ditches and lie howling there in pain!" (36744)

No wonder, then, if the duke was overcome with anger and resentment, and felt so vengeful and merciless towards them. Everyone gets ready for the attack. William's men declare that they would rather be killed than fail to wrest the castle back. The insults from the enemy, as I have described for you, as well as their temerity, gave the Normans added strength and bravery, as they went on to show that day. It was not yet midday when the attack began – a harsh, violent, painful and dangerous attack which I would be incapable of describing for you. You would have seen people busy fetching and dragging up timber to fill in the deep trenches. The young grooms had been armed also, and the Normans kept up their assault at full strength until the wood that had been thrown into the trenches caught fire. There were huge flames and clouds of smoke which engulfed the people inside the castle. Before long the stockade went up in flames, as did also the brattice platforms, and soon there was nothing left to catch fire. I can tell you for certain that there were large numbers of people burnt as well as killed, and all the others were taken prisoner. The duke had given clear instructions that the prisoners should be brought before him; he had not forgotten the insults they had showered them with earlier that day. Those responsible were not allowed to be either pardoned or ransomed or set free. No matter who disagreed with his decision or felt aggrieved, he had their hands and their feet cut off in front of the castle gate. That was his way of taking a modicum of revenge! He then had the limbs thrown in over the city walls so as to undermine the confidence of those who had revolted against him. Let them be quite certain that, if they are forcibly taken prisoner, they can expect to suffer the same fate. If, however, they surrender without more ado and gave him no more trouble, they can, safely and without fear, go off wherever they wish; he will spare them all, life and limb, and grant them free movement throughout Normandy. (36796)

After the attack, the fire, the capture of the fortress, the threats, the mutilations and the merciless killing, the people defending Alençon saw that they were in a serious, indeed dangerous situation and were heading for disaster. They had heard the treatment that was in store for them if William could get his hands on them. So well forewarned were they that they had no option but to comply. They had no confidence that help would reach them, and Count Geoffrey was still a long way off. They handed the castle over to William. The supplies it contained were worth a hundred marks, but all they salvaged was their own skins. William leaves in the castle and its keep a good number of knights, archers and men-at-arms – the exact figures I cannot give you – plus those men he can trust not to double-cross him. He wasted no time, and at dawn the next day headed straight back to Domfront. He meets up again with those of his men who are there waiting for him. They are extremely pleased to see him and delighted to hear the good news from Alençon. The people inside Domfront, however, are terrified. They can see no way out for them, and unless they receive help or reinforcements, they are in for a bad time. They will starve before long or even die; they can expect nothing better unless Geoffrey Martel comes to their assistance. Either he comes to relieve them immediately and without delay, since they can expect no help from any other quarter, or he must order them to surrender. They are already in a very bad state, since every day they are under attack, and people who lack provisions can put up little or no defence. Each individual has the same message for Geoffrey: if he fails to see to their well-being, it will be to his shame, and that will be public knowledge once it is known that the castle has fallen. It is not their fault if they have been starved into submission, and if they are taken prisoner, all they can expect is to be mutilated or hanged. The only ransom they will have is the same as the defenders of Alençon had. (36846)

Count Geoffrey quickly summoned his troops and assembled a powerful army. He is beside himself with rage at the thought of Alençon being stolen from under his nose, and of Domfront now being under siege. But he has not the slightest idea that the Normans are brave enough to confront him, and the least of his fears is that he will not be able to force then to lift the siege. With as many troops as he could ever possibly muster, he rode straight to Domfront. He came to a halt with his men close to the town next to some high ground, from where they could easily be seen, and they all camped there for the night. Next morning Duke William, on rising, summons his barons, considers the situation and seeks advice from those who are closest to him on what action to take. From amongst these he then selects three of the most renowned, the bravest, the best informed and the wisest: William, a valiant knight and son of Osbern, his household steward, Roger de Montgommery and William, son of Thierry. (36872)

"Take your horses," he said, "all three of you, and go and get an idea of how numerous the enemy are. You are experienced in estimating troop numbers. See how many thousands of them there are, and whether there are many knights among them. Tell the count of Anjou, from me, that, however small the number of my troops may be, I still have enough to control Domfront, and to restrict the movement of those of his men in it, to stop him from bringing them any help. Tell him also that there are already many among them who would much rather be in Paris than stationed here in the keep. He should know also that they have very few provisions left, and however much he might want to cherish them, it will not be possible for him to come to their assistance. We occupy the whole area around here. If he should attempt to cross our lines, the only thing he will be able to boast of is having had the roughest crossing of his life. He may possibly be brave, valiant and wise, he may well have overrun Poitou and subdued its inhabitants and made them his vassals, he may have taken Tours, Touraine and the whole of Maine and brought them within his jurisdiction, but he can be absolutely sure that, as long as I live, he will not get a single inch of Norman territory without it costing him dearly and, if I have anything to do with it, without getting his come-uppance as well. He won't find either me or the Normans as easy to deal with as his other neighbours have been. He'll be able to discover this tomorrow if he wants to prolong this quarrel. With sharp steel spears and blades of Poitevin steel we'll see which of us is behaving arrogantly. This is what I wish for and what I most desire. Tell him what I am capable of and how strong I am, and that if he takes up the challenge, I for one won't be found wanting." (36910)

Thus the duke said what he had to say to the three barons I have named and entrusted them with his message, and off they rode. They came to Count Geoffrey and were able to see his men. They spoke with him and gave their message expertly and without omitting anything. There was much recalling of old wrongs, disputes and disagreements, deceptions and failures, all of which had given rise to ill-feeling. They also spoke of how peace might have been possible, but they found the count hostile to this and it came to nothing. Geoffrey replies angrily that the castle is his own personal property, and this he will prove to be true before the end of the following day, and as the day after dawns, the duke will see which one of them will have the upper hand. A thousand sharp and upright lances and a thousand drawn swords will ensure the count, so he says, a safe passage through their lines. Only someone with no regard for his public reputation would allow his people, whom his duty is to protect and help, to be in any way harmed. "And I'll not refuse," he adds, "if there is to be a battle, to confront you in the morning with my Poitevin helmet strapped to my head. Tell your lord, he adds, that I will be sitting on a lily-white horse, fully armed and eager to fight, holding my shield with its golden lion cubs on a field of blue. I'm telling him the emblem on my shield so that he can recognise me and come and get me as soon as day breaks."* (36948)

To this the messengers immediately reply, in a proud and mocking tone, that it is not worth the count going to all that trouble, for hardly will the day have dawned before their lord the duke, fully armed and on his priceless horse, will be there alert and ready for action. They give all the details of how his varnished shield is painted, and what sort of lance and pennons he will have: that is precisely how he will find him, they say, should Geoffrey show up. There were many other exchanges not recorded in the source book, but the Normans are absolutely delighted that the battle is going to take place. They spend the whole night busily preparing with great diligence. The duke's view is that he would be very pleased to see his reputation even further enhanced if he wins the battle, for there is no ruler anywhere more honoured, so widely known, so superlative a knight. (36972)

The whole situation would rapidly have deteriorated had not Count Geoffrey's best and wisest advisers made it their business to intervene. They spent so long talking to the count that they finally convinced him, very much against his will, it seems to me, not to engage battle. As a result, before dawn had broken, they had all ridden off, leaving the region far behind them. It was [Geoffrey,] the lord of Mayenne, who had had such difficulty in getting Geoffrey Martel to leave, who clinched the matter by persuading him that the castle's defenders had actually agreed to surrender to the duke that same night. If he had not tricked the count in this way, it would not have been possible to reverse the decision to fight it out.* Geoffrey's troops were already armed and had already decided their battle order when he was tricked into leaving in this way. After the event he considered that he had been very badly treated, and for the rest of his life he bore a grudge about it. When the people inside the castle heard that the count of Anjou was going away, they had no other choice but to surrender the castle immediately. This they did without any loss of life or of limb, and they were also able to keep their equipment. The duke of Normandy had his shining gold banner raised to the top of the keep, whereupon everyone everywhere rejoiced. Never was such jubilation seen as that shown that day by the Normans: between here and the ocean, they said, there was no one powerful enough to resist them. The three wooden structures I told you about, that the duke had had built around Domfront, were dismantled. Without any delay he had all the material taken to Ambrières where it was his intention to construct a new fort. He brought thick, tall, strong timbers, ready equipped with battlements, and these were erected on huge, solid embankments. They built a huge motte and a keep, and all around such big, well-equipped and well-fortified watchtowers that there was no need for them to be wary of anyone who approached. The river ran at its feet. When he had fully fortified the place and provided it with a generous and plentiful supply of provisions, he chose the best defenders he knew, the best disciplined and the ones most devoted to him. They did not consider it likely that the Passais region would come to grief or be plundered, set on fire or destroyed for the next year or even two. Henceforth people would be able to get on with their livelihoods in peace and security. (37036)

Having brought this business to a conclusion, Duke William immediately turned to home, leaving behind at Domfront some particularly well-trained defenders in whom he had complete trust. Then without further delay he came to Rouen, joyful, safe and in high spirits, and here he did what he liked doing best: distributing costly and generous gifts. (37043)

[12] *How the count of Mortain was exiled.*

During the time I have been telling you about, when Duke William conquered Domfront, there was a count at Mortain who was called – so the Latin history informs us – William Werlenc. He was a descendant of the family of Duke Richard I, and possessed extensive estates. One day a knight of his, no fool, no coward, no mischief-maker, called Robert Bigot came to confer with him. He said: "Here I am, my lord, living under you in great discomfort and in poverty. I have no income, no means of earning a living, and no one else to rely on. I detest being poor in this land, so I have taken the decision to go to Apulia and to leave straightaway without delay. I want to see if I can earn an honourable living there through hard work and tenacity." (37068)

The count of Mortain replies by asking: "Who is it who's urging you to undertake and embark on this venture?" "It's just that I can't keep waiting and suffering. I can't put up any longer with being poor here in this land. It's hardship that is forcing me to leave. I'm not driven by any unworthy motive." To this the count replies: "Drop the idea! Circumstances will change and the situation will get better very soon. You can be sure that things will turn out well for you. Within three months from now, I tell you, in the Bessin and the Hiémois you will be able to earn yourself and get your hands on so much that you alone will be able to decide how rich you want to become. Normandy will be yours for the taking. The stronger people are, the more they'll grab. Those who can't look after themselves won't have a penny to their name. This is going to happen very soon. Keep your eyes open and wait, that's what you should do, and the news you'll hear will fill your heart with joy." This is how it came about that Robert Bigot stayed and did not leave the country. Then, through a friend of his, his first cousin Richard, a fine knight and a close acquaintance of Duke William, Robert was introduced into the ducal household. Being quick-witted, clever and a good conversationalist, he soon became one of the duke's closest companions. But what the count of Mortain had told him remained engraved on Robert's memory. He kept thinking about it, and feared that something criminal was about to take place. Short of the duke being poisoned, killed or murdered, however, he could not see what could possibly happen. But he was unwilling to keep silent any longer, and in a private interview with the duke of Normandy, he told him everything, word for word, omitting no detail. The duke understood, on hearing this, that some criminal act against him was being plotted. Being unwilling to keep quiet about it, he summoned the count of Mortain to his presence and asked him why he had said what he had. William was not willing for the affair to be hushed up: the count should let him know the truth and not hide anything from him, if he values his life and has any self-respect. (37124)

The count of Mortain did not know what to say because it was impossible for him to deny that he had uttered those base, shameful, insane and repugnant words, but there was no way of extracting from him details of exactly how the plan would have been carried out. Even though threatened with losing his life, the count would not disclose what precisely he had intended and undertaken to do. This made the duke extremely angry and very ill-disposed towards him. "There

is no room for doubt," he says, "I can see and understand what dastardly and dia-
bolical act you had in mind: you had plotted and sought to sow confusion
throughout Normandy and bring the country to its knees. I can see perfectly well
that your intention was to act illegally and commit a crime against me; there can
be no doubt about that. That is why you told Robert the knight that he could go
plundering and make a fortune wherever he pleased in no time at all. But things
are not going to work out like that, because God in his divine kindness will keep
the kingdom free from conflict for us, and maintain peace and honour, not
because this is what we deserve but out of compassion for us; this is what we pray
for most of all. As far as your intention of entering into conflict with me is concerned, see to it that you leave the territory of Normandy this instant, here and
now, for as long as I live you will never receive any inheritance, or any part of any
inheritance in this country. May all the harm that you intended to cause me fall
instead on you! It is only right that you should live to regret what you have done."
On the spot, and without further ado, the count of Mortain, downcast and grief-
stricken, was obliged to leave the country, and he set out with no knights to
accompany him and a very shabby retinue. His destination, believe it or not, was
Apulia. Duke William, according to what I find in my source, made the county of
Mortain over to his own [half-]brother Robert [of Conteville],* who thereafter
conducted himself in a truly noble manner. Those relatives on his father's side
who were malcontents and caused William a great deal of trouble, and whom he
found overbearing and resentful, he sought to keep under tight control. His more
modest relations on his mother's side, on the other hand, who would never have
thought of being disloyal towards him, he raised up, making them rich and
endowing them with valuable estates. (37180)

[13] *How [William,] the count of Eu was exiled.*

I discovered in my Latin source that the duke had another of his kinsmen,
William by name, count of Eu, who also harboured malicious thoughts against
him and was untrustworthy. Overambitious and suffering from delusions of
grandeur, he wanted the duchy for himself, and this obsession resulted in his
plunging Normandy into war, committing atrocities against the duke and inflicting grave damage on the country. Finally the duke could tolerate this no longer,
and so he raised a huge army and came at the head of his troops to besiege Eu. He
had no intention of lifting the siege until he had captured the castle by force. As

the source book informed me, William of Eu was driven into exile and expelled from the country. Filled with anger, sadness and grief, he went to King Henri of France, to whom he explained, in very pained terms, that his exile had left him feeling helpless. The king received him honourably and was ready and willing to offer him some consolation. William was a fine, upstanding knight; he had been a powerful count and came from the family of the dukes of Normandy. The king was so well disposed towards him, so we read, that he gave him the lordship of the county of Soissons as well as providing him with a wife. Subsequently the land was held by his descendants, and still is, most honourably, to this day. The Latin source records that peace reigned thereafter in Normandy, a more general and long-lasting peace than any man alive had ever before seen. (37218)

[14] *How Duke William married good Matilda, daughter of the count of Flanders.*

During this blissful period of peace and prosperity, the duke was requested, by his most influential friends and by his people, to take a wife – a wife from a noble family with whom he could have descendants and ensure the succession. There being no grounds for postponing the decision, the duke acceded to their request. The names of several candidates of great beauty were suggested to him. At that time, so my Latin source records, there was in Flanders a count, Baldwin [V], a powerful man of excellent reputation renowned throughout Christendom. He had an exceedingly beautiful daughter called Matilda, a noble young woman of elegant demeanour, intelligent and most accomplished. She was the niece of King Robert [II] of France, and grandniece to the king's mother Constance. The lineage to which she belonged could not have been more exalted. (37240)

The duke duly dispatched messengers asking for Matilda's hand in marriage. That is all I know about it: to put it in a nutshell, Count Baldwin granted his permission unreservedly. Laden with lavish and valuable presents and amazing luxuries, she was brought as far as Eu with a by no means sparse retinue: bishops, counts, barons, and the lord duke was himself accompanied by people whose names were among the most illustrious. It was here that William married Matilda with great ceremony, universal joy and merry-making. No lady of such high rank was ever held in such high esteem. So much did she love and cherish God, so great was her reputation, so far-famed was she, and so much good did she do during her lifetime, that she will be remembered until the end of time. (37260)

When these celebrations came to an end – and despite the very brief account of them I have given you here, no one ever saw anything so magnificent – the duke and his retinue came to Rouen. The whole of the following fortnight saw such uninterrupted rejoicing that it would be impossible for anyone to describe or give any sort of account of it. Within a very few years, the lady had some beautiful children. The sons, William, Robert and Henry, who had a particularly attentive upbringing, were all people of outstanding merit and with high reputations in secular matters. She also had two daughters, distinguished, intelligent and accomplished, the elder of whom was called Adela and the other Adeliza [= Cecilia].* The latter knew how to read and write, and became abbess at Caen where she protected and ruled over the nuns. Adela was countess of Blois, Chartres and Dunois, and was the wife of Count Stephen [II Henry], the most important man in the whole of the kingdom. I have no idea what more would have been needed to increase still further her reputation. She was amazingly learned, and produced many fine heirs. (37288)

[15] *The interdict under which Archbishop Malger placed Normandy.*

During this time of peace, so the Latin text informs me, several people founded abbeys throughout Normandy, more, I find, than at any time before or since. To give any description or account of who founded them, and where and on what occasion, and what lands and fiefs were granted them, would be a very long undertaking. As there remains so much of our history still to tell, we shall continue here with our narrative. (37300)

Archbishop Malger,* so I find, was a brash, untrustworthy, even unhinged individual. Time and time again he acted in an absurd manner and illegally, doing things that were both objectionable and odious. Decorated books, crosses, censers and other precious and expensive objects that belonged to the church of Saint Mary and were in the archbishop's safekeeping simply disappeared from view; they had "walked" and were lost. He placed Normandy under an interdict with the result that no mass could be celebrated there. Malger had no love for the duke and showed no affection towards him. He even went as far as claiming that William and his wife, Count Baldwin's daughter, were such close cousins that their marriage should never have been allowed, and he insisted that it be dissolved. The interdict that he imposed on the country meant that dead bodies could not even be buried. His outrages against the duke grew more and more numerous, and William, being both worthy and wise, rebuked him on many occasions and criticized his lawless behaviour. But the archbishop, rather than mend his ways, just went from bad to worse. So unacceptable did his behaviour become, and so widespread were the denunciations he was subjected to, so strident was the public outcry against his devilish deeds, his eccentricities and his acts of madness, that he was summoned to appear before the pope. Since he refused to appear, and in order to stop him committing his offences, the pope suspended him and placed him under interdict. In short, he did not do unto his neighbours as he would have them do unto him.* So finally the noble duke, who was also his nephew, called an assembly of all his bishops and brought together legates, archbishops, prelates as well as his most prominent subjects. Malger was accused of so many crimes and found guilty of so much foul wrong-doing that he was no longer fit to carry the crozier, and he was obliged to relinquish it to the duke. Because of the sin of which he was guilty, he was ejected from the archbishop's palace. The duke no longer allowed him to stay there and he drove him out. Until his death, so I find, he lived in Jersey, off the Cotentin coast. There he had numerous children with serving wenches and mistresses. Let us stop talking here about this character! A person has only as much good sense as God grants him. (37354)

Before I reach the end of my history, however, you will be able to hear me mention someone else* who was even worse and an even greater failure, someone who was the most uncourtly person ever born. For a long time I have been itching to talk about this person's character: every living creature detests him and spits at his name. In comparison with the [archbishop] I have in mind, Malger was a paragon of chivalry and a holy patriarch. Foul as Malger was, this one is worse still, and the longer he lives, the fouler [Archbishop Thomas Becket] gets. (37365)

An abbot of Fécamp, Maurilius, a native of Lombardy where he was born, a learned, wise and holy man, was made archbishop by good Duke William, who lost no time at all in making the appointment [in 1055]. Maurilius's behaviour was of the highest possible order in his service both to God and to the people. There was nothing malicious or mercenary about him, and he subsequently did a great deal of good for his church. (37374)

Duke William was deeply in love with Matilda his wife, and she loved her husband likewise. They live harmoniously and happily together, remaining God-fearing and faithful for the whole of their lives. But, as the Latin source records, they were the object of frequent criticism because of the fact that they were closely related as cousins, and attempts were made to separate them. When they found that this state of affairs had become intolerable, they sought a means of conciliation and of reaching some sort of agreement. The pope imposed a penance on them which consisted of their having to build, during their lifetimes, two abbeys, and to make provision for one hundred charitable donations to be distributed to the poor, the destitute and the paralysed – those found to be the most in need. This they were willing to consent to. They set to work, and their endeavours resulted in two magnificent and costly churches being founded at Caen, one for monks, the other for nuns. The larger and more important of the two was made in the duke's own name, and in the second it was the duchess who installed the abbess. This explains why these two abbeys are so magnificent, so beautiful and so well-endowed. If there was, in fact, any legal error in their marriage, it was entirely right that they should be forgiven for it, as they indeed were, as any right-thinking person will see, for they made extremely handsome amends for it. (37408)

[16] *The great conflagration and the battle of Mortemer [in 1054].*

Ever since the days of the wise and valiant Rollo, the first of the Norman lineage, there has always been ill-will between the French and the Normans, never-ending hatred and envy; they are always ready and willing to fight each other. Never was there any sufficiently stable peace between them that could be called lasting. On many occasions it was the French who declared war on the Normans and then came off worse. After this particular period came to an end, a number of old grudges flared up again: hatred, quarrels and great resentment broke out between several of the most powerful and most valiant Normans, and the entire situation changed. Taking advantage of such dissension, the French barons arrived, seeing what they took to be an opportunity of invading the country and of capturing land and castles and of seizing some splendidly rich booty. They encouraged the king of France to believe that he could conquer Normandy without any trouble, that it could become his personal property subject exclusively and without condition to the French crown, and that he could thereby claim to be inheriting it lawfully since the land had, many years previously, been forcibly stolen from his noble ancestors: "Now all that remains to do is take it back from them, and this will greatly increase your territory. Once they had lost Normandy, the French kings of old found themselves with limited resources. All the vast

amounts of money they had spent, all their great ventures, their greatest enter-
prises – everything they had achieved had been financed by the great wealth they
extracted from Normandy. It is for you alone to decide whether or not we are to
give all this back to you. If you do as we advise, you will find us to be your most
faithful subjects in this undertaking. Summon your vassals, your neighbours and
all those who are favourably disposed towards you! Get hold of as many troops
as you can; use all the strength and power you are able to muster so that we can
embark on this venture in such a way that Normandy is conquered!" (37456)

   This attempt at motivating the king resulted in him having a complete
change of mind: he was thoroughly converted. He devoted himself to the task,
concentrating all his thoughts and all his efforts on immediately gathering
together every single man he could, either by making promises or by giving gifts.
He announces to everyone who will listen that his intention is to conquer Normandy and make it his personal property and that of his heirs. He decided to
launch a two-pronged attack, and accordingly divided his troops into two in order
to bring matters to a rapid conclusion. The arrangement they decided on was
that the king augment his own French army with troops from Gascony, the
Auvergne, Burgundy, the Berry, Limoges, Touraine, Poitou, the Perche and the
Hurepoix. Geoffrey Martel, count of Anjou, thrilled to take part in the invasion,
added his well-armed contingents and his [Beaufort] valley archers.* These, so
it was agreed, were the forces alongside which King Henri would fight, and which
would comprise his army. Once all these had been marshalled, it was impossible
even to give a rough estimate of their number. (37484)

   The second part of the army Henri entrusted to his brother Odo. It comprised many a count and many a baron: Flemings, troops from Poix, Brabant,
Hainaut, all the fierce knights of the Liège region, the Brie, the Vermandois and
Beauvais. There had never before been an army like this: in the whole world there
was no duchy, no kingdom, no land on earth that they could not have conquered
whatever defence was mounted against them. (37496)

   Normandy was terror-stricken to see such an extraordinary military force
marshalled against it in this way. No one had ever heard of an operation capable
of instilling such fear into so many people. Count Odo was preparing to enter
the region of Beauvais with a force so great than no one could calculate its numbers. But their intention was first to invade, pillage and completely devastate the
Pays de Caux. They believe that there will not be anything left that they do not
have sufficient power to plunder, destroy or burn. The king had drawn near to
Mantes with those troops listed in our Latin source. His plan was to enter Nor-

mandy from this direction, and from here nothing will stop him, until he reaches the sea, from going anywhere he wishes and conquering the whole country, from one end to the other. Cities, castles, woods and plains, he wants to have the whole of Normandy in his hands. (37516)

It is in no way surprising if Duke William feared the massive forces of the king of France, if he were intimidated and afraid of the fierce and redoubtable army that Henri had marshalled against him in order to deprive him of his land and destroy his honour. He took the best advice available to him and came to his decision accordingly. The unanimous advice he received from his most faithful followers was for him to also divide his army into two, and this is what he did. He kept fitz Osbern with him in his own company, together with all the men from the Cinglais, the Bessin, those from the Cotentin, the Passais and Mortain, as well as all the Hiémois troops. And the king of France would do well to realise that his foragers should take particular care not to venture too far from their base unless they wanted to end up in coffins before they had time to make their getaway. (37540)

As leaders of the second half of his army, whose task it was to defend the Pays de Caux against Odo, he designated those barons who were his direct vassals and to whom he was most attached. Walter Giffard, a powerful baron, a wise and enterprising knight, was sent to head the advanced guard, followed by Robert, count of Eu, with his large retinue of knights, and in third place the everdependable Hugh de Gournay, no longer a young man, and in fourth, William Crispin. All four were highly renowned, skilful and expert warriors, and they brought along with them relatives, allies and all the troops from where they lived. From all over the country, the movables and fodder were taken out of the villages and stored in fenced enclosures deep in remote woods. There was next to nothing for the enemy to find and steal, little left to destroy or lay waste. (37562)

Odo, the French king's brother, came riding up with his army of many thousands, and the immediate result was distress and devastation. They began their outrages by laying waste and setting flame and fire to everything they found, leaving nothing untouched, nothing standing, no house, no cloister, no church. Even if they had been pagan invaders, they would not have inflicted so much damage; no living creature was spared, from the elderly right through to children: all were taken prisoner, ransomed and led away. Such inhuman treatment was without precedent. There was not one woman who was not dishonoured and put to shame. Without pausing they continued in this way until they reached Mortemer. Here the fine lodgings and the luxury living could not fail to appeal to them.

They spend the day hard at work ravaging the prosperous countryside, but at night they enjoy themselves, revelling in the fine food and the soft beds. Their stay in Mortemer was carefree and entirely untroubled. None of the Normans were willing to show their faces from dawn till dusk, since they spent all of their time in the woods until they found the right opportunity to emerge. They had spies who kept them informed of everything that the enemy was doing, and they therefore came to know exactly what their lifestyle was. Accordingly, before dawn, they left their hiding places and met together. Having armed themselves and organised their troops, they headed for the town where the enemy was lying sound asleep. So unsuspecting were they that they had not even bothered to leave anyone on watch. It was their belief that there were no longer any soldiers or knights left in the neighbourhood. Their lack of caution came from their mistaken assumption that everyone had gone off to join the duke in the battle against the king of France.* This was to cost them dearly because, before the army could get to its feet, the whole town had already been set alight. The fire was so intense and so violent that nothing could possibly protect them against it. Everything caught fire and was immediately burnt up. The French were so taken by surprise, and such misfortune did they suffer, that never since the birth of Christ was any army overtaken by greater disaster. Everyone leaps on them, hurling abuse. They are unarmed and do not even have time to dress; they cannot withstand the fire, and it is impossible for them, unprotected as they are, to rush headlong at the sharp steel blades of their attackers. Some do manage to reach their weapons and find time to arm themselves, but to what avail? Some even go looking for their horses, but there are no saddles or bridles for any that are found. The air is full of blazing cinders and sparks, and so loud are the howls of the dying that they would have drowned out God's thundering. They have no choice but to die indoors, being unable to reach as far as the door, so fierce are the flames burning them. In any case, the Normans are there, waiting to pounce on anyone who is able to escape the blaze. Outside, therefore, there are incredible fights, the fierce clashing of swords, slaughter of the most distressing kind, people taken prisoner and huge booty seized. The town continued to burn, swords to clash and the woeful slaughter to rage from just before dawn until late afternoon. What I am telling you here is but a fraction of the account of the disaster given by my written source.* (37648)

Odo, King Henri's brother, put up a defence that lasted for a considerable time. That day his bravery and his steel blade served him well. But the time came when he had to give up and flee, though never before had he left a battle as early as he did then. Anyone who escaped with his life and without injury and emerged safe and sound could consider it a spiritual as well as a physical bonus. Guy, count of Ponthieu, was taken prisoner and suffered considerable humiliation before his body-armour was stripped from him. Waleran, his youngest brother, an extremely accomplished knight, had been killed on the same day, and Guy had done everything he possibly could to avenge his death. He let many people know that day just how much anger and grief he felt, and it was Guy who put up the stoutest defence and who inflicted most damage on his opponents. It was his outstanding bravery that got him captured, and he might well have got safely away had he only been willing to flee. After he had been captured, that was the end of the fighting and there were no more hostilities. Taking prisoners was easy, and anyone could have three or four without encountering any opposition. They led away many knights, men-at-arms, squires and grooms. They found so many valuable personal effects, goblets, furs, thoroughbreds and pack-horses that even half of it would have needed seven full loads to shift. Anyone who failed to be touched by the suffering could never have seen any in his life before. No one can say just how many corpses there were, how many people burnt to death, how many were wounded, and how many led away as prisoners, but all the enemy were defeated and killed. (37688)

Pursuing and slaughtering the French, though tiring, filled the Normans with happiness and delight as they re-assembled and gave thanks to their Lord God. Everyone agreed that messengers, of the wise and valiant kind, should be immediately dispatched to the duke. William was delighted and extremely happy when he was told the story of the enemy's extraordinary defeat, the count of Ponthieu's capture and the death of his brother Waleran. No joy that he had ever experienced could have been compared, in my opinion, to what he now felt. With his hands joined in prayer, he gives thanks to the all-powerful Lord King. Shedding tears of emotion, he enquires after his vassals and his beloved friends to see whether they have survived and are safe and sound. He is overjoyed when he learns that no harm has come to them. He takes one of his vassals, the baron called Ralph [II] de Tosny, to one side: "Take your horse," he says, "I pray you, and go to the king of France's army and shout out, so that everyone can hear, the news about Count Odo, the fire and the massacre of his troops. I want the king to be told and informed of everything, and in this way this whole venture will be called off. He will go back home with his army, and a halt will be called to this agony." (37720)

Ralph jumped on his horse just as the bright moon was rising. Off he rode, and it was already past midnight when he reached the French army. It was camped in such a way that it overlooked a river, and Ralph came galloping up onto the wide top of the cliff that towered over the camp. He was itching to be able to give the message that his lord had entrusted him with. From the top of the cliff he began to shout out, his voice resounding down through the valley: (37732)

"Sire, are you asleep? Listen to me!* The duke has sent me to give you some bad and unwelcome news that can no longer be kept from you. Yesterday, within one day, your army was destroyed by a fire and your men overcome and killed at Mortemer. No army in the world has ever been seen to fall victim to such a massacre. Odo managed to escape by fleeing, but our troops captured your count of Ponthieu and made him their prisoner. They killed his brother Waleran along with many many others. Every day you live henceforth will be a day of grief." (37748)

The knights who were on guard heard all this and took due notice. They were truly amazed as well as suspicious. To get more information, they asked him who he was and why he was relaying news that sounded like someone talking in his sleep and having a dream which, like all dreams more often than not, was completely nonsensical. "Just listen to what I'm telling you, please," he said. "My name is Ralph de Tosny. Go and fetch some carts to transport the corpses you will find at Mortemer, and it won't be easy for you to get hold of as many of them as you will need. Tell your French king that he will find it no laughing matter. Your comrades will have learnt, I think, what sort of men the Normans are when it comes to defending their country. While we're thinking about what happened back there, the only prospect you have here is the same as that of your comrades who got beaten and killed, because it is wrong and unlawful of you to be attacking us." (37770)

This whole incident was reported to the king, whose only possible reaction was one of loud lamentation: it almost broke his heart. Immediately and without a moment's hesitation, he had his soldiers gather together their weapons. From the mightiest to the humblest, all were disconsolate. King Henri goes off with his vast troops and without delay returns to France. This battle and the fire took place 1054 years after the birth of Christ, as I find recorded in the written sources. (37784)

[17] *Who William fitz Osbern was and how he met his end.*

My task here is to tell you what happened after the battle of Mortemer where so many people lost their lives, as you have already heard at length – namely the duplicity King Henri was guilty of and the policy he adopted when he destroyed Tillières and demolished it, and then fortified it again and held it as his personal property. In this he acted most improperly, since, despite Duke William having specifically requested him to do so, he refused to relinquish the castle and instead placed his own garrison in it and used it to wage war on the surrounding countryside. It was in order to counter such highhandedness, so we read in our Latin source, that good Duke William had Breteuil fortified, a large, handsome and solidly built castle, well-sited and set in appropriate countryside. The duke appointed William fitz Osbern as castellan for the whole year, winter as well as summer, since he was someone William could trust unreservedly. The source book gives ample proof of the sort of man he was and how he behaved, what a brave knight and what a loyal vassal he was. He married a lady called Adeliza, and with her, I discover, he had two sons: one was called William the Red [of Breteuil] and the other Roger the Arrogant [of Breteuil].* According to what I read, Adeliza was the daughter of Roger [I] de Tosny. William fitz Osbern was the founder of two abbeys, in which he took an extraordinary interest. I am able to name them as Lyre and Cormeilles. When Adeliza died, she was buried at Lyre, whereas William's resting place was Cormeilles. William showed himself to be extraordinarily brave, strong, courageous and intrepid, when he accompanied his lord in the conquest of the kingdom of the English. He subsequently became earl of Hereford, and occupied a position of considerable power in the kingdom by virtue of his intelligence and his experience. What happened next, according to our reading, is that Robert the Frisian, with a powerful company of armed men in addition to a large number of German troops, came to dispossess Baldwin [VI,] count of Flanders, the nephew of good Queen Matilda. At the time this was happening [1070–71], Philippe [I] was king of France, and he, without hesitation or delay, came to confront this great military force that you have heard me describe. He brought William fitz Osbern along with him with some handsomely armed companies. On their arrival in the region, they were taken unawares in some way or other, and the king of France was forced to flee, with the most unfortunate result that his nephew Baldwin, so I read, lost his life in the retreat along with many other valiant men, much to the king's immense grief. It was on this occasion that William fitz Osbern was killed, and throughout France as far as the Alps at Mont-Cenis he was mourned and grieved over for a very long time as someone especially highly honoured in worldly affairs. (37858)

[18] *How Duke William conquered Le Mans [in 1063].*

At this time, then, the French were neither attacking, fighting nor entering Normandy. Good Duke William, on the other hand, had not given up his fight against Geoffrey Martel. I can tell you for certain that there were many fierce clashes and confrontations between them. The violent resentment between them lasted for a very long time. This was why the duke kept waging war against Maine until he finally made it entirely his own. (37868)

As I understand it from what I find written in my source, Count Geoffrey had waged numerous wars, embarked on wholesale invasions and undertaken violent persecutions against Le Mans and the surrounding country, where he inflicted grave suffering. At that time Hugh [IV] was count of Le Mans, and Geoffrey committed many outrages against him. He persecuted the city's inhabitants by setting fire to it on several occasions. There was nothing left to plunder, and even the vines had been stripped bare. Geoffrey had subjugated a large part of the country, subjected it to his will and brought it under his jurisdiction. Hugh, so the Latin source reveals, had a son called Herbert, and because he was the eldest, his father handed on to him not only the county but also the hatred and the hostility he had against Geoffrey Martel. Hugh died [in 1051], and Herbert [II] accordingly inherited the county and assumed control. Besides being handsome, valiant and clever, he was a very young man with relatively little experience. He took steps to defend his position, and out of fear of count Geoffrey and in order to ensure that he had the military aid and assistance he needed, he became the vassal of the lord of Normandy. He recognised William as his overlord and held his fief and all his other lands from him, on the understanding that, should Herbert be unable to have children and then die childless, William would be his heir. To cement their friendship and their alliance, and so that the arrangement they had come to and the bonds between them would be strengthened, they agreed that the duke would give his daughter [Adelida] in marriage to the count – a noble young lady, extremely beautiful, elegant and clever – as soon as she was of marriageable age. The objective was that their union produce a lineage that would henceforth hold and rule over the county. This, however, they could not accomplish, since it transpired that Herbert died before the marriage could take place. He had insisted, on his deathbed, and made his men swear an oath, on threat of excommunication, using entreaty and arguments and appealing to their sense of fidelity, that if ever he could no longer govern the county, they would accept no other lord but the duke of Normandy. He promised and assured them that, if they followed his instructions, they would find William an easy-going lord to serve, one who would be considerate and not overly exacting. If, on the other hand, the duke was ever obliged to subdue them by force, they could be absolutely certain that they would suffer a great deal as a result. "As well you know, his qualities are strength, power, glory, valour, intelligence, a sense of justice and honour, and what you should wish for, more than anything else, is that he be your lord; that is the best way of ensuring that your lands are safeguarded. Just look at the sort of noble family he comes from! Don't let yourselves be misled at this particular moment! Do as I say. More sincere and loyal advice than this I could not give you." (37938)

Herbert died [in 1062] after only a short life. Listen to what happened next! His men were unwilling to follow their lord's urging or obey his instructions on how to ensure the future of the Maine estates by becoming vassals of Duke William. Instead they turned to Walter of Mayenne, which proved to be a very grave error on their part. As we learn from our source text, Walter had married Herbert's aunt [Biota], the sister of Hugh [IV], and this is why they made him their lord. But they never got to know just how bad a decision they had taken, because Duke William, as soon as he learnt what was happening, became indignant and extremely angry: Herbert had designated him as heir, and he would be exceptionally unhappy to lose the lands. Consulting the records, he discovers and understands that formerly, in the distant past, the whole of Maine had been under the exclusive control of the lords of Normandy. Without wasting a moment, he calls up his army and sets off, with all the troops under the sun he can muster, to besiege Walter in Le Mans. Even if he cannot capture the city by attacking it, this will not stop him from laying waste to the whole of the countryside around. He could not, in fact, succeed in taking Le Mans by storm, so he built and fortified two fine, tall wooden siege-towers. One of these was called Monbarbé, though I cannot tell or even discover why it was named in this way. Eventually, however, William did succeed in taking Le Mans, and all the surrounding castles – all, that is, except Mayenne, despite the many efforts he made to capture it. It had a keep, ditches and walls – a secure stronghold with many knights, sergeants-at-arms and fine archers in it who conducted themselves valiantly and put up a brave defence. Finally, however, the castle was taken thanks to a clever stratagem. The Normans trained two young boys, telling them exactly what they had to do and how they were to behave. These infiltrated the local native children of Mayenne and innocently joined in their games without drawing attention to themselves. During the early hours of the night, when it was already pitch-black and people were at their least vigilant, the boys set fire to two houses. Immediately the whole town went up in flames, and soon there was nothing left to catch fire. The townspeople had immediately to open the gates to save their skins, though there were many who lost their lives. The castle was destroyed and captured in exactly the way I describe. I never before heard of any town or stronghold that was captured in this particular fashion. Before the duke left, the castle was rebuilt and reinforced with much better fortifications than it previously had. The duke had this work carried out unhurriedly and peaceably. Thereafter he also arranged for supplies of food to be made available. In addition, he installed valiant and trustworthy knights whose task it was to closely and loyally guard the great gates in the city walls. William kept Mayenne in his possession for a long time. Some havoc the Normans wrought on the good count of Anjou's land, while the people of Mayenne caused a great deal of trouble for the Normans and inflicted much suffering on them! (38014)

When the duke had conquered Le Mans in the way I have described to you, his wish was that this new situation be continued without any opposition or conflict so that subsequent generations could govern in total peace. He made provision for future heirs and the succession like the great and wise statesman he was. The author of my source informs me that, on his mother's side, Herbert had a [half-]sister, a young German [= Breton]* lady, clever, refined and very beautiful. Duke William wished to marry her to his own son in order to further consolidate his position and to prevent anyone finding any reason to seize the town illegally or mount a surprise attack on it. His son [Robert] was still very young and not yet of an age to marry the young girl. In the meantime, until he was old enough, Duke William saw to it that she enjoyed a lavish upbringing and was looked after just as if she had been his own daughter. As the Latin source records, her correct name was Margaret. She was one of the most beautiful creatures that any man on earth had ever set eyes on, loved and made a fuss of by one and all. But her life was all too short, for it came to an end and she died before she could marry. And even if she never had an earthly lord and husband, she found one in the Lord of Heaven. No young lady of her age was more intent on serving God and doing his holy will. Every day, morning and evening, she was at her prayers, and she had even put a hair-shirt on next to her skin that stung her bare flesh. She was wearing it the day she died and was buried with it on. The duke was distraught at her death, and nothing else could possibly have saddened him more. He could be heard loudly grieving and lamenting. He had her buried at Fécamp. Thus, as you have heard me tell, did Duke William take Le Mans and add Maine to his personal possessions in a series of events that went on over a long period of time. (38062)

[19] *How Duke William got the better of the king of France crossing the river Dives [in 1057].*

Following the huge damage that the Normans had inflicted on the French as a result of the fire and the slaughter, King Henri became so infuriated that he would never again find any enjoyment in life until he had exacted his revenge. For him it had been an insult, a source of shame and self-reproach. He would not feel at peace again until he had crossed Normandy, until he had occupied and seized the land and left nothing of value there. He also needs to make the duke lament the loss of the glory he had derived from having defeated the French. Henri swears that all the power he possesses will be directed at proving his point. His mind necessarily goes back, time and time again, to the slaughter he suffered at Mortemer, and his heart aches and bleeds at the memory. But there is no reason for him to be hesitant or to hold back in taking his revenge in the most brutal of ways, since the whole of France expects him to do so. He summoned his troops and by proclamation ordered all his numerous soldiers to come and join him. Now, it seems to me, things are beginning to look bad, for Henri has assembled extraordinarily powerful forces. The count of Anjou has also mustered his companies whose numbers are excessively large: a powerful and numerous cavalry, infantry, sergeants-at-arms and common foot soldiers. The count's army alone was a huge one. They joined forces with the king and entered Normandy. No country had ever been invaded in this way or subjected to such grievous mistreatment, for the enemy spared no one, not even the humblest. To put it in a word: they destroyed everything. They cross the Hiémois and the Bessin without meeting any resistance at all until they come to the ford over the river Dives. If they had been allowed to continue unchallenged, only the sea would have stopped their advance. Had they succeeded in getting that far and then returning, far from incurring displeasure they would have earned praise and glory for such an exalted victory, which would have led to their indulging in never-ending boasting, bragging and bluster at having laid waste to the whole country, captured, plundered and destroyed it, with impunity and without encountering any opposition. This is precisely what they hoped would happen, but they were on the point of suffering a very serious setback, for Duke William was not prepared on any account to see them turn their boasts into actions and to do what they alleged and swore they would do. Never will the French have returned home in such ignominy, such grief and such despair as they are about to in the very near future. William is devastated to see the country burnt, damaged and destroyed in this way. He was in the vicinity of the French army with seven hundred knights, but, intelligent and experienced as he was, he had no wish to join battle, fight or engage them until it was the right time to do so and circumstances were favourable. (38132)

In high spirits, King Henri crossed the ford at the point where the wide, deep sea, stretching away into the distance, comes pouring in and fills the river to overflowing. Although he did so at low water, there were so many people to get across that only half of them had reached the other side before the sea-tide turned. Their adversaries – the duke, that is, and his Normans – who were champing at the bit could not wait a moment longer. They donned their helmets, snatched up their shields, and, with their sharp blades in their hands, attacked the French with such ferocity that since the birth of Christ, so I believe, a massacre like this had never been seen to happen in so short a time – no more than the time it takes me to tell the tale – and no body of men had ever been wiped out with such brutality. For the French to put up any defence is useless: the tide is coming in behind them, cutting off any possibility of turning back unless they are willing to be swallowed up and drown. This is enough to make them panic, but seeing the steel blades drawn in front of them means that they are now staring death in the face: no quarter will be given. You would have heard the howling and the screams of pain, but no one could possibly begin to describe the slaughter and the carnage unhesitatingly meted out to them. All this happened under the very eyes of the French king who was literally trembling with fury and anguish and punching his fists together. No one person could ever show such grief. By this time, the high tide had covered the ford that had separated the two sides. This episode, now over and done with, was a hundred times more distressing even than you have heard tell here. (38170)

Anyone who succeeded in escaping from the steel lances or the clashing swords was at the very least taken prisoner. There were very few of these who emerged unwounded. They were dragged across the whole of Normandy and thrown ruthlessly into many a desolate prison where most of them subsequently died. (38178)

King Henri of France was exceedingly angry, sorrowful and dejected, and it was little wonder if he was deeply depressed at seeing the misfortune that had befallen his men. He had no wish to stay in Normandy and wasted no time in going away. The only reward he had reaped was shame, disgrace, defeat and insult. As the proverbial saying goes: "Someone imagines he is avenging his shame only to find he is increasing, even doubling it." The king goes off but with a heavy heart, as is acknowledged by the fact than never again in his life – if our written source is to be believed – did he set foot in Normandy or do any harm or damage there. Moreover, some prominent figures, upright and wise people, undertook talks in order to reach a peace settlement whereby they might bring about a reconciliation between the duke and the king. Their disagreement had been a source of grave hardship and suffering for both of their countries. So many people had had to pay the price for this that it would take more than a hundred years for the losses to be made good. But for the moment the conflict was at an end. So that the peace between them was equitable, the king gave back Tillières. This, for William, had been the crux of their dispute, its sore point, the main issue at stake. He was, therefore, very happy and content that the castle was now back under his control. This was how the bad feeling between them, that had lasted for so long, was finally dispelled. (38212)

This Henri was a good-humoured king, a valiant paragon of chivalry. Though he was a strong and powerful man of action, he was also very benevolent. As I read the history of his life, he had married the daughter of the king of Hungary [Conrad II], a most worthy lady called Matilda* who had three children with her husband: Philippe, Hugh, the younger, and a daughter whose name I do not know. He was an extremely courtly and generous king, and his reign lasted for twenty-five years. A worthy medical doctor of high repute and intelligence had concocted a particular potion for him to drink. But things turned out badly on one occasion when the doctor had to go away. On leaving the king's chamber, he had left two of his own chamberlains there to take good care of the king. Henri, however, became extremely thirsty. He asked for something to drink, and the chamberlains administered the potion to him. This was an extremely serious error on their part, for on that very day the king was to die because of it, and there was nothing to be done about it. So rapidly did the illness strike that he hardly had time to make his confession, be given absolution and take communion before his soul left his body. As was necessary in the interests of the kingdom, Philippe [I] was anointed king [in 1060]. He was crowned and became king in a seemly and harmonious fashion. He was still a young boy. Baldwin [V,] count of Flanders was his regent, and he whole-heartedly undertook to instruct his ward on how to live a virtuous life. (38248)

[20] *How several Norman barons were deprived of their inheritance.*

The Latin history informs me that at exactly this time there arose a despicable incident contrived by jealous, underhand people who, by means of false and treacherous allegations, succeeded in poisoning relations between the duke and his barons, just as such people still do to this day. The result was that it was impossible to restore peace, friendship or goodwill otherwise than by the duke banishing the individuals from the country. Among these, so I find recorded, was brave Roger de Tosny, Hugh de Grentemesnil with all his sons and nephews, together with Arnold [d'Echauffour], so I discover, son of William Giroie. These were admirable knights, powerful and experienced people from the most noble of families, people whose accomplishments were many and whose acts of bravery numerous. Either because they were forced to do what they did, or because they acted out of compulsion, or perhaps as a result of their own recklessness, they dared no longer stay in Normandy, and it became necessary for them to go into exile. Had it not been for the duke's very powerful position, the situation could not have failed to cause a great deal of damage. The whole country came very close indeed to disaster and collapse. But the people in question stood in such awe of William's ability, and the power and strength he had, that they did not dare defy him and engage combat or declare war. There was, at that time, no leader in the whole world who was more redoubtable, more feared, no one more implacably opposed to evil, no one more committed to sovereign justice. (38286)

[21] *Which Normans first went to Apulia and then conquered it.*

I have no wish to pass over or omit anything that I read and find in the Latin history, anything that others before me have written and which deserves to be repeated, for there is great benefit in knowing the noble deeds of our ancestors. It is altogether right that the honour, the glory, the heroic exploits, the valour and the prowess of the illustrious people of Normandy should be spread abroad throughout the world. It is right for me to recount and tell you which men of Normandy it was who conquered Apulia and Calabria and who achieved domination over Sicily. It is right for me to give you a brief account of this here and now, but without my being long-winded or holding up my narrative. (38302)

At the time of the Emperor Henry [III] who ruled over Germany, a high-ranking, powerful and much feared man who had been crowned at Rome, and at the time of Duke Robert [I] of Normandy – so the history of his life informs me – a certain knight by the name of Osmond Drengot was the first Norman to go to Apulia. He was bold, strong, brave and wise, and he took along with him the most prominent of his family members. And I will tell you on what pretext he went there and why, as I understand it. Duke Robert had a companion, a resident in the ducal household, a brave, experienced and upstanding knight by the name of William Repostel. He and Osmond Drengot had a long-standing and implacable hatred for one another, and the ill-will between them was to be explained by the arrogance and stupidity of each of the two parties. No one could bring about a reconciliation between them. When the duke went hunting one day with his personal retinue, before his very eyes Osmond killed William, hacking him to pieces with his sword. The duke had not been able to come to the victim's assistance, since, like William, Robert was himself unarmed at the time. But if the duke had been able to get his hands on the perpetrator, Osmond would have regretted committing such an insolent, foolish and deranged act, for Robert would have had him hanged, drawn or otherwise put to death. There would have been no other course of action possible. Together with some of his closest allies, Osmond was obliged to leave Normandy with his brothers, nephews and cousins; there was no question of their staying. Travelling in lavish style, they made their way straight to Apulia where they entered the service of the men of Benevento as highly paid mercenaries. Their bravery led to their being held in great esteem. There was, at that time, a fierce and intractable war going on between the Lombards and the Saracens. It would never have come to a peaceable conclusion until the Lombards were beaten, since they are still to this day a people to whom bravery is unknown. The Saracens kept on plundering the Lombards' land before their very eyes, and the whole country was on the verge of collapse. Drengot and his relatives opted to get involved in this conflict, since when they decided to settle at Benevento, being skilled in the arts of war, as is customary among the Normans, they were eager to cover themselves in glory, as strangers are in a foreign country. The operations they undertook were on such a scale that it was often very demanding and difficult for them to bring them to a successful conclusion. But so often did their swordsmanship allow them to emerge victorious from repeated battles, encounters, combats and violent skirmishes that the Saracens, pagans and Greeks found the Normans to be so brave that they were never able to stand their ground against them unless they were willing to forfeit their lives in the process. Vanquished and overwhelmed, the invaders abandoned all the territory they had won and fled out of the reach of the sharpened blades. Once all the Lombards' enemies have been defeated and they now no longer have to go in fear of them, they begin to treat Osmond Drengot and his fighters with utter contempt. They cut back on their pay and allowances, and begin to subject them to all sorts of bad treatment. The Normans, anticipating the shame and the abuse that the Lombards were about to oppress them with, and judging that they would not accommodate them any better in the future, had no alternative but to elect their own leader and lord from among those of their companions whom they considered to be the most worthy. This was the risk they were willing to take. Even though it was an extremely difficult undertaking, and one that put them in mortal danger, they found a certain satisfaction in being courageous enough to defend their own interests and strengthen their position by conferring the lordship of the country on themselves. This led to their incurring enmity and loathing and to their being frequently attacked, to which they responded by drawing their nielloed swords, their trusty blades of engraved steel, and dashing out their enemies' brains, gouging out their entrails and intestines. They captured strongholds, fine, strong, upstanding and well-fortified castles. By the use of force and by imposing justice, they made the common people and the peasantry subject to them as their vassals. Never did any people need to use such force and make so much effort to conquer a land in which they and their heirs could live. (38408)

The duke of Salerno, Valmache, who reigned for sixty years and more, had taken on a number of Normans as mercenaries, and these had risen to positions of power. They were led by one Thurstan Scistel, a fine, upstanding and wise knight, not only brave, courageous and valiant, but skilful and enterprising also.* Just listen how bold, strong and forceful he turned out to be! One day when he had come to the palace, he found there was a lion there that had caught a goat – or it may have been a sheep, for all I know – and was on the point of eating it. Bold and brave, Thurstan came rushing up and attacked the lion, grabbing it in his bare hands in full view of everyone there, and forcing it to let go of its prey. What was truly astounding was that, in front of all and sundry, he hurled the lion over the palace wall with the greatest of ease and as if it was no trouble for him at all. The animal was smashed to pieces and dismembered, and its two eyes came flying out of its head. This caused the Lombards to regard him with fear and suspicion; they became extremely jealous of him, and took such an active dislike to him that, every time they met together, they would discuss how best they could bring about his death. This led them to think of one particular place in the country where a dragon lived in a cave under a rock. A devil of a monster it was, so ferocious and horrendous, such a terrifying colossus spitting flame, fire and toxic fumes, that it was feared, reviled and loathed in equal measure for the unspeakable evil that it was capable of doing. This is where these despicable Lombards took Thurstan, straight here. He had absolutely no idea of how deviously they were acting or that there was a dragon here. When it hears all the noise they are making, the horrendous monster suddenly appears in front of them, baring its fangs and spitting fire and flame. Terrified, the Lombards take to their heels and make off as fast as their horses can carry them, leaving Thurstan all on his own. He is greatly surprised to see them all run off and leave him in the lurch and alone except for his groom. Then he suddenly catches sight of the devilish dragon, but cannot get away from it quickly enough to prevent the beast from seeing him. Anyone witnessing the extraordinary sight of Thurstan battling against the beast would have had every reason to be panic-stricken, for the dragon spewed forth so many flames onto him that time and time again he could see absolutely nothing in front of him. Who is the man who would not have been frightened to death seeing the whole of his shield catch fire? Never was there such a horrendous and long-drawn-out combat. But finally, after great exertion and suffering, Thurstan killed it with his shimmering mottled sword. No man alive, be he Saracen or Christian, had ever achieved such an extraordinary exploit. It cost him his life, however, and because of the burns he received and his poisoned wounds, he survived for only three days more, according to what I find in my written source. His burnt and battered shield had turned to cinders. This is how he was betrayed and deceived by the Lombards. Had he lived a longer life, he would greatly have enhanced the fame of his lineage. He was the founder of the city of Aversa, and his name was known as far afield as Persia. (38492)

His death was the occasion of much mourning, and he was greatly lamented by his friends and allies. Being unwilling to remain without a lord, the Normans designated two leaders from amongst their number; they were called Richard [Drengot] and Rainulf [Drengot], both valiant and enterprising individuals. Everyone swore publicly that they would not rest or find peace until Thurstan was avenged. The harsh treatment they meted out to the Lombards grew so oppressive that never a single day passed without their country being involved in warfare. (38504)

This state of affairs continued for a long time until finally Drogo, a noble knight and son of Tancred de Hauteville, who had come to Apulia from the Cotentin coast, was made leader by the Normans who had settled there. They could not have made a better choice, for more than anyone before him, so I read in my source, he was of great worth and prowess, fervent in his Christian faith, praiseworthy and steadfast. (38518)

The count of this country was called [Waszo],* a powerful, influential and forceful man. This vile and deceitful Lombard, an untrustworthy and dangerous individual, had made Drogo a cherished companion of his, but only in order to deceive him and the better to betray him. He had befriended him as if he had been one of his closest and most intimate confidants, but in reality his word was totally unreliable, for he treacherously and perfidiously killed him in the church of Saint Lawrence without any of Drogo's fellow Normans realising what was happening. They had all gone to the church, as good, dear and faithful friends do, to celebrate vigils. As Drogo, kneeling at the altar, was saying his prayers – it was dark outside and the sky was overcast – this oath-breaker took his life, and he died what I would call a glorious death. His brother Honfroi became the Normans' leader thereafter. He took such cruel and vicious vengeance for his brother's murder that as many as a thousand heads – I exaggerate not – felt the effects of his sword as brains came gushing out in a stream that no bandage was any help in staunching.* Honfroi waged many a violent battle and conquered the whole of Apulia and established law and justice there. He was yet another extraordinary figure. He had a son by the name of Abelard, and his [half-]brother was Robert Guiscard.* (38550)

Robert was someone whom no one could possibly praise less than he deserved without immediately being castigated for doing so. However much may have been written about him, and however much you may have been told about him, there would still be more than a hundred times more to tell. Before Honfroi died, and when he sensed that his end was near, he bequeathed Apulia to him, without any qualms, as his beloved brother, as well as to his own son Abelard. Robert was to be Abelard's guardian and regent, and would retain lordship until the young man was old enough to be knighted. In this way Robert Guiscard became supreme leader and as such had lordship over his brothers as well as over the people. His brothers were individuals of great prowess, and all of them had positions of wealth and power, the poorest among them being a duke or a count. No one advanced the interests of his family as much as he did, though he excelled them all in intelligence and merit, so outstanding were his qualities. Many a castle and many a town he captured, and he conquered Apulia, Calabria and Sicily by the sword and steel. There was no one ever to compare with him, no one to equal him, no one even like him, since people first took to the sea in ships. He took land from the pagan Arabs in the region, and even conquered extensive parts of Greece. He married a beautiful, noble and intelligent wife [Alberada], but because of the fact that they were closely related, he separated from her. They had a son together who was a person of great merit and very knowledgeable. His name was Bohemond. There was no one in the world to match him. I know of no one with more qualities than he had, no one whose fame and worth were greater than his. His extraordinary achievements will be recounted in stories in both French and Latin until the end of time. Robert Guiscard married a second wife [Sichelgaita], the daughter of the prince of Salerno, Guaimar [IV], son of Gaitel-grima.* Her elder brother gave his consent; this was Gisulf [II] who had inherited at the death of his father Guaimar [IV]. I find written in my source that Prince Jourdan [I] of Capua, whose ancestor was the valiant Rainulf [Drengot], one of the Normans' first leaders, was an ancestor, had as his wife Gaitelgrima, a young lady of great accomplishment and the sister of Robert Guiscard's wife. Again according to my written source, Robert Guiscard had three sons and five daughters with his second wife. The daughters were so attractive that in the whole world there were no young women at that time who could rival them in accomplishments or intelligence. They married into the best families and were extremely well provided for. One of them [Olympias] even married the person who at that time was emperor of Constantinople [Constantine X Doukas]. It would take me all day and into tomorrow simply to tell you of Robert's personal exploits. So much did he do to enhance his family name that it was amongst the most celebrated in the world. The author of my written source informs me that in one year he overcame two powerful emperors in pitched battle: one was Alexius [I Comnenus]* whom he defeated in Greece, while the other one was [Henry IV] a man of very high rank who had been crowned in Rome. He had come as far as Lombardy in order to attack Robert. No one ever did anything so foolish, and no one ever will, I should think, for a thousand of Henry's men were left to finish their lives on the battlefield and die unshriven, while the rest of his army took flight. The most conservative estimate of the booty that Robert took put it at more than a hundred thousand marks. I cannot imagine how there could have been anyone in the whole world who was so feared and dreaded. To everyone's great grief, he died while still vigorous and in the prime of life. (38638)

His son Bohemond, that fine, valiant and intrepid man, acceded to the crown. He sent to Normandy for some first-rate knights and to France to enlist those that could be of most use to him. He was not content to rely on all the honour accumulated by his ancestors, or on the kingdoms and lands liberated by them and from which they had ejected the Lombards; his one desire was to have his share of the cities occupied in different parts of Romagna by the pagans. With his household troops, more highly esteemed than anyone else's, he attacked and waged war against them, either slaughtering them or harrying them to such an extent that they either fled or were overcome, put to death and killed. By armed struggle he won many a fine castle, many a city, many a mighty stronghold from them. No one at that time enjoyed greater fame. He accompanied the powerful body of knights that went off to conquer the land of Syria, and more than held his own among them. When it came to conquering Antioch, no one inflicted more damage on the enemy and no one covered himself in more glory and honour after suffering such great hardships. He was made prince of Antioch [in 1098] and defended it with great valour against the masses of the pagan army. He married a lady by the name of Constance, daughter of Philippe, king of France, and they produced a son, another Bohemond [II], a valiant and highly praised knight, noble-hearted and most energetic. When his father died, he succeeded him, but the only heir he had was his daughter [Constance], a very beautiful and knowl-edgeable young lady who inherited the entire kingdom. Raymond, son of the count of Poitiers, a fine, upstanding and wise man, married her [in 1136] and thus came into possession of the land. He was so great and valiant a prince that stories will be told about him for a thousand years to come.* (38686)

Roger Borsa, the son of Robert Guiscard and his second wife, reigned over the kingdom of Apulia. His reign was a long one. He also married and had a daughter and heir, but the truth is that they all died within a short space of time, and many a tear was shed over them. (38694)

Roger, the brother of Robert Guiscard, became count of Sicily. He was a very shrewd knight who inherited the land as his share of the inheritance. This Roger had a son, another Roger [II], whose inheritance comprised the whole of Apu-lia in addition to Sicily. I could not find a finer person to write about. His rule was high-minded and noble and extremely peaceable, and he did not relinquish as much as a square foot of his territory. Indeed he went further by taking advan-tage of the ugly and degrading schism between the two popes, the legitimate and rightful one, Innocent [II], and the usurper Pietro Pierleoni [Anacletus II]. Hav-ing backed the winner, Duke Roger was then in a position to ask permission to be crowned king. This is the reason he became king, as I understand it from what I read. He was the first person to be called king in the lineage into which he was born, and he was the first king of Sicily. As we read in our source, exactly 1130 years had elapsed since the birth of Christ when this great schism arose, and it lasted, I find, all of eight years. At this point, I am not willing to say any more on this topic in order not to digress from my subject matter, to which it is now time for me to return. For anyone who might now wish to hear how Duke William conquered the land and the kingdom of England from Harold who had had himself crowned, I will tell the true story of what happened. (38732)

[22] *How Duke William conquered the kingdom of England from King Harold.*

It so happened that the will of God was that Edward, the legitimate and true king who ruled over England in peace, the supreme and truly Christian king who was filled with kindness and goodness, should be childless and without heir.* His intention was to make William, duke of Normandy, his heir. Edward loved no one in the whole world as much as William and had set his heart on this as something he desired more than anything else. Some years earlier, as my story goes, he had sent the most distinguished figure in his kingdom, [Robert,]* the archbishop of Canterbury, over to Normandy to confirm his intention of granting the whole kingdom and the crown to William. This was how things stood at this point. He now wished to reinforce the arrangement so that things should be more certain and more transparent, and no problems should arise. He therefore sends Harold [Godwineson] over to William in Normandy, this earl being by far the most powerful of all the earls in the kingdom, to swear homage to William in respect of the entire kingdom as delineated and including all crown appurtenances. Edward's instructions are that Harold ratify the grant by swearing an oath on holy relics recognised as such. Harold set out immediately and, without losing a moment, made his way straight to the coast and the boats. His plan, and that of his companions, was to set sail for Normandy, but the crossing was exceedingly rough, and a violent storm and strong gales made it impossible for them to land on the Normandy coast. Instead they were driven further up the coast straight into Ponthieu, where they reached port half dead and so exhausted that they would rather have been in Sicily than where they ended up. There they were taken captive by Count Guy d'Abbeville who threw them into prison in the hope of securing a ransom for them. The price of their release would be the amount they themselves considered they were worth. (38780)

Harold was, then, detained as a prisoner. But he has a message sent to Duke William to inform him of the situation, to tell him where he is and what position he is in. As soon as William gets to know what is happening, he takes the whole matter very seriously, immediately sending word to Guy that he will be very distressed if Guy were to detain Harold for a single day more. He requests him to be kind enough to release Harold, exonerate and hand him over, but not at his own expense or at any cost to himself or to any of his men. Guy, however, would not go along with William's request and, being so greedy for payment, was very evasive. William immediately summoned his troops, hundreds and thousands of them, and set off for Eu, incensed at Guy's refusal to hand Harold over. Very soon Guy's luck would have changed for the worse,* and he would have suffered the sort of losses that would have taken him a whole year to recover from. As it was, he was wise enough to see sense, and before any sort of harm came to him, he brought Harold safely to Eu and released him to William. Even if he did refuse the duke's original request, Guy nevertheless got his own way in the sense that he never ended up out of pocket. This, then, was how Harold came to be freed, and the duke went with him directly to the town of Rouen where, in amity and good faith, he gave him the warmest and most honourable welcome that he could possibly extend to him. Even though Harold had been through a somewhat unpleasant experience, he now had everything he could possibly ask for and was made to feel very comfortable indeed. William took Harold with him to war when, with a vast army that he had assembled, he marched against the Bretons who had wronged him by unlawfully refusing to submit to him. William showed him such affection on this expedition, and Harold had been so much in his element there, that he could think of nowhere else where he had enjoyed himself so much. When this interlude came to an end, the duke called a council meeting at Bonneville, according to what I read in my source. It was here that the oath that Harold himself devised was sworn,* namely that for as long as King Edward was alive, he would keep the country in peace for him, insofar as it lay within his power and his capacity, without deception and without corruption. And on Edward's death, until such time as William took possession of the kingdom, Harold would hold it on his behalf against anyone else until William was crowned, and from that day on he would offer him every assistance in all matters. He would immediately hand over the keep and castle at Dover in proper and correct order, suitably provisioned and with its defences intact, and it is to be placed under the safekeeping of those of the duke's men whom William will designate. And should William wish to construct strongholds elsewhere along the coast, Harold will supply financial resources, subsistence and everything else necessary at his own cost. With his hand firmly on the reliquary that people brought forward for the occasion, he swore to keep his word without any deception or evasion. (38856)

The duke, in order to be sure of having Harold's fealty without any false pretences or deception, and to guard against the earl changing his mind, grants him his daughter [Adelida], an altogether admirable and clever young woman, in marriage, in addition to half the kingdom once William is in possession of the crown. Harold was more than happy to signify his fealty by kissing William's foot.* Such was the agreement between them. William gave Harold so many presents that it was a wonder to behold: huge and magnificent precious objects, horses, arms and armour, gold and silver, and many other expensive items of equipment and clothes. Having equipped and fitted him out in this way, William accompanies Harold directly to the coast from where he will cross the Channel. Harold says his tender goodbyes and expresses his thanks to a person he now treats not only as his dear friend and overlord, but as king as well. Harold had a younger brother called Wulfnoth – a finer young man you would not hope to find – who was both courtly and clever, and he left him with the duke as a surety. I do not know, and have no way of finding out, whether Harold was already planning his criminal act when he left his brother behind in Duke William's safekeeping. In any event, Harold never honoured his agreement with William, he never abided by his oath, kept faith or observed the law, and, as far as I can see, this is going to cause him to come to grief. (38884)

King Edward grew weaker and before the end of March he had passed away and died [in January 1066]. He was buried with great pomp. His was a holy and glorious death, and he was widely mourned with many tears of grief. Harold, consumed with greed and without pausing to reflect on what he was doing, lost no time in taking over the kingdom. The duplicitous law-breaker declared himself king without either the unction or the consecration that, according to correct protocol, should be administered to a king on the day of his coronation.* (38898)

This is how, without any further explanation, this rapacious and duplicitous law-breaker had himself illegally crowned – actions that would lead eventually to his undoing and to his death. He failed to keep his word to the duke, failed to honour the arrangement they had come to, failed the surety he had left behind and simply forgot his brother. This is how he secured the kingdom and made it his own. (38906)

The way Harold had treated William, seizing and taking over the kingdom, was immediately reported to the duke. Harold had no fear of God punishing his crime or his perjury, or of what other people would think of him. It never occurred to him that there were some additional steps he should take, or that no one in the whole world would hate him more than William will do for the rest of his life. When the duke got to hear of what had happened, he was both astonished and furious. He was, however, not too apprehensive, for he firmly believes that no one can deprive him of something that God is willing to make available to him. He desires nothing in the whole world, nothing he might acquire himself or receive as a gift from someone else, unless it be in accordance with God's will. He informed his bishops and prominent clerics of what had happened, and those of his barons who were dearest and closest to him, his faithful allies by whose advice he set great store. (38928)

Robert, count of Mortain, William's good and trustworthy [half-]brother who had no time for any sort of malice; the valiant Robert, count of Eu; Richard, count of Evreux, valiant, brave and well-informed; Roger, count of Beaumont, a most shrewd knight; Roger de Montgomery, whom it would be wrong to omit; William fitz Osbern, to whom William subsequently proved to be so benevolent; and Hugh [de Montfort] the valiant viscount – these, as I record them, are the names of his counsellors, and they were unanimous in advising William to demand that Harold tell him and let him know what his intentions were with regard to the crown and the kingdom. William's decision on what to do then will depend on Harold's response. Let William in the meantime dispatch his messengers straightaway and begin to assemble his fleet. He should also summon, from all over Normandy, his neighbours, friends and allies, and those who owed him allegiance in such a way that so great a fighting force will never have been mustered by Normans, and such an invasion, that for them could be a matter of life or death, never before mounted. (38960)

The duke is very happy with this outcome: the fact that they are ready and willing to help him defend his right to conquer the kingdom of England means that they will put all their resources, their strength and their power, as well as themselves, at his disposal. He sent his messengers to Harold, valiant, well-trained and experienced men, to inform him of what steps he has taken since hearing that the earl had seized the crown. He should not, he said, have acted illegally as he did, since it was common knowledge that the kingdom had been granted to him, William, and Harold had been the first to acknowledge this by swearing an oath in public. Let him not commit perjury and break his word, but let him honourably hand the kingdom and the crown back, as his duty demands and as justice and right require! And let him know for certain, and let him be in no doubt, that, as long as there is breath in his body, William will never rest or give up until he gains possession of the country. This was the message sent to Harold as it was relayed to him. But the answer he gave was little more than arrogance, contradiction and contempt. The only way he could get people on his side and be willing to accept him would be to provide guarantees and offer impressive sureties and promises of land. (38992)

Having declared himself king, Harold declared war against the Welsh. I can find no reason for this or discover what the cause of contention was. But the Welsh lord, King Gruffudd [ap Llewelyn],* fell on the battlefield. Harold killed him then seized his wife Edith, who was the daughter of Ælfgar, the good earl [of Mercia]. This caused her much anguish, and being an extremely virtuous lady, she refused to sleep with him and would not allow him even to touch her, day or night. She was heart-broken and incensed that her husband had been killed in the way he was. This was how and by what means Harold went about winning a wife for himself!* (39006)

It was during this time that there appeared, high in the sky, a brightly shining heavenly body, a dazzling comet with three huge tail-like rays emanating from it. I read and understand from my source book, and I know it to be true, that it remained visible for a full fifteen nights.* The astronomers said that it signified a change of reigns, of kings or of dignitaries. (39016)

This, then, is how Harold behaved, taking no notice of the fact that he was being called an oath-breaker and a traitor, and remaining indifferent to the charge as long as he had possession of the kingdom and the rank that went with it. There was widespread outrage at his crime. At Rome the pope at that time was Alexander [II], a just, most pious and sincere man who maintained a lasting peace within Holy Church. King William sent him word of what was happening to the kingdom, telling him how it had been granted to him and how Harold has acted disloyally by breaking his word to him. He requested the pope, being someone not only pious and wise but also having the requisite power, to lend his authority to his claiming and establishing his legitimate rights, as this was something very dear to his heart. (39034)

The pope was extremely pleased to see the duke being so deferential to him. By the power invested in him, he granted William papal approval and instructed him, both orally and in writing, not to hesitate to acquire what he was requesting. Together with this he sent him a special standard, the Standard of Saint Peter,* as a token of his willingness to offer him assistance. It will be a sign of authority and a pledge that what William is seeking to acquire is his legitimate right and the crown which belongs to him. It will also give all those who accompany him the additional assurance of knowing that no misfortune or serious accident will befall them. (39050)

Harold had a younger brother called Tostig. I can find no clear explanation of why there was bad blood between them. Tostig came to see the duke who gave him a warm welcome, cherished and honoured him, and showered him with valuable gifts. Tostig, who was a good, brave knight, noble, sincere and loyal, was extraordinarily keen on going to war against his brother and capturing his castles and strongholds, for Harold had treated him extremely badly. Following the advice of his principal counsellors, the duke was ready and most willing to provide him with everything he needed: boats, troops and as many arms as he wanted. Tostig immediately rushed off to cross to England with his huge army. But Harold had placed the ports under close guard to prevent Tostig from landing; he was thus denied the right to make landfall and was unable to get into England. He would have liked to sail straight back to Normandy, but the winds were against him. Instead he had to make his way to Norway, despite the sea being extraordinarily rough, and he somehow managed to reach a port there. Humbly and modestly he appealed to the mighty and powerful King Harold [Hardrada]* to deign to receive him, as he came in peace, without any dishonest intention or deception. He also asked – if he were to be so bold – if there were any possibility of the king providing him with some help – if it were no trouble – against his brother who was treating him so unfairly. For the rest of his life, he said, he would recognise the king unreservedly as his liege lord. The king granted Tostig everything he asked for, and before the end of the month had called up enough troops to make an army and assembled a fleet powerful enough to conquer Saxon England. Thereafter things gathered pace: they issue a challenge to King Harold and plan to mount an attack against him that will be a crushing blow and place him in great jeopardy. (39100)

In the meantime, while Duke William was busying himself with preparations to cross the Channel, with bringing troops from afar and calling up the local ones, with making sharp, pointed swords with broad, cutting blades, with seeing to equipping the boats, Count [Conan II] of Brittany* was bent on forestalling him. Envy prompted him to act in the most disgusting and criminal way by attempting to stop William carrying out his operation. He sent him messengers, clever, eloquent, knowledgeable and experienced people, who delivered Conan's message in such a way that everyone could hear it. "Count Conan," they said, "is extremely pleased to know for certain that you are going to cross the Channel to attack the English, and that the kingdom is to be yours, thanks to your glinting swords of Viana* steel and your steel lances, in order that you may be crowned there. However, without resorting to insulting language or any sorts of threats, he humbly begs and requests you to hand over Normandy to him, since the duke you consider to be your father, when he left for Jerusalem – and no great joy or any good came of that – entrusted the land, the country, the entire heritage of which you have made yourself lord and guardian, to count Alan, my father, his kinsman and friend. It was you, together with your perfidious accomplices – renegades, traitors and scoundrels, all of you – who killed him at Vimoutiers, a murder which still makes Count Conan's heart bleed to this day. The poison you tricked him into taking in order that you could get absolute control of the land drove his soul from his body. Our lord, who was still a young child at the time, was criminally deprived of his inheritance. But by now he has been waiting for it long enough: he is quite willing to take possession of the land by force unless you hand it over peacefully. For him this is no impulsive raid to grab land. He intends to bring with him a thousand mounted and fully armed troops, each one girded with a sword and carrying a sharp steel spear, and ready to smite and strike, and who would be willing without hesitation to lay down their lives rather than see Conan fail to win the land outright." (39156)

Hearing this sort of threat could only cause Duke William extreme annoyance, for the last thing he would have needed at that moment was to experience any setback or hold-up. The crossing is poised to start, and his equipment is already in place in the various ports and on the beaches. This latest development puts him in a very difficult position, for he has no wish to leave Normandy under present circumstances with his power in such jeopardy. There is no one who would happily advise him to leave the country when he is under such threat. He could see no way out, not knowing which advice to heed or what decision to take, when God was good enough to provide him with a solution, as I am now able to reveal to you. (39172)

A powerful Breton castellan – of whose name I can find no written trace – a skilful, experienced and ingenious man, who had sworn fealty in public both to Duke William and to Count Conan, served as ambassador, carrying messages from one camp to the other. He had concocted a potion of venom and poison.* Listen to what he did with it! He used it to poison Conan's saddle and reins as well as both his gloves – I can tell you no more than that. Having once contaminated his hands then brought them into contact with his mouth, Conan had no need of any doctor to attend him: the long and short of it is that death was a foregone conclusion, such was the power of the concoction. He had just finished besieging Château-Gontier which had already surrendered and been captured when, in the presence of all his barons, Conan breathed his last. So great was the people's grief that its like had never before been described. He was a fine, valiant and generous man, a brave and accomplished knight, noble-hearted, a stranger to wrong-doing, an unequalled lover of justice. It was said subsequently, and it was entirely true, that had he been able to live a longer life, his family would not have produced so worthy a leader for a hundred years and more. The castellan, as soon as he saw Conan give up the ghost, was wise enough not to stay around or dawdle, as he would pretty soon have been subjected to some harsh treatment. Without waiting to see the outcome of his actions, he quietly left the army and slipped away on his own with only a small retinue. He lost no time in telling Duke William what had happened and how things had turned out. William was greatly upset, very sad and sorrowful, for Conan had been someone of great merit. If he had not shown such hatred for the duke and acted so contemptibly towards him, no one in the world would have been as upset to see him die, as William's reaction clearly showed. (39218)

[23] *How Duke William and his army cross the Channel, and the battle that follows.*

The duke's great enterprise, then, is underway, as the written history recounts. Now that Brittany no longer threatens his security, he has no fear that the invasion will not take place. Now there are no problems to be anticipated from that direction, and William has no concerns or misgivings. He can leave his kingdom in such a settled state, and in the hands of such faithful friends of his, and those of his dynamic and shrewd wife, that no harm can possibly come to it. His resentment is now focused on the English. Provided he has sufficient forces and the power to do so, he will inflict such slaughter on them that their descendants will for evermore bemoan it. He understands all too well that there is no point in waiting any longer, since Harold will be securing reinforcements and additional assistance. When the Norman troops had all arrived, and when all the boats had been rigged, provisioned, loaded, listed and named, there were – so the author of our source assures us – at least three thousand boats. All the troops that William had summoned assembled at Saint-Valéry: Normans, Flemings, French, Bretons and others from many different places. Eustace, count of Boulogne joined the expedition with a large number of troops; fitz Osbern also, the valiant, brave and wise steward; Aimery, viscount of Thouars, strong and good-natured; Count Hugh [of Montfort]* the marshal, a noble, valiant and loyal knight; Walter Giffard, who enjoyed great fame and was a person of outstanding merit; William of Warenne, than whom no man alive could possibly find a better knight. These are the people who will cross to England and see to it that, before the midday hour has passed on the following day, the crown is restored to good Duke William. (39260)

The boarding and the loading passed off without any upset or upheaval, for the wind was light and mild, making few waves on the sea. By the time night fell, everyone was on board. The winds being in every way favourable, they hoisted the sails and set out, commending themselves to the King of Heaven. In good spirits and with the weather fair and fine, they reached land at Pevensey [early on 28 September 1066]. There, overlooking the harbour, they immediately constructed an impressive, strong defensive fortress, and the duke garrisoned it with a large enough number of proficient knights from among his army to ensure its defence for two years. After which, so my written source recounts, he at once made his way to Hastings, and there he promptly and within a short space of time had another fortress built. They took care, in constructing it, to make the walls high enough to withstand any attack, from whatever direction it might come. Here again he installed guards of maximum reliability and whose loyalty to him was beyond question. (39284)

A rich and prosperous nobleman,* a native of Normandy but resident at that time in England where he led a life of luxury, had totally reliable and genuine information on how the battle had gone in which Harold had killed his brother Tostig. He hired a highly trustworthy messenger whom he immediately sent to Duke William without anyone else knowing. Having told him who he was, where he came from, and whose message he was bringing, the messenger told William the whole story that his master had entrusted him with, of how Harold had gone to war and overcome the people from Norway, killing his brother and the king together with more than twenty thousand others that he had brought with him. Harold was at that moment, he told him, on his way back from this battle, emboldened and all proud of himself, with more than a hundred thousand armed troops such as no one had ever before brought together. "So keen are they to engage battle with you," the messenger said, "that they are worried they will not get here in time. Watch out, think carefully, don't be complacent, because there is difficulty and danger ahead! Take care not to get yourself caught out, even though you have in the past won so much honour and fame! Do not rush into war, or expose your troops, or end up in a situation where they might get killed, or you yourself might be humiliated or come to grief as a result of some ill-thought-out operation!" "Many thanks for that, my friend," replies the duke. "Your lord did well to send me this message, and he very much deserves our thanks for it. My reply to him is this: someone who has God as his protector, who is led, guided and supported by God, whose cause is a just, upright and well-founded one and undertaken for God's honour and glory, should, if he places his trust in God, have advantage, power and victory. This is, I think, precisely my case, for I am in the right and am claiming my right, and I call on him to be my protector in all things. And God will emerge victorious, for no one has the strength, the merit, the power, the protection or the means of defence to withstand him. And now may his will be done!" (39334)

After Harold had killed his brother, as I have explained to you, and defeated and killed the [invading] Danes and won a victory over them [at Stamford Bridge on 25 September 1066], he came triumphantly to London with his army, happy in the belief that henceforth he would find no one capable of offering him any resistance. He nevertheless takes extremely seriously the fact that the Normans have come to attack him. Learning how numerous the Norman fleet is, and how many fierce, courageous and intrepid enemy knights there are, he has no desire or inclination to spend his time hunting in the woods or along the river banks. With all the troops he can raise, summon or conscript, and without waiting or losing any time, he rides off to confront the Norman army before idle rumours start to circulate.* (39354)

Harold was strong, valiant, courageous and audacious, and there would have been no point in looking anywhere else in the world for a better knight. He cut a fine figure of a man, was an eloquent speaker, a lavish giver of gifts and a generously hospitable person. His mother [Gytha], as far as she could judge and insofar as she was able, had tried to dissuade him from the life-threatening and distressing venture that he had undertaken. Earl Gyrth, his brother, spoke in moderate terms to a meeting of Harold's most intimate followers, and said to him: "Sire, everyone knows that you are more valiant, braver and more audacious than anyone else. But the Normans have come to attack you, to challenge you for the kingdom and take it from you. What is needed in such circumstances, and what is absolutely necessary, is for you to show intelligence and moderation, and to respect justice and the law in all matters. Anyone who makes a false move will soon reap the reward in shame and contempt. You are tired, and your men even more so from the fighting and from the battle that they have just got back from, and it would be a wise move by you to allow them a short rest. One other thing:

you would do well to remember what you consented to, and to be aware of the promise you made in Normandy to King William regarding the kingdom and the crown. Are you forgetting that, by so doing, you became his sworn vassal? Take care not to lay yourself open to the charge of perjury, and bring about your own undoing, and that of our people and our prestigious families, by this sort of unfortunate accident and serious judicial error. Unless you take the right decision, the legitimate and honourable one, they will be ruined, and you yourself, powerful and valiant as you are, will incur widespread disgrace into the future and be cursed as the cause of our destruction and the author of our downfall. As far as I personally am concerned, I have sworn no oath to the duke, come to no agreement with him, issued no challenge to him. I owe him nothing, have done nothing to him that I could ever be accused of. If, sire, you instruct me to do so, I will go into battle at the head of your great army, for it would be wrong for me not to stand by you. The moment I see the need to act, I shall strap on my helmet, take my sword in my hand and go and fight for the land and defend your right to be its ruler. I make it absolutely clear to you and grant that never through any fault of mine will I commit any offence or crime against the enemy. You see the difficult position we find ourselves in. If we emerge victorious, all our problems are solved: the kingdom is yours to rule over in peace. If we are crushed on the battlefield, you would not necessarily be a defeated king. The greatness, power and authority which the English have always enjoyed in this kingdom will not necessarily come to an end. Take care, then, at this particular time, not to fall into a trap!" (39424)

Hearing Gyrth's declaration and what he had to say in front of everyone put Harold into a foul temper. He did not want to listen to any advice. He accused his brother of interfering, pouring scorn on him and condemning him for being foolish and naïve. He was extremely hostile to his mother whose heartfelt wish it was for him to hold back and not proceed. She went on making her case for so long that Harold finally pushed her over flat on her back with a kick to the stomach. In the meantime, with all possible speed and over six days, his combat forces came together from all over the country. Harold then set out for where the Normans were camped. He did so by night, under a moonless sky, with the intention of taking the Normans by surprise as day broke. To do this, he saw to it that his troops were armed on the battlefield and drawn up into battalions. He had some of his soldiers take to the sea to capture and detain any of the enemy that might flee the battle and try to get back on their boats, of which there were more than three hundred there. The English believed that, by doing so, it would be impossible for Duke William to escape, and that he would either be taken prisoner or killed in the heat of battle. (39454)

The duke had taken every step possible to prevent being taken by surprise. That evening, under the cover of darkness and in order to be on the safe side, he had had all of his troops armed in anticipation of an attack at first light. It was a Saturday, as I discover from my Latin source. William next took three of his huge divisions which he organised into three battalions. The rest of his troops, archers, sergeants-at-arms and foot soldiers, he also drew up in ranks. When everyone was in place, the standard which the pope had sent from the Holy Church of Rome was unfurled. To cut a long story short, the Normans made their confession, were given absolution, then took up their shields and rode straight at their deadly enemies. The wise, valiant and thoughtful duke had already addressed his men:* they were to bear in mind the many honourable victories they had won since he had been their lord, and the fact that nowhere had they ever been beaten. Now the time had come when they were to increase still further their valour – redouble it, flaunt it, and take it to a still higher level. It was no use pussyfooting around.* They had to defend themselves and save their lives with their furbished steel blades, for that was the ultimate point of all their hard work, fighting and suffering. This was the way to earn the great rewards which are due to all good knights: lands, fiefs, all sorts of property, and in greater quantities than their ancestors had ever had. Great wealth, great estates and fiefs will follow as the recompense for their valour and their acts of prowess. But it is an extremely dangerous gamble to take: if victory is not theirs, if they do not end up winners, they are dead. There are no two ways about it. It will be no use fleeing, no use seeking shelter, be it in castle or woods. Let anyone who intends now to act as a valiant and experienced fighter should act, show himself in his true colours! His help in all manner of ways will be welcome: as leader, as defender, as simple warrior. And a moment's reflection will show everyone that the English have never in the past been able to defend their country when anyone has made the slightest effort to conquer it. Another thing they should bear in mind is that they can be absolutely certain that Harold is guilty of committing perjury against him. Harold enters the fray as an oath-breaker who has lapsed into sin, bearing all the burden of his dishonour. Whilst he is already beaten, dead and gone, they will live on in the honour due to the great conquest they are about to carry out, the glory of which they will share with Duke William. All that remains to be done now is the fighting – to smite as only brave men can, so that, before night falls, the battle has been won. (39520)

Harold brought his troops up so close that they almost came into direct contact with the Normans. He had divided his army up into so many different companies that it would be impossible to enumerate them. The troops were so splendidly and so expensively armed that the whole countryside around was glinting with gold and silver weapons. As they rode forward, they unfurled so many richly decorated standards and pennants. The two sides clashed with such violence and ferocity that you will never hear tell of such a devastating massacre. The armies came to grips, with arrows and spears raining down in such profusion and so unremittingly that everyone kept their eyes tightly closed. The sound of horns, the hue and cry could be heard from miles away. So ferocious was the encounter that the ground was soon swimming in blood. Unhesitatingly and in little or no time, they throw themselves at one another in a deadly onslaught. With broad-bladed Danish axes and steel-tipped lances they lash out at one another with such force and venom that the crimson blood comes gushing out of ribs and spines, heads, arms and chests. There are an unbelievable number of people lying prone and lifeless. Then comes the turn of the swords – terrifying, sharp swords seen relentlessly smashing against ten thousand shields, shattering and shredding them, splitting open sturdy coats of mail, sending not only bright crimson blood but also bowels and entrails spilling onto the ground where already two thousand men lie pallid in death. No laughing matter this, as the violent clashing of steel swords against helmets rings out, bringing grief and suffering to those who come crashing down from their saddles, their faces split open, their brains dashed to the ground. On and on goes the fighting until the two sides finally merge into a single mêlée, cowards confronting heroes, foot soldiers and mounted knights face to face. So indiscriminate is the struggle right up to the midday hour that no one thinks they will ever emerge or escape from all these furbished spears, all these gleaming blades, all these keen-edged swords, all these well-honed axes, all these steel-tipped arrows. Everyone is resigned to dying as they see how savage the slaughter has become now that they are wading up to their knees in both corpses and bright blood. Never in a single day were so many anguished voices heard or so many grisly shrieks from dying men. (39586)

I will tell you of one advantage the English had, and which caused our boys great anxiety in this savage and bitter carnage. The part of the battlefield where Harold's troops were positioned was higher ground than the rest and consequently difficult to reach. This explains why the English were able to hold out all day, because getting to them was so strenuous. Had they occupied flat terrain, the battle would have come to an end much earlier, but our boys suffered a great deal that day from being denied the chance to fight on a level battlefield. They found it a great disadvantage to have to attack a position from which the enemy were able to mount such a stout defence. So much so that, on the left of the battle-line from which our boys were fighting – and my written source is clear on this point – there was a sudden, deadly panic as a number of people, as a result of an event that must presumably have been very dire – though I have no idea what it was – said that they thought that Duke William had been killed in the fighting. This was enough to make a thousand warriors turn their backs, take flight and head straight for the coast. The reaction was extraordinary, for nothing like it had ever been known to happen in so short a time: the English launched an attack against the Normans, pitching in to them and forcing them to break ranks. The result was distress and consternation. There would have been no way of stopping people from fleeing and of being able to continue the fighting if God had not worked a miracle. (39619)

Seeing some of his troops dead, others overwhelmed, yet others shirking or scattering unless God comes to their immediate assistance, William is deeply upset and cut to the quick, and in his frenzy almost loses his mind. He is aware that his men believe him to have been killed, and that it is because of their believing him dead that this calamity has befallen them. In the midst of the battle he bares his head, removing both his helmet and his visor. With so many good fighters dying around him, and in a place where his own life is in mortal danger, he wishes to show his face openly so that his men can see that he is, beyond the shadow of a doubt, alive and well, and convinced that everything will turn out well. With drawn sword he overtakes the people who are already fleeing, so violently upbraiding them for having fled the battlefield and their post that no one could possibly find words to describe it. You would have heard him shouting out: "What did you hear that made you run, you of little valour? Can't you see your lord, safe and sound and well able to help you, and certain that victory will be ours? Come back and enter the fray, and you'll soon see them trounced!" Up gallops Count Eustace, who proceeds to threaten the duke and attempts to unnerve him, saying that William is without any doubt a dead man unless he abandons the battle, for his men are now incapable of retrieving the situation. Count Eustace is holding himself up to ridicule and shame, for what he has just said soon turns out to be most ill-advised and extremely foolish. (39656)

The duke's men take heart from William's encouragement, and he inspires them to rediscover their valour. Seeing him safe and well dispels all their fears. They turn their horses' heads towards the battlefield, and the good and valiant duke leads the way back. Such are his knightly exploits and such great deeds does he accomplish this day that, with the blade of his decorated sword, he splits the enemy's armoured knights in two right down to the knots of their baldrics. He strikes and fells, cuts and kills, and his great army takes fresh heart. They find the English in disarray, for they had already broken ranks to pursue the fleeing enemy and kill them. There followed such a huge and grievous massacre that thousands, so I read in my source, fell and ended their lives there. By the time the Normans had got the upper hand again, they were up to their knees in blood. Before this carnage had come to an end, King Harold had been struck down and had died, wounded by three large, steel-tipped lances through each of his sides, and by two sword-blows to his head, splitting his skull right down to his ears and staining the weeds crimson.* His death was not noticed immediately, with the result that, for a long time, his men carried on resisting in the most extraordinary manner. (39689)

In the course of the struggle that I am describing to you here, I can tell you that Robert [of Meulan], son of Roger de Beaumont, proved himself to be such a valiant, brave, energetic and dynamic knight that the history I am translating records his name on numerous occasions. Count Eustace and his men forcefully reoccupy terrain that had been lost, whereas William fitz Osbern defies the enemy's iron and steel: any Englishman he gets his hands on, however well-protected he might be, can be certain to die. He is a strong, hardened, dependable knight, experienced, resilient and steadfast. The good viscount of Thouars, the one named Aimery, no slouch, no boor, covered himself in glory that day. Walter Giffard, we know for certain, found himself in dire need that day when he was knocked off his horse. Five hundred enemy knights had already ridden past him, and he was beyond the point of rescue by anyone when the good duke of Normandy, his furbished steel sword in hand, came to his assistance and saved him by getting him quickly back up on his horse. Such a demanding exploit as this in such circumstances by any leader anywhere in the world will never be heard of again. No one would deny or dispute that in that particular battle on that day it was William who won the prize in terms of fame, so fearless and so regardless of his own security had he been in rescuing Walter Giffard. Hardly anyone, either, acted more laudably that day than Count Hugh [de Montfort], while that courageous knight William, count of Warenne, made an outstanding contribution to the conquest of the kingdom. A certain Taillefer,* as my written source recounts, acquired a great deal of prestige, even though he was killed and lost his life. So intrepid was he that he slipped into enemy lines with as much confidence as if he had been enclosed within walls. He performed such deeds of prowess, even after he had been mortally wounded, that no knight of however noble a lineage inflicted such damage on the enemy as he did that day. (39742)

Just like the original author who wrote the Latin history, I cannot give the names of all those who played a prominent and courageous role in this grim, gruesome and mortal struggle. If I wished to list their deeds, it would take far too long to recount, and even after filling three quires of parchment, I would not have reached the end. The reason I should finish writing my history expeditiously is because some people – perhaps many – become restive, inattentive and distracted and quickly get bored with listening; often they turn their minds to anything else at all rather than listen to such fine exploits and learn from them. (39756)

From first light when battle was joined until late in the afternoon, the fighting raged on without flagging and without anyone withdrawing. But when it was realised in the English camp that Harold was well and truly dead, and that the majority of his army had been killed, including his brother and a number of his barons, they could no longer hope to save the day. They are weary and exhausted, weak and pale at the loss of blood pouring down from their bodies. They see their ranks broken and scattered, overrun on all sides, their troops slaughtered and dead. Nightfall brings a sense of hopelessness when they see the Normans revitalised, their strength increased and greater than ever. They realise they cannot now offer any defence. Anyone unable to save his skin by hiding, fleeing or riding off can be absolutely certain to die. They turn their backs; it is all over. Their men stop putting up any defence. Such were the losses they had suffered and so disheartened were they that huge quantities of them were overrun, and this was followed by so great a massacre by the sword that I am incapable of describing it to you. This painful carnage went on as long as daylight lasted, and night brought no end to the suffering until Sunday dawned. What caused even greater slaughter among the English was the fact that the battlefield was difficult to negotiate, being criss-crossed with trenches and full of prickly bushes, which prevented anyone from getting away, however hard they tried. People kept stumbling and falling over, and the foot-soldiers could simply dispatch them. I have never known, never been led to understand, never read, nor have I found it written in any history, that such a vast army was assembled only for it to suffer this sort of treatment and be destroyed and annihilated in this way. The battle was won, then, on the first day of October, to be precise.* Estimates of the number of English found dead on the main battlefield alone, following their defeat there, are as high as five thousand, so it is firmly believed. This is not counting the protracted slaughter and killing that took place during the night that followed. You would have seen much rejoicing from our boys when they made their way back through the corpses, though Duke William was greatly moved by compassion,* and the tears came streaming down his face when he saw the number of those killed. Even though they had all been his mortal enemies, and those of his men as well, even though they had killed many of his best fighters, and even though he should have been extremely happy at having defeated a deceitful and disloyal tyrant who had broken his pledged word to him, nevertheless he was moved to pity at the thought that the finest and the best warriors, the flower of the kingdom's military might, should have perished and died as they did because of Harold's crime and through his fault. They searched out his body and found it to be covered with more than thirteen wounds. There had been, I believe, among his peers no better knight than he. But he had not been God-fearing and had not honoured his pledged word, and that was why things turned out badly for him. The bodies of his two brothers were, I believe, found next to his. They had been unwilling to abandon him, and all three of them had to die. This is what happens to someone who pursues what he thinks he deserves: he who wants everything loses everything. (39836)

This most grievous slaughter which the Normans inflicted on the English was also what they had deserved from their past when they committed the enormous crime of killing Alfred [Ætheling] and so many of his good Norman companions. Thereafter the Normans never ceased to harbour a hatred against them, and to look forward to making them pay for their great crime with the sort of defeat that they have just now meted out to them. Their wickedness had gone unpunished for long enough, but now all that is a thing of the past. All their military might has disappeared, and they have reverted to insignificance. From now on, the lordship of their kingdom will be handed down to heirs of Norman extraction. It is theirs by conquest, won by true knights with their sharp iron blades and steel. (39854)

Early in the morning, after he had eaten, the duke had people search out those who had died. Quantities of feet, hands and entrails were found, but all the weapons and other remains were ordered to be collected together. William had all of his men buried. King Harold was also buried. My written source informs me that his mother was willing to pay a large sum of money to the duke in order to have the corpse, but William refused to accept a single penny or hand over the body for any reason whatsoever. He granted it to a certain William Malet who had asked him for it. He was no young upstart, this William, but a hardened and valiant knight, and he was given permission to bury Harold's body wherever he pleased. (39872)

And here's something quite extraordinary: there is a comparison here, and a very revealing one, with Agamemnon* and the Greeks who, with even more than forty kings, were not able to capture Troy in ten years, however hard they tried. Duke William, on the other hand, with his Normans and other fine helpers, conquered a whole kingdom and its inhabitants – a strong, warlike, unusually hostile and very numerous people – in the space of a single day between dawn and dusk. And just see how extraordinarily magnanimous and kind Duke William was: after his conquest he was unwilling to seize the crown on the spot without due process.* He was also unwilling to cause damage to the country, to burn, rob or impoverish it, or to eliminate its most powerful leaders who had shown him such enmity and whom he could have put to death or done away with. On the contrary, he has them summoned, telling them that they could come in complete safety, without fear or any apprehension. In this way he can both reassure and convene them. He also acted in an admirably pious manner by insisting that the bodies of those who had been killed be properly buried. This work was entrusted to the locals, and they carried out the task scrupulously, seeing that they were burying their own friends and relatives. No more than 1066 years had elapsed since the birth of Christ up until the day when King Harold was killed, and the kingdom seized and conquered. (39910)

William had Hastings garrisoned with his very best knights, and the fortress further strengthened. Then he made his way to Romney, which he intended to destroy utterly and completely. Some of his troops, for a reason I am not aware of, had already arrived there, and the vicious and dastardly English had been guilty of killing them. This greatly angered William, and he made them pay for it in the most ruthless manner. Thereafter, and without stopping anywhere, he made his way to his fortification at Dover, a fine building that he had constructed at the foot of the cliffs. The English were up on the top in a well-fortified position. In it they had secured all their possessions from the countryside around, and a huge force of men had gathered there. Because the stronghold was so easy to defend and out of range of any war-engines, they had constructed strong enough fortifications for them to think that they could successfully resist the duke from there. Within such a sturdy enclosure and one so tall, with so many towers and walls, it would be no simple task to capture it as long as their provisions held out. The duke spent eight days besieging it. Attack after attack was launched day after day: violent, ferocious, vicious and damaging assaults by foot-soldiers and squires. The people within the castle began to realise and then convince themselves that, even if they could continue holding out, they were all on their own and could expect no help. They are well aware that King Harold and the best part of the English army are dead. To a man, they realise that in all the kingdom there is no one left to come to their aid. Given that their prospects are so unfavourable and so dispiriting, they no longer have the will to keep up their resistance. They understand that for them there is nothing to be gained in the long run, so they have no choice, no alternative, but to surrender their fine, strong and powerful castle to the duke. Their lives, and their possessions, however, were spared. All the people from the surrounding region swore fealty to the duke and did everything he required of them. William stationed a valiant and courageous garrison there. Before he left, he received the visit of the people of Canterbury, both nobles and commoners, who swore homage to him and handed over suitable sureties. Stigant was archbishop of Canterbury at that time, so I read in my source.* More than anyone else in the country he derived power from his personal fortune and the number of influential friends and allies he had. The English consulted with the most powerful and prominent people in the kingdom, including Earl Ælfgar's sons. While recognising just how serious the defeat of the English army had been, they were unwilling to contemplate the Normans taking over the country. They therefore elected as their lord an outstandingly noble young knight from the same family as good king Edward who was called [Edgar] Ætheling.* They made him their king, whether out of fear or as a precaution, for the last thing they could have tolerated was having a king in England who was of foreign extraction and born abroad. (39984)

All the most prominent people in the country had assembled in London, prepared – to put it bluntly – to give their support to the Ætheling as lord of the realm. The duke determined to go and seek out as many of them as he could find in one place. After several days' journey he arrived in London, where he encountered a hostile group of people intent on denying him entry. The most brash among them armed themselves and came riding out of the city gates to show how little they feared him, and that they did not intend to defer to him in any way. Fully armed, as I have already explained to you, they drew up their troops against William's army. On seeing them and the posture they were striking, William attached so little importance to the threat they posed that he ordered no more than five hundred or so of his troops to take up their arms. These Normans, their helmets strapped on their heads, contemptuously but no less furiously and ruthlessly, charged their adversaries at full gallop. You would then have seen heads flying in all directions, spears piercing breastbones, ribs and armpits. In less than no time, they had driven the English back into the town, forcing them to leave many of their companions expired and lifeless on the ground. They then set fire to the houses, and so fierce was the conflagration that everything round the Thames was utterly consumed by flames within one day. There was great grief throughout the city, and the people were exceedingly despondent. Their losses had been great in terms of both human lives and possessions, and this was very painful for them. The Norman troops, both on foot and on horseback, crossed the river together and proceeded to Wallingford, and they did not rest until the castle there had been surrendered to them, and they had set up their tents. Great jubilation followed. Archbishop Stigant and several others of the kingdom's dignitaries arrived to swear fealty to William, who accepted their homage and the sureties they provided. Edgar Ætheling, whom the English had inadvisably made their king, was brought before William, and after the moving intercession of Stigant, the duke forgave him for having incurred his displeasure. He then brought the whole of his army back to London with the intention of capturing the city, but the English leaders and people did not dare put up any resistance. Instead they immediately came out to meet him and surrendered everything to him: themselves, their possessions, their city. They will be his faithful vassals and henceforth do everything he requires of them. They swore fealty to him and handed over satisfactory sureties. Despite being advised then to have himself crowned, William refused to do so until his wife arrived. He said this while fully recognising that, without having been crowned, he could not rest assured that the kingdom was in fact his. This is why he finally decided not to postpone his coronation any longer. Accordingly he had London made ready for the ceremony, preparing halls and chambers, erecting enclosures and walls, having meat, poultry and game brought in, wines from Lorraine as well as from the Île-de-France, and they spent the whole month laying in stocks. (40060)

The duke was tireless as he travelled round besieging and capturing strongholds that refused to submit to him, with the result that people lost the will to resist. Many of the strongholds he pulled down, but many he took control of himself, and by the time Christmas arrived, Normans and English collectively, commoners as well as nobles, were willing for him to be crowned king. On Christmas day, therefore, without any further delay or postponement, the crown was placed on his head in Saint Peter's at Westminster. Far from there being any sign of reluctance, his coronation that day was greeted with jubilation, with joy and with love.* Blessed was the day William was born, attaining such greatness and eminence after suffering so much adversity and so many cruel hardships. Nor did he ever break God's law or grow contemptuous of the service he owed him; he became, on the contrary, a thousand times more merciful, and more zealous and more determined to carry out his holy wishes. He embodied justice and truth, and no one cherished peace and righteousness more than he; these were his greatest aims in life. He did not seek to amass wealth, and no one gave more generous gifts than he. From his coronation onwards and right from the start of his reign, gifts were distributed in such abundance that in the whole of the kingdom of France it would not have been possible to find as many. He gave not only to his dignitaries, his barons and his noble companions, but also to nations' churches and to holy religious orders. No one could calculate all the wealth he sent to the illustrious Saint Peter's in Rome, but both the pope and the clergy were extraordinarily pleased and overjoyed to see his great victory. In remembrance of this victory and to further glorify his great triumph, William had presented and sent to the pope a trophy he had won during the battle: a large banner of great value, portraying a knight embroidered in gold and precious stones, which was certainly worth an enormous sum and which Harold had had in the battle.* There was no major monastery in France, Aquitaine or Burgundy, nowhere in fact this side of Saxony, to which William did not send fine, expensive and handsome gifts. Nor did he forget, as was abundantly clear, the Norman monasteries. He sent out a great deal, he gave away a great deal. It was a wonder to behold, and William performed wonders. (40124)

Thereafter William lost no time in constructing a fine, magnificent abbey, which he generously endowed, on the site where the battle had taken place. The monastery was founded under the glorious, beloved and precious name of the Holy Trinity and under the order of Marmoutier. The name that was given to the place, and the name it will be known by forever, was Battle, in commemoration of the battle fought there in which Harold was defeated and died. God will be for evermore served there in memory of those who gave their lives there. (40138)

William spent little time in London, but did issue from there many useful statutes and ordinances which were necessary for the government of the kingdom. He spent whole days and nights deliberating on the common good to be shared by those whose peace and love he wished to ensure. We will not here go into the detail of the ordinances he passed, the laws and taxes he introduced, the grants of land he made, or the other arrangements he came to; it would take far too long to list them all. (40150)

The most powerful and the most influential people in the kingdom, so I find in the Latin history, were Earl Morcar [of Northumberland] and Earl Edwin [of Mercia], both sons of Ælfgar. They came to swear homage to King William and to carry out his orders. Copsi, [earl of Bamburgh,] a noble and valiant earl who had always been a supporter of the Normans, put all his energy into doing whatever William required of him, and no one was a more devoted servant than he. To these people William, magnanimous, benevolent and compassionate, gave back as many of their estates and lands as their ancestors before them had had. Edgar Ætheling, whom the English, as I have explained to you, made their king, he endowed with vast lands, fine, splendid and magnificent fiefs, because of his connections with King Edward and because he was a member of the same family. This is why William, for the whole of his life, was particularly fond of him, and Edgar for his part always remained loyal to him. In the marcher lands, the cities, the forts and the strongholds, William stationed valiant and noble knights, French as well as Norman, to act as guardians. He provided them with everything they needed, an abundance of all sorts of goods and provisions. Anything that was the legitimate property of the English, however, he refrained from confiscating to give to his own people. (40182)

Although Winchester was a particularly magnificent, and at that time an extremely rich, city, its inhabitants were devious, untrustworthy and arrogant, villainous, obstinate and duplicitous. Whenever they became involved in any sort of hostilities, they would call in the Danes, being not very far from the sea. From keeping such company they had grown accustomed to committing all sorts of acts of cruelty and many an unsavoury practice. Here, within the city walls, in places he judged to be the most secure and best able to withstand the threat posed by the town's inhabitants, William erected towers, walls and gates in order to make the area safe from insurrection or armed attack. He installed William fitz Osbern as governor and made him supreme commander of the entire region. The king had no more dependable friend than him, no one he could have more trust in, no one better able to safeguard the entire kingdom and all the business of the crown: the enforcement of rights, the raising of income, the collecting of fines, the administration of justice and the oversight of judicial proceedings. It was entirely right for William fitz Osbern to love the king, as it was he who had made him into such a rich and powerful baron. (40212)

The king entrusted Dover to his [half-]brother Odo, the widely renowned bishop, in addition to Kent and the surrounding country. Odo was a man of great merit, highly skilled in worldly matters. A wise and astute man of great subtlety, he took his responsibilities extremely seriously. The king left Odo and William fitz Osbern in charge of the entire country and kingdom. (40222)

[24] *How King William returned to Normandy after his coronation.*

Having made these appointments and these arrangements, and having issued his instructions, all of which he did properly, skilfully and appropriately, William came straight to Pevensey where his fleet was waiting in readiness. There he called together his barons and the most powerful people in the country whom he had sought out and summoned, because his intention was to take them with him. He did not dare trust them enough to leave them in England, for he would soon live to regret it. They are very powerful and influential men, and he is unwilling for them to stay behind and have the opportunity of plotting behind his back or causing him trouble. Among these, I find in my written source, were Archbishop Stigant; Edgar Ætheling, the ex-king; and three other powerful earls: Waltheof, Edwin and Morcar. William was particularly wary of these people, knowing that as long as he had them with him, they could not do him any great harm. They were so fearful of incurring his displeasure that they did not dare disobey him. Even though they were afraid of what he might do to them, they never gave the appearance of being in any way reluctant. And William nevertheless shows them great affection and treats them with great honour when he is kind enough to take them along with him to Normandy to hold his celebrations and to distribute honours and generous gifts. What calms their fears and reassures them is that the power that William exerts over them and the protection he offers are benign. (40258)

To the knights he had hired as mercenaries he gave magnificent and expensive presents, dismissing them properly, amicably and with high honour, with the result that for the rest of their lives they would never hold anyone in greater affection. William was thus able to embark in high spirits and without experiencing any resentment; everything he had undertaken had gone smoothly. They landed in Normandy without a hitch or mishap. William was welcomed back with such joy as had never before been heard, never before described or recounted. Nor did any individual ever heap so much honour on his people or give them so much wealth. The good Duchess Matilda knew more joy than she had ever experienced, for no wife in the whole world loved her husband more than she did. William had been away from home no more than from the feast of St Michael [29 September] to the beginning of March. He straightaway began active preparations for holding court at Fécamp, where it was his intention to celebrate Easter by calling together all his barons, the flower of Normandy's nobility. Here people have the opportunity of seeing their lord again and of showing him how happy he has made them and how much they love him. Everyone is at pains to serve him. In the first week of June he was present at Jumièges for the dedication of the abbey-church that was particularly close to his heart. Present also at the consecration celebrations was Maurilius, archbishop of Rouen, a most benevolent man who passed over and died in that very same week. He was a highly intelligent and very learned person, a man of nobility who had led a chaste and holy life. Appointed in his place was John [of Ivry], bishop of Avranches, a worthy, wise and benevolent man who was consecrated as archbishop. He was the son of good Count Rodulf [of Ivry]. (40305)

My written source informs me that the mother of Richard [I], son of [William I] Longsword, was Sprota. It is a matter of common knowledge that, during his childhood, this Richard was for a long time detained in France and prevented from taking possession of Normandy as heir. During all of this time his mother, Sprota, a fine, worthy woman fair of face, remained unmarried and alone, without anyone to take care of her, and extremely anxious about her son. With no one to advise or support her, she had no choice but to take a husband – a rich, powerful, well-to-do man called Esperling [of Vaudreuil], a self-made man and well provided for, but nonetheless a reputable citizen and modest person. He had the lease and tenancy of the water-mills at Vaudreuil, from which he made a staggering profit. He successfully asked for Sprota's hand and married her. He treated her honourably and was genuinely in love with her. The first offspring they had was the Rodulf I have already referred to, followed by some beautiful and much-admired daughters, who subsequently greatly enhanced their status by marrying into the nobility and then producing children who, in their turn, reached exalted positions. When later Duke Richard came to assume power in Normandy, from which the king of France – according to what I read in my source – had wrongly and illegally excluded him, it so happened, I discover, that one day, when Richard was back in command, his hunters and archers went hunting in the forest of Vièvre.* One of their number was Rodulf who, as I have already explained to you, was Duke Richard's half-brother. Though he was not yet old enough to be a knight, he was a tall, powerfully built young man. He was, then, out hunting with the others and in pursuit of one particular animal. They all rode down into a large valley where they suddenly stumbled upon a bear. The beast had been startled by their arrival, and there was no one brave or foolhardy enough not to immediately turn his back and flee. Everyone panicked at the prospect of being killed by the savage bear – everyone, that is, except young Rodulf. He finds himself suddenly presented with an opportunity – albeit it a terrifying one – to show his prowess. It would be a perilous undertaking even for the strongest man to be found between here and Rome. Rodulf, however, is more afraid of shame than of anything else, and would not lower himself to run away. Despite being so young, he goes straight up and grasps the bear, this ferocious monster of a wild beast, in his arms. There is nothing more that I can say. The struggle ended with Rodulf killing the bear stone dead where it stood. The hunters returned grief-stricken, believing Rodulf to have been killed, but there he was, safe and sound. Everyone was aghast at this wondrous exploit and crossed themselves. They were ashamed at having left Rodulf on his own. The adventure was reported back to good Duke Richard, who was extremely happy and pleased to know just how brave, valiant and admirable Rodulf was. Using his gloves as a token,* the duke invested him with the lordship of the forest and all the fiefs that went with it, wherever they were located. And this is the reason, I can tell you, why the place where this happened was known thereafter as Val-Ourson, and Rodulf was also thereafter known as the count of Ivry after the fief he was granted. My Latin source also tells me that Rodulf married Eremberge, the daughter of a rich knight from Quevilly in Caux, and with her he had sons as well as daughters. Their two sons were outstandingly intelligent thinkers and became bishops: one, Hugh, at Bayeux, the other at Avranches, and as we know, the latter, John, became archbishop of Rouen. They had two daughters as well, both of whom gave birth to persons of high nobility: one of the daughters was married to Osbern – the very opposite of an ill-assorted match – and she and this Osbern produced William fitz Osbern. The other daughter married Richard de Belle-Faïe. I do not wish to continue with this subject here, because there is too much to tell, and it is not right for me to hold up my narrative any more. (40408)

[25] *How Count Eustace was defeated at Dover.*

The history of the king's life* records that, during the whole of that summer and part of the winter, William did not cross the Channel but stayed in Normandy to put his affairs in order. This he did in a most majestic fashion, thoroughly, fittingly and justly. Over the whole of Normandy the good people were able to live in safety, without extortion or lawlessness, corruption or denial of justice. The country was, accordingly, prosperous, productive and well-favoured. (40420)

During this time the two governors* that I was telling you about and whom the good king, having no confidence in the natives, had left in England, were there ruling and watching over the country. They ran into a great deal of trouble which, unless it were eliminated, would have resulted in the death of thousands. These people were united in their aims and had a mutual understanding enabling them to bring help and assistance to one another, for they were frequently in need of both. The vast majority of the English were impulsive, perverse and fickle, and incapable of living in peace, nor could they be either bullied or cajoled into abandoning the perfidiousness they always had in mind. They were not brave enough to initiate an attack or to revolt openly in such a way as to disclose what plots they were hatching in secret, for their behaviour was frequently threatening. They were often in cahoots with the Danes, the Scots and the Irish. Many went abroad to plan and hatch their plots. The notion of having the Normans as their overlords does not appeal to them at all. (40448)

At this period and during this precise time, as became all too clear later, there was no love lost between Count Eustace of Boulogne* and King William. From before the Conquest, I find in my history, there had been bad blood and a great deal of hostility between them. They made peace, however, before crossing the Channel to the extent that Eustace, before being allowed to join the expedition, handed his son over to William as a surety to pledge his good faith. I have no idea whether his son was ever returned to Eustace. The count's intentions regarding William, however, were malicious in the extreme. The English had made overtures to Eustace and promised finally to see to it that he got possession of Dover. Let him have no fear, and let him not delay! He should set sail for England just as soon as he sees their messenger arrive. Eustace was well known to everyone as a strong and valiant knight. (40468)

They agreed on this venture, but it was one that was to prove very costly, and rightly so because they were very much in the wrong. Bishop [Odo] and Hugh de Montfort had gone to the other side of the Thames to attend to some other business, taking with them the greater part of their contingent of knights. The English immediately informed the count of Boulogne of this, who, without wasting a moment and taking advantage of a favourable wind, coolly crossed the Channel at night under a bright moon, reaching port at dawn next day. The count's troops took up their arms to launch a surprise attack against the castle's defenders who were guarding the keep. The English, race of Saracens that they are, came together from all the surrounding country to confront them. These hateful, villainous and duplicitous people, without hesitation, all set about attacking the towers and walls. This they did with such ferocity and with such force, and their charge was so unexpected, that the defenders were still fast asleep when the assailants were already climbing the castle walls. I do not know of anyone waking up in more consternation and distress. But there was no question of their hanging around; general alarm was unavoidable, and they lost no time in snatching up their weapons to concentrate on defending themselves. In the places where the attack was most intense, most alarming and frightening, they put up a valiant defence and killed a large number of the enemy. This all-out attack lasted the whole day without any let-up, and there was a huge amount of slaughter. Count Eustace was told what was happening, and he understood that, try as he might, he would never be able to take the castle. Since it could not be captured by means of a surprise attack, or its walls breached by an assault, there was no point in persisting, and of necessity they had to withdraw from the castle. But just listen to the distressing and terrible disaster that overtook them when they left! The Normans defending the castle would not allow them to simply leave and get off so lightly. With great ferocity, bravery and daring, they emerged in a body from the castle, bent on wiping the enemy out. With their broad-bladed Danish axes they blocked their path, forcing them either to cross Norman lines or to jump over the cliff and end up shattered, crushed and dead. This is how the Normans sent them on their way, on the receiving end of their huge, sharp-pointed spears. Then another catastrophe overtook them, as I will now tell you. When they boarded their boats, there was further grave loss of life: on loading they were unable to organise themselves in such a way as to distribute their weight evenly. Instead, in their panic they all piled aboard en masse, and because there were far too many of them, they sank to the bottom and perished. In this way many of those who were already aboard drowned in the absence of anyone to save them. All those who managed to escape did so by swimming out to safety. Some good knights died later from deadly wounds they had received. Count Eustace made his escape by being picked up in a boat, but his nephew, a highly renowned warrior, was taken prisoner. The Englishmen, who were familiar with the neighbourhood, managed to make off as best they could. Many of them, however, were caught, and there were few to mourn their passing. The whole episode came to an even more murderous conclusion than I have told you here. In this way, as he does in many others, God thwarts endeavours that are inspired by evil. (40558)

The king had been receiving news – some important, some less so – and many other messages from his people in England, and he had finished all the business for which he had returned to Normandy. He had made all the arrangements and brought everything to a successful conclusion, including transferring the whole of the lordship of Normandy to his son Robert. So he had his fleet made ready, having decided to leave without any further delay, because it was not only useful but also necessary for him to do so. He left the duchess, his household and his sons behind. His crossing was a perilous one, as the weather at the time was extremely stormy. He was returning to England in mid-winter, and the winds were far from favourable. Nevertheless they reached port safely and made a good landfall at Winchelsea.* There the common people gave him an enthusiastic welcome, and he made for London where he stayed until it was time to celebrate Christmas. What happened then was that he organised and held a sumptuous court which the bishops, barons and all the most prominent people from far and near felt obliged to attend. William extended a cheerful welcome to them all with hugs and embraces that warmed their perfidious hearts. He pretended to take their petitions and requests extremely seriously, and although he knew just how duplicitous they were and, should they have the opportunity, just how treacherous, he took care not to let it be seen on his face. But he earnestly warned his own people, those looking after his castles, strongholds and fortified towns, to be ever-vigilant and on the look-out for the fiendishly treacherous tricks they were capable of. (40600)

Meeting together in several different parts of the country, the English had planned a major conspiracy: on Ash Wednesday [1068/9] when the Normans, like all good Christians, were due to attend mass, they were to be cut to pieces and killed, and the whole country liberated. If the king had still been in Normandy, the plot might well have succeeded, but both William's presence in England, his strength and power, and the bravery of his people, meant that the plotters failed. And when the conspiracy was discovered and became common knowledge, the conspirators dared not stay around but fled. They made for Northumbria, so I find, and its wide wetlands and woodlands, for at that time the countryside there was extremely wild. The English set about strengthening and enclosing Durham and worked hard at fortifying the town. It was clear from the scale of their defences that they did not wish ever to make peace or seek any truce with William. It was no concern of theirs and of no importance to stay on good terms, since they would henceforth, so they said, miss no opportunity of causing him trouble and strife. The locals all pledged their word, joined the insurgents and provided them with assistance. Everyone, the great and the small, the good and the bad, brought so much food and so many provisions to the town, and filled it with so many men and soldiers to form a defence force, that they did not believe it possible for the town to be captured. These forsworn traitors, with the agreement of everyone, elected as their lord and ruler a young nobleman by the name of [Edgar Ætheling].* The king was highly annoyed when he heard this, and set out with his Norman companies – his good, valiant knights – to quell the rebellion which he had no intention of tolerating. Even before he began besieging the town, there was an encounter that left five hundred men bleeding to death, for the traitors defending the town emerged and made an armed sortie attacking the king's troops, but in a disorderly fashion and without keeping any formation. William's men, brave knights all, welcomed them with their burnished blades, splitting open so many chests, ribs and breastbones that, all over the place, streams of blood were spilling onto the grass. The English retreated back behind their walls, subdued, in silence and in great distress. But even there they did not reach safety, for the Normans had pursued them so closely that they managed to enter the town at the same times as they did. They immediately set fire to it, and everything in it went up in flames. Everything burned right down to the very ground, and the distress and misery were enormous. There was not a single person, child or youth, peasant or noble, who was not burnt alive or cut to pieces. Only some of the treacherous insurgents escaped by way of the Humber in small boats that they had fitted out. (40674)

King Harold had had two sons – fine, valiant and brave knights – who were hostile to King William and had left the country, taking with them a good number of their father's troops. Dermot, king of Ireland, an extremely powerful man in his own country, responded to their requests and entreaties by providing them with sixty well-armed and well-equipped boats. In these, the devilish outlaws, these savage Saracen killers, returned to England where, to William's great exasperation, they set about burning, robbing and killing people. They left a trail of destruction behind them, laying waste to everything and leaving nothing standing, to the distress of the whole population. (40694)

That fine, experienced knight Brien, son of Eon, count of Redon, with as many armed men as he could muster, launched a ferocious attack against them, twice in a single day. They inflicted losses on them totalling one thousand five hundred, and among the number of casualties and dead were all the rebel barons of the highest nobility. The day was won, and not even the smallest fraction of the enemy would have escaped with their lives had not night fallen at that point. The few that did emerge alive went back to their homes covered in shame, furious and grieving. The news they returned with brought tears to the eyes of their closest friends. (40712)

[26] *How Queen Matilda was crowned.*

This time, King William stayed in England until shortly before Rogationtide [in April 1067]. At the request of a number of people, he summoned his wife to cross the Channel so that he could have her crowned at Whitsun, if such was God's will. Duchess Matilda was extremely happy. With knights of noble heritage, with high-born ladies, with well-born and well-bred young ladies, with bishops and with abbots, with wise and learned clerics, with joy, with pageantry and with great ceremony, and with a lavish baronial escort, she crossed the Channel to join her husband. He very much loved her, and his love was a genuine love; this was as it should have been, for no king had a more praiseworthy wife, nor one with more good qualities, more intelligence, more merit or more godliness. (40734)

At Whitsun the king assembled a full-scale court in such a way that the most powerful, the most valiant and the most important people were present. To everyone's delight and to universal rejoicing, William marked the day by wearing his golden crown, while good Matilda was consecrated and crowned queen. Her head that day, adorned with gold and precious stones, sparkling and awe-inspiring, was blessed and crowned. She had completed all the work on her abbey at Caen in Normandy, a superb building, generously and richly endowed and decorated in the most priceless fashion. She was a queen of such reputation that, as I recall from my reading, there was no lady to match her in merit and worth between here and Greater India. (40754)

England is a large and extensive country consisting of many different regions, and whose people have, since time immemorial, been greater devotees of change and novelty than anyone else on earth, and there is no people less able to be consistent or stable in what they think. This explains why it was such a difficult and contentious task for the newly crowned king to win complete and unrestricted possession of the kingdom. As is recorded in my written source, subsequent to William being crowned king and declared lord of the kingdom, he was the object of a great deal of harassment. William sought and demanded of [Malcolm III] the king of Scots that he serve him as his vassal just as his ancestors had done to the English crown, and as was incumbent on him as monarch. The English had always had domination over the Scots, so much so that no sooner were they in a position to do so than English kings would invoke the mutually agreed convention. (40774)

The king of Scots did not dare demur. Given his power and military strength, he had no choice but to accede to William's demand and do as he wished. The operations that followed, so I read in my source, were conducted by Earl Ælfgar's sons, Edwin and Morcar, though it was very much against their will. Acting on King William's instructions, they took with them to Scotland some noble French knights, and in the most impregnable sites they could find, they erected strongholds and castles, well-fortified and surrounded by robust defences. The king's intention was to take all necessary precautions to maintain peace. (40790)

Ælfgar's sons were very powerful figures, and King William was convinced that they were in no way insincere or capable of deceiving him. They were the most prominent and important people in the whole kingdom, more so than any Frenchman or Norman, however close to the king. William showed them great affection and admitted them to his inner circle. Their trustworthiness, however, proved to be very short-lived. For two years they succeeded in concealing their resentment and the shameful crime they were preparing. What they did was to take prisoner the Normans they had brought with them to man the strongholds, and who were not in the least mistrustful of the two Englishmen in whom they had more faith than in anyone else. The good turn and the honour the brothers did them was to clap them in chains and throw them, still living, into prison where they held them, in the most appalling conditions, naked and without food. They enlisted help from all around to put their deadly plan into action: these deceitful and mendacious peoples, wallowing in debauchery and floundering in drunkenness, so difficult for anyone to keep under control, sought to inflict damage on the king. The rebels had families and many relations, households, people working for them, and servants. And all those who had been lying low grew bold and seized the opportunity of flouting the law and giving vent to their vicious malevolence. All the land north of the Humber was in turmoil and oppressed. The rebels occupied the foul and disease-ridden bogs, the vast, deserted woods, and the strongholds of the region where they felt secure, and they plundered all the surrounding country. (40828)

The citizens of York, the knights and the peasants, are going out of their minds with foreboding, and despite anything their most saintly archbishop can say to them, they can find no relief and cannot be made to see sense. They frequently attempt to bribe the Frenchmen guarding the towers with generous bribes of gold and silver, but the soldiers could not be moved; whatever the offers or the promises, they can never be won over. These brave rebels dared not engage open battle; each of them was afraid because of the great strength and power of the valiant, wise, courageous and audacious King William. He inspected and studied the countryside around, and in all the places where he needed to do so, he constructed well-fortified and secure strongholds to confine and destroy these forsworn traitors and bring an end to their lawlessness. (40852)

William was staying at Warwick where he was strengthening the castle when Morcar and his brother Edwin came begging for mercy, seeing that their foul conspiracy and their shameful imprisonment of the king's men were growing less and less effective by the day. The king granted them his pardon after each of them had accused the other of having forced him to start this damaging rebellion. They and their closest allies then swore fealty to him in full public view. Next the king constructed a splendid, strong castle at Nottingham. Meanwhile the citizens of York, fearing that some disaster might befall them, that they might come to some harm or other, or be put to shame, sent their most diplomatic messengers to the king, surrendering the keys of the city and begging for mercy. William, however, was well aware that they were untrustworthy and intractable, and he accordingly had little faith in them. He constructed a fortress within the city to keep them under control, and in it he placed knights he could trust to look after it. Inside this enclosure he built a tower, a keep, a wall and ditches. He did the same thing at Huntingdon and, on advice, at Cambridge also, and in other places where attacks could possibly be expected. He then decided to stop holding court in order to lighten the burden on the country, as there was not sufficient food to go round and the country was very much impoverished. He dismissed his soldiers and his serving men – I have no idea how many – and they went off carrying valuable gifts, very anxious to come back one day, for he had treated them extremely well. (40894)

William granted Durham and its county to the valiant Robert de Commines,* one of the best of all knights. Before the end of summer [1069], and accompanied by five hundred choice knights, Robert had already taken up quarters in the city. They had no reason to be afraid or feel unsafe anywhere at all there. One night, however, their hosts and the peasants from the surrounding woods and the plain strangled and killed them; only two people were able to make their escape. It is obvious why they were betrayed: it was because they were all separated in different places, and their efforts at defending themselves came to nothing. And just listen to what a scheme the madmen of York dreamt up! They gathered together a large number of people and, thanks to their sorcery, were able to hatch a plot that resulted in their treacherously cutting to pieces Robert fitz Richard as well as his companions who were on guard in the fortress. That is how they behaved, giving further impetus to their lawlessness and not giving a tinker's curse for the oaths and pledges they had sworn or the sureties they had handed over. These people were savages still, almost semi-Saracens, their evil ways a relic of the past – lechers, serfs, pagans. But there are more crimes to come. They attack the splendid castle the king had built. Several of their leaders, base criminals and traitors, are involved in this: Mærle-Sveinn and Gospatric, highly malicious individuals, the Ætheling and Arnkell, and the two sons of Karli the Red, as well as several others from round about. William Malet straightaway let the king know what had happened. The attack was such that there were few means of defence. If the king did not bring immediate help, he would lose Malet and all his people. Little wonder if William flew into a rage, and he showed it by leaving that very moment to sort things out. He set off like a maniac, impossible to restrain, to cut them to shreds and kill them. The price he made them pay for raising his ire was to attack them unawares, besieging them and either capturing or killing so many of them that hardly a quarter were finally able to make their escape. In this way they got what was coming to them! (40954)

In the eight days that he stayed there, William built and fortified another castle as a defence against these Judas-like renegades whose capacity for evil was inexhaustible. I know that he placed William fitz Osbern in charge with orders that, if he should need to do so, he should send for him wherever he may be. Leaving everything well-defended and well-provided for, the king set out for Winchester, and here clerics and barons assembled to celebrate the Resurrection of our Lord and Easter. King William, like any good king should, contributed to the joy and splendour of the occasion by bringing together a court so magnificent that never in the whole world, as far as I know, was there any better. So many costly gifts were distributed: decorated goblets, cloaks, fur-lined robes, gold-embroidered cloths and clothing, gold- and silver-mounted jewels. To churches he sent quantities of different sorts of vestments. He was never too busy with affairs of state anywhere, never too preoccupied with troubles or emergencies, to carry out his personal devotions to God, his Father and Creator. It was his constant priority to serve God in word, in deed, and in good works. (40984)

Only a short time elapsed before the English, our dread and deadly enemies, began again to muster their troops. They will continue fighting until they cap-

ture the fortresses at York and flush out all those inside them. They demand that
the two Williams leave the city, failing which they will immediately besiege them
until they capture them by force, in which case they will all be hanged and drawn.
This ultimatum the Normans ignored, but at midnight, when everyone was
asleep, they came stealthily out of the city and, taking cover in a steep valley,
waited for the enemy to come charging down. When they came, the English suffered the ignominy of being cut to pieces and killed, and hardly a single one of
them escaped. The valiant and shrewd William fitz Osbern was in fact in the habit
of getting the upper hand in this way, so I find in my source, every time he fought
against the English. So many of their heads did he succeed in chopping off that
for some time to come peace reigned in the country. He had captured one of
their leading figures, and the English had promised to pay a large ransom for him
on condition that he was handed over unharmed. But William was in no mood
to show clemency or consideration, nor was he sufficiently interested in money
to prevent him from cutting off the man's testicles, ears and nose and gouging
out his eyes.* This was not altogether surprising, because if the English had been
able to capture him, they would certainly have tortured him to death. These
events and the huge loss of life had the result of re-establishing peace in the city,
the castles and the countryside around. William fitz Osbern immediately went off
to court, where he frequently used to deputise for the king.* (41025)

It was not long after this that King William, because of certain very serious,
difficult and unusual events, decided to send his fair and beloved wife, valiant
Queen Matilda, back over the Channel to Normandy where her children were.
She would have less trouble and less worry over there, since in England she kept
hearing reports of many incidents that she found upsetting and distressing. In
Normandy, back home in their own land, she will lead a more peaceful and less
troubled life; things will go much better, and the people and the country will fare
better also, when no violence is likely suddenly to flare up. Their son Robert
[Curthose], much loved, popular and highly esteemed, was ruler there, though
being a youth, he still governed under guardianship. The queen, then, had been
sent back over the Channel, and she was welcomed with such joy and honour as
cannot be described. At that time the king of France was enjoying good relations
with Normandy, and there was no bad feeling, resentment or hostility between
the two. The whole country was going through a period of carefree prosperity.
The fair-faced queen acted with greater benevolence and more honourably than
any lady ever had. She was devoted to God and to his service, and this was the
highest of all her priorities. (41058)

The wife of King Edward, [Edith,] Harold's sister and Earl Godwine's daughter, was an outstandingly good woman who underwent many trials and tribulations in her quest for Heaven. If she had had her own way, the battle of Hastings would never have taken place. She had done absolutely everything in her power to restrain Harold and to stop the battle happening, but was unable to prevent it. She had great affection for Duke William before he became king, and it was very much against her will that Harold did what he did. This was why William loved and cherished her, and he would not in any way tolerate people treating her dishonourably or badly or causing her any harm, for she was a loyal and God-fearing lady. But her mother [Gytha], Godwine's wife, when she understood that it had been Harold's destiny to die, immediately left the country, taking her fortune with her and crossing the Channel to France. Here she stayed, she lived and died; she never again returned to England. Had she not fled, good Duke William would never have permitted any harm to come to her as long as she lived. (41088)

Swein [Estrithson], king of Denmark and lord of the Danes, wanted to get his hands on some of the great wealth of England. The lands that his ancestors had once had would be his. He was so closely related to the royal family that it would have seemed base and dishonourable on his part not to have been seen, sooner or later, to be claiming his share of the country. He was exceedingly sad and angry at the losses his people had suffered, and at the death of Harold and of his friends and allies. Swein represented a great menace to King William because of the military strength of his kingdom. If he needed, he could also call upon the huge armies of Saxony, Poland and Frisia, and many other sorts of peoples. He had won several victories over the pagans, and had even triumphed over the Lithuanians, a very belligerent people and so aggressive that it was on hostile terms with all of its neighbours. He was not, however, minded on this occasion to rashly embark on a formal battle, but surreptitiously and stealthily sent an armed fleet over the sea with the mission of capturing and plundering English cities. The fleet was large enough, menacing enough and carried enough knights to surely have the power to lay siege to London. (41122)

King Swein had two sons, excellent knights, a brother who was a marvellous warrior, three courageous earls, and no fewer than two bishops, and to these he entrusted all his troops; they were to act as their lords, their leaders and their commanders. They speed over the sea, heading straight for England. They attempt to stop at Dover to take on water, but people are able to stop them disembarking. All the way along the coast they did a great deal of damage and harm.

Their intention was to attack Norwich, take it by storm and set it alight. But the valiant Ralph Guader had assembled all his knights and all the other troops he could enlist, and went to attack the Danes. He claimed five hundred victims and forced them back into their boats, where another seven hundred of them drowned before they could get under way and leave port. Waltheof,* Siward [Bearn] and the Ætheling, like untrustworthy Saracen oath-breakers, came to join them in response to the invitation they had made. They had come down the Humber, and it was there they met up with the Ætheling who, with his troops, was plundering whatever he wanted throughout the region. He met no resistance. The slaughter and the grief were enormous. (41156)

King William's troops were in Lincoln, and when they saw the shameful and unlawful things that were happening, they strapped on their helmets, leapt on their horses and went to attack the marauders. Within one day not a single person from the Ætheling's company, of whatever condition, was left alive, except their humbled leader and two lone soldiers. The Danes arrived at York, guided there by the English, by Waltheof, Gospatric, Mærle-Sveinn, Arnkell, Elnoc* and Karli's sons – all foul, criminal individuals. With as many forces as they could muster they came and attacked the fortresses. The defenders made the mistake of coming out to confront the rebels, and of not taking sufficient precautions as the engagement began. They found themselves attacked with so many fine-pointed lances, so many sharp arrows, so many shining, furbished steel blades, that they could not organise a retreat or find any way out of the fray. As they came back in through the city gates, they let their deadly enemies in with them. They succeeded in taking very few of the rebels prisoner, though, because so many of the Normans tragically lost their lives that day. Not one of them, neither fair nor foul, survived, and so the fortresses were captured. (41188)

When the king heard of this misadventure, he found it hard to bear and took it badly. His advisors led him to understand that he could fully expect there to be a pitched battle with the rebels, whatever the outcome of it might be. The king was very upset at having lost his men in this way, but he did not hold back from taking revenge, so straightaway he set out to capture them or to destroy them utterly. The rebels, however, did not dare wait for him to arrive. If he had found them all grouped together, they would have suffered the ordeal of seeing their ranks so smashed apart that never again, for the rest of their lives, would they have been capable of attacking another city. They crossed over the Humber into country where they had little to fear. Nevertheless among the bogs and wetlands the Normans managed to track down no fewer than seven hundred of the English, not a single one of whom, however strong he might have been, got away with his head still on his shoulders. (41210)

It was here that the king received what must have been very welcome news for him: a huge Saxon army had put together a military campaign more than seven thousand strong, and had come over to England. They were there at the invitation of the inhabitants of Dorset and Somerset – God's curse be on them both! – to capture and occupy the land. They were already busy attacking Mont-acute* when they were spotted. All the people of London and Winchester, and those of Salisbury also – no shirkers here – having no prince or king at their head and only [Geoffrey,] the bishop of Coutances as their leader, armed themselves with axes, bill-hooks, lances and sharp swords, and succeeded so well in splitting open the invaders' heads and slashing their ribs and their arms that there was never so remarkable an encounter, such slaughter, so many prisoners taken, so much booty in terms of powerful, well-equipped boats and other valuable pos-sessions. When this most welcome and providential news reached King William, he was hugely relieved and overjoyed, and on hearing it he gave thanks to God. This is how he kept possession of the kingdom he had conquered. Had he been lazy, indifferent, niggardly, mean or inadequate, he would have added little to his own territory, but in his time there was no one, Christian or Saracen, to match him as far as hard work and diligence were concerned, no one capable of more endurance or patience, or more generous in sharing out material possessions, no one more used to going without food or sleep, no one more lethal with his blade of steel. (41252)

To deal with the invading Danes I have been telling you about, the king left [Robert,] the count of Eu in charge with a large number of knights, and his brother Robert, count of Mortain, a true and entirely trustworthy friend of William's, to guard against the Danes plundering and any attacks they were threatening to launch. The invaders were already able to cover their living expenses, since the English in the neighbourhood supplied them with all the pro-visions they had, even to the extent of their taking their meals and drinking together with them. The debauchery and the drinking bouts they indulged in were staggering, and their like unheard of between here and India's land of indigo.* Leaving these two counts behind with their bold and courageous troops, the king had to set off on urgent business to Scotland, taking with him a large and mighty army. He went as soon as he possibly could and successfully com-pleted what he wanted to do. From there he made his way back to Wales, a jour-ney that turned out to be extraordinarily violent and horrific. In Wales he stifled the locals' revolt, wiping out their ferocious resistance. If anyone were to tell you how he went about this and how he achieved it, you would dismiss it as incredible. He went all the way up and down the western shores facing Ireland before moving on to Arthur's Cornwall.* This was no peaceful or uneventful campaign, because the Welsh are a bunch of wretched pagans, a wild and savage people. William built many fine and easily defendable castles there which he strongly fortified and garrisoned, and were guaranteed to keep the natives subdued and under control. Thereafter the Normans fought many a battle and had many a violent skirmish with them until finally the country was pacified. (41296)

When this troublesome episode was over and done with, William made Stamford his base.* Here were brought all those condemned to die for having unlawfully caused the death of his men, all the oath-breakers and liars, all the people who had set fire to his lands, all the fugitives from justice, all those who had acted treacherously towards him and engaged in hostilities against him. Their punishment was for them to put one another to the sword, so that the others would hear tell of it and be deterred. But their being criminals and perjurers had served no purpose. They and all their families had been irresponsible, perverse and disloyal from birth, and they lacked all discernment and judgement. It is a well-known fact that they were at that time still semi-pagan. (41314)

The Danes were very happy and content when the king left England,* and they immediately returned with the huge English army to start a new invasion. But the two counts and their troops were there to prevent them from doing so. The Normans fell on them by surprise when they were off guard, casually eating and drunkenly swigging away in open country next to a little copse. They suffered a dreadful calamity: before their tables could be set, they were splattered with the blood dripping from their blond and flaxen heads; a thousand chests, a thousand foreheads belonging to the bravest of the warriors were split open, and they were left for dead on the ground. The Normans went on relentlessly pursuing and killing the invaders as they fled back to their boats. On this particular occasion, then, the enemy emerged with no more than half their army having survived the sharp, pointed lances and well-honed blades of the Normans. (41338)

The king undertook other expeditions to the northern regions: such difficult journeys, so full of danger, and in many places so arduous that, if you read the poignant and daunting accounts of them given in our genuine historical source, you would think that no army ever suffered as much as they did or achieved what they achieved. They crossed forests and marshes, climbed high, steep and sheer mountains, trudged through freezing and melting snow which left their prize horses without fodder, went through a thousand and more places where men walking three abreast would not, for anything in the world, have ventured to pass. In such places they flushed out criminal fugitives, outlaws and rebels who thought their hideouts would have kept them safe even from the Day of Judgement. But these renegades were not clever enough to conceal themselves or keep out of sight or flee to hiding places among the rocks or in scrubland* without their getting dragged out by their throats, like dogs but worse. An expedition of this sort was extremely useful, a great act of charity, a great way of liberating the country and of delivering it from oppression. (41366)

When it was convenient for him to do so, King William left his entire army with instructions to stay vigilant and on their guard against the Danes. He then ordered his royal paraphernalia to be brought from Winchester: his cloak, his coronation robes, his crown and sacred vessels – no king on earth had finer. At Christmas [1069] he wore his crown at York, with decorum but in great pomp and splendour, in a way fitting both to God and to the king's subjects. From this moment on, the whole situation improved considerably. All the barons from throughout the country who had formerly acted as traitors, and had supported the Danes and facilitated their arrival, now came offering peace and begging for mercy. They provided the sureties they had been asked for, that is their eldest sons and their nephews. The fact was that their circumstances were no longer at all favourable. Their Danish allies were in a wretched state: they were living under the threat of the sword, of being harassed to death, in constant danger of being slaughtered, their stomachs distended with hunger, hunted and pursued everywhere. No army ever ended up in such a sorry state. To stay alive, the only food they had was stinking rotten meat. They did not dare leave their boats and come ashore to look for food. The freezing winter winds so lashed them in their boats riding out at sea that they fell on the deck swooning and their faces distorted. The few that escaped death sailed off home with such glory, such nobility and such wealth as I have just described to you. All the Danish king had to smile about was the fact that less than one eighth of the whole of his original fleet managed to make it back home, and even then few, if any, of the men were able-bodied. A fine return indeed for his investment! The grief and suffering that gripped the whole of Denmark was beyond description. (41414)

In this way England was delivered from its deadly, criminal enemies, and at peace. Thereafter King William rebuilt his castles, improving them, making them finer, stronger, more secure and better equipped. When he left York, he took with him the sureties that he had required and demanded. He had brought peace to all the regions and purged them of undesirables. Here is not the place for me to tell you – it would be too long-winded an undertaking, both boring and boorish of me – any more than a small fraction of what King William accomplished, where he went, and the hardships he had to endure. I will not tell you of the violent destruction he wrought on those evil enemies of his, nor the castles he fortified in order to control and keep watch over the land, nor of the fiefs he distributed or the gifts he made to his powerful barons, nor of the allocations he made, in so many places, to churches and the improvements he made to them, nor the laws, the rights, the judgements and the excellent statutes that he introduced and enforced for as long as he lived. No more than a small fraction of this has been described in this book, for we have already devoted a great deal of space to all that. So complete was William's mastery of the kingdom that not one of his neighbours ever challenged anything that was his by right. From now on, he could do just as he liked. For many years more he reigned over the kingdom in peace, prosperity and blissful tranquillity. I will turn now, following what I find written in my source, to how his enterprise came to an end, and what destiny held in store for him thereafter.* (41454)

[27] *King William's last days and his death.*

Long-standing rancour and hatred between the French and the Normans suddenly flared up again with sweeping and deadly consequences. There was a series of military confrontations leading to lands being plundered and towns being mercilessly set alight. The poor people came close to ruin, and the situation reached a stage where no one, cleric or lay, was spared. To cut a long story short, Hugh Tavel together with Ralph Mauvoisin and the castellan of Mantes, as well as many other Frenchmen, began committing acts of rebellion against the realm of King William. In the dark in the dead of night they would often come across the river Eure and ride through the country around Evreux, and it frequently happened that, before the next day dawned, they had taken a large number of prisoners, oxen, cows and sheep, leaving the country exhausted and impoverished. When King William heard of this, he was exceedingly displeased and troubled, sentiments that he was determined, if he could, to make widely known and felt. In front of his own people, he complained bitterly about the insolence of the invaders: "I absolutely demand that from now on I have full control over the

Vexin. If not – to put it bluntly – I, with my mighty army behind me, shall renounce my allegiance to the whole of the kingdom of France, and, whether the king likes it or not, I will occupy Mantes, Chaumont and Pontoise, all of which, after all, legally belong to me. These people are in for a hard time once again. It was quite wrong of my son Robert to desert me and go over to the other side, for never had a father been less ill-intentioned towards his son. If I have not been willing to put up with his disloyalty or to approve of his silly behaviour, this is no reason for him to do me harm, because he will always turn out to be the loser." (41498)

He sent word to King Philippe, via some select and well-informed messengers, that he should hand back to him the lands in question that were legitimately his, for if he kept them, he would have to pay a high price. William is not willing to tolerate any more delay in having his rightful inheritance restored to him. He has been making this request, that I have just referred to, for all of twenty-one years, ever since the king of France first took over these lands and began ruling there. The king of France, however, regarded William's claim as spurious and so much hot air and took no notice at all of his threats, believing that he would take the matter no further. King William, for his part, brought together vast numbers of eager troops who were quite prepared, under the right leader, to march on Paris. The prospect did not worry or overawe them. They set out in the last week of July [1087], making directly for Mantes and without stopping on the way. They took the French so much by surprise that, before the gate could be shut against them, they had set fire to the town, and the whole place immediately went up in flames. There had also been a great deal of fighting, some violent assaults and a hard-fought battle. The French losses were extremely high, the town was burned to the ground, the troops taken prisoner or hacked to death and killed. It was unbelievably hot, and William had full armour on that day. In addition, he was corpulent, overweight and no longer a young man. Just hear the extraordinary calamity that ensued! Either because of the fumes given off by the conflagration, or because the intense, boiling heat penetrating his body, already dripping with sweat, caused the fat to melt and infiltrate his stomach, the result was that he fell ill soon after.* The illness was so painful that no one ever suffered a more excruciating one, or such great distress or so much agony. He spent six weeks in bed at Rouen, much to the joy of the treacherous and malevolent perjurers, and much to the dismay of all those who loved peace and who were disconsolate in the extreme. Just as during his lifetime William had always been someone of high intelligence, great benevolence, with an infallible memory, a fine intellect and an unerring sense of judgement, so he remained until the day he died. His voice remained strong, as did his mind; he never became incoherent and always had his wits about him until the moment his soul left his body. When his condition worsened, he summoned his bishops and his barons in order to share out, from his sick-bed, his land as well as his prodigiously vast wealth. He called both his sons, Henry and William Rufus. The third, Robert, who was duke of Normandy, was not there, for in a very minor fit of antagonism, he had gone over to the king of France, having quarrelled with his own father and having on several occasions been guilty of bad behaviour towards him. (41572)

Good, noble King William did not want there to be any dispute, after his death, about his legacies or his gifts, so he divided up his wealth in full view of his bishops and barons. He did so as he saw fit, recording the various distributions in writing, until not a single penny of his remained. He made generous gifts for the repairing, re-roofing or rebuilding of the churches at Mantes that had been destroyed, burned or demolished, making thereby ample compensation. He made his confession at many different times, both in company and in private, then asked those of his clerks in holy orders who had gathered in his presence to pray for God to grant him full pardon, and that he, if such was God's will, by his clemency and grace be saved. "I have," he said, "greatly loved and cherished all of you.* I have protected and defended you so that no wrong or harm has been done to you in either word or deed. I have never in any way or anywhere shown any disrespect to Holy Church, but have honoured and enhanced it, safeguard-ing its rights and always avoiding simony. I have even embellished it in many places with holy and righteous men, and granted it so many lands and fiefs that the nine abbeys of monks, not to mention those with canons and the one for nuns, that my ancestors before me had founded, have never deteriorated or been in any way diminished by me. Indeed, since I acquired land and power, I can claim that on both sides of the Channel at least eighteen abbeys of monks and six convents – if our information is correct – have been created and built. I know for certain, also, that I have never confiscated anything that people have wanted to give to these churches as offerings or as benefactions, nor have I ever challenged or disputed such donations. I am the creator and founder of all these religious houses, their adviser and their supporter, and all of those whose bishops I appointed have thrived and prospered. There is no darkness or foul air in these holy houses: they are illumined by God's rays. In them, confession and salvation are remedies for life's disorders. So thoroughly is the Devil conquered there that neither his wiles or his assaults have any purchase or relevance. God will be served there for ever more. I have drawn up sealed charters and documents recording the income and allocation of fiefs of those houses that I founded on my own initiative, and those founded by others also, each one separately. I have ratified them all with the sovereign authority vested in me. This is how I wish to leave things for my heirs and those who come after me: in the name of God I order them henceforth to respect these dispositions. (41648)

Fair sons, I wish to beg you most earnestly and request you in all sincerity to follow my example in all of these matters, to observe and maintain the way I have arranged things. In this way you will live and reign in peace, and with true nobility in the eyes of God and those of your subjects. If you keep company with good and sincere people and heed their advice, you will live a noble and honourable life. It was thanks to those for whom I had particular affection, and whose values I came to know best, that I have enjoyed honour and been able to accomplish everything I set out to do. Because of them I have been able to govern the country and be victorious in so many great battles. They took revenge for me on those traitors who, had they been able, would have driven me out or killed me on countless occasions. And the most important of all the recommendations I make to you is that first and foremost you love God, and then love your good subjects. Tell good from bad, and cherish justice above all else. Never act arrogantly or criminally. The humblest loves God best of all. Bring low and destroy unlawful and perverse tyrants. Take care not to despise the poor or the common people. Send your gifts and your wealth to families who are destitute or to religious communities that are in need; this will be true Christian behaviour. Remember always to attend church to hear God's service, for without love of God any wealth you have amassed, any worldly power or strength you have, are but worthless, transitory and irksome vanities. You will find yourselves honoured and strengthened if you do as I say, and may God grant you the courage to maintain these values, as I wish and desire you to. (41692)

As a result of the great crimes committed against me – and today is not the time to list them – I have killed many men with my own hands. My conscience is, therefore, not clear; it is troubled and in need of repentance. May God now show me how truly merciful he is.* And because I acquired the kingdom [of England] and took possession of it by means of much killing and dire tribulation, I would not be so rash, nor would I dare, to grant or concede it to anyone except to God. May he who distributes everything that is truly good in the world grant the kingdom and crown to my son William, for this is what I want! Never has he intentionally shown any defiant attitude towards me, nor has he ever acted against my interests. May God grant that he be crowned king of the kingdom, and that he live in honour in the world! To this I myself give permission." (41712)

In the midst of all this major sharing out of power, these donations and arrangements – and no one standing round the king could fail to marvel at his wonderful memory and command of the situation – with everyone present weeping and wailing, William's [third] son Henry appeared before the king, his face wet with tears. He had not heard his name mentioned, only those of Rufus his second brother and [Robert] the eldest. The king had left him nothing, given him nothing, and had made no worldly provision for him. In tears he said to him: "Fair sire, what arrangements do you intend to make for me? In Heaven's name, am I not your son? Am I so different from the others that I should have nothing or take nothing away with me? They certainly have so much power over me now that it leaves me apprehensive. It is clear that you have very little love for me, unless, of course, you have something else in mind." (41732)

The king replied with composure: "You, fair son, will have five thousand pounds of my good sterling silver. Take care, though, never to enter into any conflict or hostilities with your brothers that would put you in the wrong. They will be mighty figures with vast power, able to do you great harm and force you to leave the country." (41740)

To this Henry replied:* "But even if each and every penny of this money were gold instead of silver, what use would it be for me to accept or take it if I have nowhere to spend it in?" "Fair son, replies the king, "be sensible! Concentrate and keep focused! Do not be unreliable and keep changing your mind! Listen to God, be patient and accept the fact that your two brothers have lordship over you; that is the law, and it is right, reasonable and fair: William's share is England, and Robert's Normandy. I am sure that soon enough you will have it all for yourself and outdo both of your brothers in nobility, power and wealth. Have no fear, do not be alarmed or apprehensive! All the land I have ever owned will one day be yours. You are destined for greatness, only love God, believe in him and in his guidance!" (41762)

One thing the king was afraid of was that there might be trouble in England, some sort of disorder, discord or disturbance, for he knew such things to be commonplace in the kingdom. He therefore has a writ drafted and sealed in which he lays down the provisions that are to be made, and tearfully hands it over to his son William Rufus whom he knows he will never see again. Embracing him a hundred times over, he orders him to cross the Channel immediately and without delay.

Let him take possession of the property he receives from God, the kingdom and the crown! His departure was the cause of great grief: people tore their hair out and their beards, shouted out in cries of sorrow. Rufus, sighing and moaning, swoons repeatedly in anguish and distress so that his heart almost breaks. Tears still streaming down his chest, he mounts his horse, because he cannot wait now to get possession of the kingdom. Before he had arrived at the coast and before he had time to dismount, indisputable news reached him that his father was dead. Without waiting any longer, they crossed the Channel in broad daylight, and even though the next week was one of mourning for Rufus, happiness was just around the corner: when he came into possession of the kingdom, he forgot all his grief. His coronation took place without any impediment worth me telling you about. (41798)

Henry did not neglect to take delivery of his money; he had it accurately weighed up and he collected exactly what he was entitled to, to the nearest penny. The bishops and the most notable of the barons had intervened on behalf of the prisoners who had been thrown in jail. Powerful men of noble origin and from prominent families had been arrested and condemned for a very long period for their crimes – some with little justification. When they had spoken to the king about them and made their humble requests, William had responded sympathetically except in the case of his [half-]brother bishop Odo; all the others could be released from prison on condition that they took an oath promising for the rest of their lives to respect any period of peace that was decreed. (41818)

On hearing this news, Count Robert [de Mortain] was very upset to learn that his brother was to remain in prison where Odo was becoming angry and despondent, complaining bitterly that he would never be released. Before long representations on behalf of him and his companions were being made to the king, who waited an inordinately long time before finally agreeing to forgive him, grant him his peace and free him. It was a request that they should never have made, for surely they knew that nowhere was there a more evil and untrustworthy person, a more disloyal individual, someone more hateful to God and to Holy Church; nowhere was there anyone who had done the king more harm. "Never once in his life has he done anything good. He has never shrunk from any shameful, ignoble or base act. Many a time have I instructed him to mend his ways, but he will never give up his corrupt practices. Never have I regretted more having consecrated a bishop: he observes no law, he has never acted in good faith and never will. It is a calamity and a cause of great sorrow that he should still be alive and not die. He lives a life of shame and woe; this saddens me more than anything else, and the grief it causes me is real and genuine. But I cannot, and should not, continue to turn a deaf ear to your request. Let it be granted as you wish! But one thing is certain: if Odo lives, he will continue to cause a whole lot of trouble, because he would rather court disaster than simply live a quiet life."* (41858)

In this way King William released those he had had arrested and kept prisoner. He forgave them all the crimes they had committed against him. He is willing for them all to benefit from his peace, to have their rights restored, retrieve their rents and the incomes from their forfeited properties. Just as he hopes for God's forgiveness, so in his turn he forgives them in all sincerity, without any residual bad feeling or any wish to see them come to harm. Thus he continued to act rationally and with discrimination until the end when his soul was to leave him. This happened, as is recorded in the Latin history, exactly on the tenth day of September [1087] in the morning as the first service of the day could be heard chiming at Saint Mary's church. William asks what it is and remains fully conscious. He then turns his face in that direction and looks up at the sky, his face contorted and bathed in tears. With joined hands and with trembling voice he prays to the glorious and holy mother of our Saviour, her son, that by her great and holy mercy she reconcile him with Jesus and so appease him that the Devil has no dominion over him, and that he bring his soul up into Heaven where his dear ones are. After this prayer, his soul separated from his body so decorously and so serenely that no one present, young or old, was aware of it. Everyone thought that he was tired after the exertions of talking to settle the affairs of state, and that he had fallen asleep, and that was why there was no outburst of crying or wailing. Before the evening none of those around him could realise or know that he had died. Some people even say that they were unaware of it for the whole of the following night. It was exactly in this way that God's will was done. Everyone, the whole population, was dismayed and apprehensive; they wept, became despondent and grew fearful. No one had ever known such great grief or such strong emotion. Off gallop the barons at break-neck speed in their desire to take whatever precautions they can against all eventualities, so frightened are they all. The staff of William's personal entourage left absolutely nothing behind; they removed and carried everything off so that not a single object was left. The vast majority of them abandoned the body and made off in all directions. (41916)

You can clearly see, if you care to reflect a moment, how ephemeral and unsubstantial a thing fealty is in this world, and how quickly people forget the person they have loved most. News quickly spread, and it was soon known, across a large number of lands, that King William had died. Our source book recounts that even in Calabria and in Rome several people knew – by what means I cannot say – the exact day, hour and minute that he died, as they later themselves verified. (41932)

Ah! Worldly glory and splendour, all material riches, imperial power, you deserve nothing but our contempt, since all your raising up only results in things falling down again and reverting to nothingness, for even those who in life are the finest of people, the most invigorating, the cleverest and the most innovative, return to ashes and to dust in more or less no time at all.* Of all the land an individual owned and of all that he acquired in his lifetime, only a few feet remain for him – you know which they are: those he is invested with to lie there alone on his back and to be devoured by worms and lizards. Happiness in this world is nothing: like the bubbles of a babbling fountain, it is over and gone in a trice. Everything that is in nature becomes exhausted, everything passes away and comes to naught. (41953)

Just listen to what transpired in this particular case! Someone who had been so powerful, noble, rich, had carried out so many conquests, and had been served by hundreds, sometimes thousands, of knights, could not even muster ten people to accompany his body and bury him. But the archbishop, clergy and monks did come, with great emotion and in solemn procession, to perform the commendation prayers. William's body was carried to Caen in conformity with his instructions. He had wished to be laid to rest in the abbey he had founded and had built. Everyone, his relatives and well-wishers, his closest personal attendants, were now scattered all over the place, with the result that there was no one to take care of the body. Accordingly – the Latin history informs me – a certain knight, one Herluin, a native of the surrounding area, when he saw William abandoned in this way, was overcome with pity and grief, and together with his sons and his friends, nobly undertook the task. With his own money he paid for the wherewithal to transport and deliver the body and do everything else that was necessary. Before evening fell, the body had been placed on a boat on the Seine, and with a very modest procession they made their way downstream towards the sea under a fine, bright sky. When they reached their destination with the body, the monks disembarked first, with the abbot,* duly robed, at their head. Such a great outpouring of grief as greeted William when he was taken into the town will never again be seen. But just hear what the Devil, that enemy of everything good, contrived to do! When the common people had gone up to the body and shed their floods of tears, a sudden fire swept through the town. No one could possibly stay with the body then, except the monks. The event caused great commotion and considerable disturbance. The body was then carried to the abbey, by which time more than half the town had burned down before the fire could be put out. (42006)

The Latin history and the life record how, before the actual burial, time was left for the bishops, abbots and prominent members of the nobility to arrive from all over Normandy. William's son Henry arrived, pale and ashen-faced with grief. Only twelve abbots and six bishops – seven if you count the archbishop – were present at the burial. It was an extremely solemn and splendid ceremony with full honours. The ground in which the king was buried was purchased on that very same day. A local by the name of Ascelin had been repeatedly claiming ownership of the plot, maintaining that the ground on which the abbey was built was part of his inheritance. Before today he had never received any payment for it, but on this occasion his request was finally granted, and this gave him great satisfaction. The ceremony came to an end, and many a tear was shed before the time came for people to leave. (42033)

I can state in all truthfulness that I have translated and recounted this history exactly as I found it written down. I have added nothing false or untruthful. Since the fruits of my labour have cost me a great deal, I pray to our Lord God that the work be pleasing to my lord [Henry II]. This is what I seek and desire more than anything else, for his approval would stand me in good stead. (42042)

[28] *Here ends the history of King William [the Conqueror], and here starts that of King Henry [I], King [William II] Rufus and Duke Robert [Curthose] of Normandy.*

Now that, by the gift and by the leave of the almighty King of Heaven, who makes little children into skilful and intelligent beings capable of reasoning, and gives the deaf and dumb eloquence, hearing and understanding, I have been translating the history of the dukes of Normandy* – a very voluminous history in which I have found a great deal of material to treat, much learning and many different subjects – and have now come right up to Henry who is to be the eighth duke and one of the most important, it would not be right for me to stop at this point and give up writing. My task is to keep going straight ahead in an orderly and uninterrupted fashion until I come to good King Henry II, the place on which my heart is set. May God be willing to grant me the opportunity of recounting his illustrious deeds! I am sorry that it is taking me so long, but in the same way as people apply plaster and colour to the wall on which they are painting, so that the brush strokes are better-formed, more delicate and richly coloured, so I have taken a long time to prepare the plaster for my painting without being lack-adaisical or allowing myself to be distracted.* The reason I am so assiduous, deter-mined and persistent is so that the work can be brought to completion this side of Judgement Day.* (42071)

Now is the right time for me to tell you that the first King Henry was a very valiant, brave, wise, discerning and just person, and the subject of praise through-out the world. In his time no ruler on earth did more good or acted with greater honour, none loved serving God more, or maintaining peace and justice; no one gave valuable gifts more open-handedly, nor lavished such generous allowances on people, no king's household was better cared for or a happier place. Any good act was permitted,* as was any form of beneficence, with the result that no king had a greater reputation or was honoured more or was more celebrated for such qualities. This is what he will be remembered for throughout the world for ever and ever. (42089)

The Latin history requires me not to pass over his brothers in silence. It is right that everyone should know that after King William Rufus had been crowned, the life he led was that of a great man. We have still to tell the story of his end and the manner of his death that was so violent and horrendous. Still to be told also is the story of the eldest of the brothers, the senior, Robert who was duke of Normandy – a true lord and a flower of chivalry. Even if my account of these two is brief, I am fully aware that this can only add lustre, distinction and splendour to the achievements and the deeds of the noble King [William]. If each of these two were, in themselves, valiant and brave men of high worldly renown, I find that King Henry's merit was as much as seven times greater than theirs. (42109)

It has been demonstrated beyond a shadow of doubt that what King William Rufus* wanted most in this world was to acquire possessions and then distribute them. No one loved spending as much as he did, no one was more energetic and enterprising; he was the least timid of men, the least faint-hearted. His mind was, however, set on doing things that earned him universal criticism, and that no consecrated or anointed king ever needed or was ever required to do. He had a quite unheard-of attitude towards Holy Church: his behaviour towards clerics, those in religious orders and to all religious houses was ill-intentioned and hos-tile, to the extent that, time and time again, protests and complaints about him were made and voiced directly to God. (42126)

Robert [Curthose], duke of Normandy, a valiant and brave knight, highly skilled in warfare, had an outstanding reputation as a fighter which enabled him to further increase his stature.* He never, however, cared for matters of state. Even though he was good-natured and a worthy and just man, he did not know how to govern his country and, through his own fault – sad to relate – he could not be as effective a duke as his ancestors had been. This is why I tell you that King Henry was superior to both of his brothers in merit, intelligence and in reputation. It transpired that it was he who finally acquired everything, not only taking it all, but holding on to it. Even if, when his father lay on his death-bed and the kingdoms were being divided up, Henry had been excluded and got nothing, nevertheless later he acquired everything, in accordance with God's will. Later he was to reach the pinnacle, as the greatest of the three, as I shall now proceed to recount to you. In so doing, I exclude the possibility of my adding to the account anything that I do not find in my written source. (42148)

Following William's death, therefore, of which I have already written, his son William [Rufus] reigned after him, and in his turn took possession of the land and of the kingdom. Robert had already gone over to the king of France, having unadvisedly got into some sort of antagonism with his father, because during his lifetime William had not allowed him to have free rein in Normandy and in his great county of Maine, and had gone to great trouble to enforce this. It was true that Robert was the legitimate heir to Normandy and Maine and had been invested with the lordship of both. This is clearly established by our written source in the person of Count Herbert [II of Le Mans'] daughter [= half-sister Margaret], a very beautiful, worthy and wise lady who, most unfortunately, died before Robert could marry and take her to his bed. It was on this basis that Robert wished to have both Normandy and Maine and have free rein there. His father, however, would not allow this, because on many occasions he had been displeased with his son whom he had forbidden to do what he then did, much to the detriment of a great many people. (42174)

When his father was still alive, Robert held a great muster of knights featuring Normandy's most celebrated knights at Abbeville in Ponthieu. People deliberately and somewhat rashly flocked there expecting to see a display of Robert's new lordly power as well as to satisfy their own ambition, as is the custom and convention. At places like this, people who have the opportunity of making trouble, and who have the desire, inclination and intention to do so, can easily become greedy and acquisitive, forget their duty and fail to keep their word. So much disorder was, in fact, stirred up there by these sorts of people that Normandy's marcher lands, which were close by, were badly ransacked and repeatedly plundered. When, however, Robert knew for certain that his father was dead, he quickly made his way to Rouen where, calmly and without encountering any opposition, he declared himself lord of the city and claimed all the relevant property rights. (42198)

He once again accepted the acts of fealty due to him. Thereafter he was urged insistently to cross over to England, drive his brother into exile and have himself crowned king, since, being the eldest son, both the kingdom and the crown should, by rights, be his. He swore to those who urged him to do this, so I find in my source, that if he had been far away in Germany, Alexandria or Spain, the English, however distasteful it might be to them, might possibly have waited for him before submitting to or accepting someone else as king. He did not think or expect that it would ever have occurred to Rufus to be so foolhardy as to have himself crowned king on his own individual initiative. Such an act of arrogance did not actually take place, but if it had, the price to be paid for it would have been very shameful.* However the situation was, in reality, quite different: Rufus had known right from the start exactly how things stood, and that he was the one who was to be consecrated and anointed king. After that, there was such hatred between them that no greater had ever before been seen between brothers. (42226)

Henry kept company with Duke Robert and was very happy to serve him. He travelled over the whole of Normandy with him, and proved to be most loyal and quite without guile. As the Latin history reminded me, his father had left Henry five thousand pounds sterling. I do not know if it was as an outright gift or as a pledge, but I do know that Henry was given the Cotentin in exchange for this money. His brother readily granted him possession of the county before finally taking it back from him in the most scandalous fashion. On the specious advice of some criminal individuals, Robert made an accusation against Henry who, unsuspecting and quite unaware of what was happening, found himself taken prisoner by the duke at Rouen. Robert kept him there until he had made him hand back everything that he had originally agreed to – either as a gift or as a pledge, I have no idea. This was extortion of the most contemptible kind, even though Henry might not have committed an actual offence against his brother. From then on, so I find, not a day went by without relations between them deteriorating,* and Henry became much less of an ally of Robert's and much less of a friend. (42252)

The fact was, then, that King William Rufus had the land and the kingdom of England, and Duke Robert was not at all happy about it. But people get what they deserve, and if Robert had loved, served and obeyed his father, he would readily have been given the kingdom and everything that went with the crown. Through his own fault, however, he found himself excluded and completely debarred. The two brothers [William and Robert] did, however, come to an agreement [in 1091]. If the duke had played his cards as cleverly and as wisely as the situation required, he could after all have got the whole of the kingdom, and all his wishes would have been granted. (42268)

A very significant campaign had been launched [in 1088] in which Eustace, count of Boulogne, who was in continual and relentless conflict with the king of England, [Odo,] the bishop of Bayeux and [Robert,] the count of Mortain, together with a number of other barons whom I do not care to name at present, crossed the Channel to attack England with as many troops as they could muster. Within the first two weeks they had, without any great effort, occupied Rochester and the castles in the country around Canterbury. They kept on summoning Duke Robert to come and take control of the land, but he was always busy, out hunting, taking things easy, sleeping in late in the mornings. This gave rise to frequent murmurings, often extremely insulting, since his own principal estates were in pretty poor shape at the time. If the invaders continued their occupation for any length of time, he could not be of any use to them, since he was unwilling to cross the Channel and come to their assistance. In any case, the incursion came to nothing, since King Rufus was continually harassing them and threatening their lives, with the result that they vacated the castles, leaving them wrecked and in a severely damaged state, and withdrew altogether from the land they had occupied. They were obviously extremely shamefaced when they returned to Normandy. Subsequently, as I find recorded in my source, there was an agreement signed at Caen between the duke and King [Philippe I] of France after the latter had come to Robert's aid when Rufus crossed the Channel with his fleet, consisting of a large body of well-equipped knights, to conquer and seize Normandy. Rufus had assembled his troops at Eu, fully expecting total victory, when it was decided that peace negotiations should take place. According to the terms of the reconciliation that was agreed between them, Rufus came off best with Duke Robert very much the loser. King Rufus was not willing to withdraw; no one could see to it that the castle he considered his and had taken over from those left occupying it would be given back, and it was handed over to him. The duke, as his contribution to helping Rufus win the war and gain total victory, was occupying Fécamp,* the county of Eu and a number of other powerful castles that his close friend Count William [of Evreux] had made available to him. Another firm and stable ally of his was Stephen of Aumale, son of Odo, count of Champagne, and cousin of good King William [I]. There were many others in the same category, and they were not the sort of people to stay out of the fighting. King William was unwilling to let them go, and in spite of his brother's reluctance, he retained them in his own service as worthy fighting vassals. (42338)

A strange event took place during this peaceful period I am telling you about – an unusual and most unseemly episode of violence. The two brothers, William and Robert, had a discussion together which resulted in their affirming and pledging that Henry would not be allowed to continue living in any of the territory that they held between them. They would not tolerate his presence among them any longer, however much other people might object, and they did everything in their power to ensure this. It is true that between them they ought to have avoided acting so maliciously as they did towards him. Henry had land at his disposal, and possessed castles, towns and several other holdings capable of ensuring that he could lead a suitably honourable life as their beloved younger brother. But they let him know, in a most vindictive fashion, that they wanted all that property for themselves, and they ended up besieging him at Mont-Saint-Michel [in 1091] where he had fled to seek refuge. Their intention was to starve him into submission until he gave himself up. This might well have been the outcome, but the siege was abandoned when a dispute arose between William and Robert, and this enabled Henry and his people to emerge without any harm having come to them. It was shortly after this that Henry skilfully managed to secure Domfront through the intervention of a man of his who was guarding the fortress. They were living under duress there and their lives were being put at risk by Robert de Bellême. No one had ever had a fouler or more loathsome christening than this man, no baptism more alien to our Lord God, less imbued with love and faithfulness, more obsessed with perfidy. The person in charge of the castle could tolerate it no longer, so he invited Henry in and installed him there. Henry was delighted and all too happy to take over the castle and thereby be in a position to protect the surrounding country. This was in such a deplorable state that no peasant ever left a farmland ox free to roam and lost a single penny without making loud protestations or causing an uproar. Henry held the castle in such affection that for the rest of his life no one else – we can be absolutely certain of this – ever had control of it or took it out of his hands. (42390)

According to the Latin history, John [of Avranches], the good archbishop of Rouen, a holy and worthy man, died during this particular time [1079]. William [I Bonne-Âme], abbot of Caen, was consecrated archbishop in his stead within the same year, and he presided over the church as a great peace-maker. (42398)

King William Rufus had returned to his kingdom in England, and thereafter Henry so skilfully arranged and organised things that he succeeded in taking back under his lordship the whole of the county of Cotentin right up to where the Bessin starts. He did not do so without a struggle, but did, I find, have the consent and the agreement of his brother Rufus. It was Duke Robert, whose behaviour had, on many occasions, been deplorable, and who was exceedingly weak-willed and frivolous, who had taken the Cotentin away from him. Richard de Reviers had been an ally of Henry's in this, as had been also Roger of Mandeville, an excellent knight of great nobility. Because Earl Hugh of Chester could not have been a better friend to him, a better supporter or a better helper, Henry wanted to give him, in fee, the castle which we know as Saint-James-de-Beuvron.* Previous to this, there had only ever been the wardenship of the tower there. It had been founded and constructed by King William [the Conqueror] as a defence against Conan, [count of Brittany,] who was no friend of his, I can tell you, in order to prevent the invasions that the Bretons would often attempt in the border regions there when no one was taking notice. The command of it had been given by William, sometime before the Conquest, to one Richard, a worthy and wise man who was the scion of an excellent family, whom he had installed there. This Richard [Goz] was the father of Hugh [of Chester] whom I have just referred to. (42436)

The people of Maine saw and understood the meaning of the various difficulties and setbacks that were causing Duke Robert to be suffering such losses on several fronts and to be falling into obvious decline. Hating, as they did, having the Normans as overlords, they began negotiating with a baron of considerable repute, who was also a brave knight, called Hélie [de la Flèche]. A generous, noble and much praised man, he was the son of John de la Flèche, and his mother [Paula] was a lady who commanded great respect. Hélie was a prominent figure in the region in terms of lands, possessions and friends. The people of Le Mans had proposed that he marry the daughter of a count of Lombardy [Azzo of Este], niece of the elder Herbert who had been count of Le Mans. It was Herbert's daughter who was this lady's mother. The negotiations had been taking place because it was for them unseemly and unacceptable that Normandy and the Normans should be their overlords, and their most cherished wish at this time was to put an end to this situation. Deliberations continued until finally they appointed Hélie as their lord. He came to hold Le Mans, the county and the rights appertaining to it; this is what was decided and what happened. As I have recounted elsewhere, the whole of Maine had formerly been under Norman lordship and control, having been conquered, as I read in the history and the life, by force of arms by King William the Conqueror and his allies, and left unconditionally to his heir. Now, however, the heir can be quite certain that the county's most worthy figures have as good as thrown him out. (42476)

[29] *How Duke Robert joined the great movement to conquer Jerusalem.*

In the second year of this particular period [1095], Pope Urban [II], as our written source informs us, came to Clermont in the Auvergne to teach the truth and justice to which Holy Church bears witness, and with such spiritual understanding and so effectively did he preach to the public at large about the journey to Jerusalem, Antioch and Bethlehem that a large number of people, including the most powerful and the most prominent, took the cross to expel the pagan people from the great land of Syria where, at that time, they all lived. So magnificent a journey had never before been undertaken, and in my opinion never will again until the Day of Judgement. (42494)

In the following year, therefore, without further delay, dukes, princes, counts and castellans, and the entire nobility of the West all the way to the Urals, set out to liberate the Holy Temple at Jerusalem. Duke Robert was so enthused by this sacred, holy pilgrimage that he was ready to depart and took the cross. He consequently summoned his brother the king to Normandy and begged him to come to his immediate assistance with financial support. Robert agreed to make over to him his duchy and all the land he held, as well as all the revenues that accrued to him: let him take and hold everything until he comes back home again. (42512)

The king was extremely happy to accept; he found no reason for further delay, and immediately crossed the Channel. What I can tell you for certain is that he made Robert a loan of 10,000 marks of silver, the understanding being that, for as long as Robert was absent, Rufus would receive all the income due to his brother without any restriction whatever. All profits would be his unconditionally, and he would make no outgoing payments until Robert came back. If Rufus's money is paid off and returned, Robert will get his land back in such a way that he will not find himself placed in the wrong or engaged in any war, or have anything done to him that ought not have been done – these are the conditions that the duke agrees to with Rufus. Well provided with money and a rich supply of goods, and accompanied by elite companions whom he greatly values, he joyfully sets out on God's service. This body of knights later proved so useful to him that none was ever so highly prized, more honoured and more revered than they were, and such was the duke's outstanding personal valour that everyone referred to him as good Robert of Normandy. Never again, I have been led to believe, will his high deeds be surpassed by those of any other crusader. (42542)

It was in this way that Rufus found himself in possession of the whole of Normandy. Count Henry remained his ally, as there was a great bond of love between the two of them. Henry had set his mind on serving Rufus and on doing everything his brother wanted. In return the king retained him in his service, and they were constantly in one another's company. Rufus readily made over to Henry the great county of Cotentin as well as the Bessin, though he retained Bayeux and Caen for himself. It was not long, in the course of this same year, before King William Rufus established Gisors[-sur-Epte] as a fine, strong and well-endowed castle, in order to acquire more security in relation to the kingdom of France. But after he had become king of England, his brother Henry strengthened and reinforced the fortifications in such a way as to make it impregnable. He had towers constructed and such high walls built that no attack against him would have been likely to succeed. King Rufus carried out a great many military operations which many people considered to be repugnant, though he remained a redoubtable force and one greatly to be feared, more so than I could possibly tell you. He declared war on the Welsh because he could never come to terms with their resistance. No one inflicted so much slaughter on them, and nothing exerted such powerful control over them as this did. On many occasions they rebelled against him, and for this they frequently had to pay the price. (42576)

King Malcolm [of Scotland] was another one who acted foolishly when he came down to attack Rufus with his Scots. His intention was to ravage England by occupying, laying waste and plundering the country. He had brought a large number of troops with him from several far-off countries. King Rufus, however, fearlessly engaged him with his army. Inevitably Malcolm was obliged to submit to Rufus's will, such was his strength. He threw himself humbly at his feet in submission. In this way Rufus subdued all his ill-intentioned neighbours. No one would have rebelled against him without having to pay dearly for it. (42590)

Hélie [de La Flèche], as I was telling you, was in control of Maine. He held Le Mans for a long time until finally, out of fear of King Rufus, the townspeople and others ousted him and handed the city over to the king's men peacefully and without any argument. But what happened afterwards, as I am able to tell you, is that Hélie sought help and summoned a large number of troops, including Count

Fulk of Anjou who, together with foot-soldiers and knights, came and laid siege to Le Mans with as many men as they could muster. They launched a great many attacks such as to cause those guarding the fortress considerable alarm. So hard-pressed were they, and such was their need, that they were forced to send word overseas to England and inform the king. On hearing the news, Rufus was not in the least pleased and not at all happy. Immediately and without losing a moment, he made straight for the coast. He took only a few knights along with him, but any inaction or delay would not have been acceptable to him. He gave orders for his people to follow him as rapidly as they could and, as soon as they reached the coast, to cross over after him. (42620)

Rufus himself had set his heart on making the Channel crossing, and was extremely keen to do so. The wind, however, was not in his favour, and the sea was rough and stormy. The sailors strongly advised him against setting out in such conditions, as did all of his closest friends; not one of them would intervene to urge him to cross in such a storm and with the sea so choppy and violent. Anyone would have to be mad, they say, to set out in such bad weather. To which the valiant and intrepid king replied by declaring to all and sundry that he had never heard of any king drowning at sea, and he would certainly not be the first to do so. The sailors were thus obliged to do the king's bidding despite the storm and the raging sea, and they set sail from the port fully convinced they were going straight to their death. From now until the end of the world no people will ever expose themselves to greater danger. I have no idea how they survived, but the fact is that they succeeded in making landfall. No king ever, in his entire life, undertook such a reckless act. Everyone thought it was a miracle. Without waiting for his army, troops or companions, he rode straight to Le Mans, spurring hard at top speed and in great haste. He was expecting to find the two counts [Hélie and Fulk] there, but they had no intention of staying around. From the mightiest to the humblest, everyone had disappeared rather than wait for the arrival of Rufus. (42658)

Whatever tales anyone else might tell, I can find nothing more about Rufus in my written source, and I have no wish to write anything down that people might possibly be able to contradict. But the sort of deeds I have been describing were entirely typical of him, for no knight was ever born in this world who was more venturesome than he. His reputation would have been particularly high and distinguished had he not undertaken to wage war against the clergy, Holy Church and all things religious. But he had a most malicious nature and never showed any respect towards the religious, and this is the reason why he fell victim to such a severe judgement. This is our firm belief, beyond a shadow of doubt. I intend now to end my account of his deeds, and I shall turn to King Henry. This is someone who loved and served God so well, so honourably and so truly, so my written source recounts, that no king on earth who was so esteemed and enjoyed such glory would have been more worthy of being commemorated. (42680)

As I read and as I understand it, Rufus was still on the throne when [in 1093] a kinsman of Robert of Mowbray, by the name of Morel, a fine, valiant and powerful knight and a man of considerable influence in Northumbria, assembled a large army. What he did thereafter was simply attack King Malcolm and his sons and the formidable army he had brought together and that had crossed over from Scotland to England, as they were used to doing with such regularity. Morel won the day so resoundingly that all the Scots were either captured or killed, and King Malcolm himself was killed and his eldest son also, together with an enormous number of other fighters.* It was Robert of Mowbray who orchestrated all of the events I am recounting to you here, and it was he who was subsequently to pay the penalty with his freedom for the great losses that were suffered. He had seized the king's castles, crown property that he had in no way gained legal possession of, which he then fortified, made secure and properly garrisoned. He wished to add these to his county holdings, even though they should not rightfully have been his. Because he refused to return them to the king, Rufus ordered his men to take him prisoner. He was clapped in irons and thrown into prison, where he was treated with the greatest contempt. He was still being held prisoner when King Henry [I] was crowned [in 1100]. What I find is that, before he could be released or pardoned or granted the king's peace, it was unavoidable that he should be put to death, because people had not forgotten that he had conspired to have the king of Scotland, the father of [Henry's] Queen Matilda, killed in the most violent manner. This is why the written story records and requires that his punishment was never again to emerge from prison until his dying day. It is not unknown for events such as this to happen. As I find in reading my written source, part of Robert of Mowbray's county of Northumbria and his Normandy holdings – these were fine, attractive, productive, extensive and well-endowed lands – were given in fee by King Henry, into whose possession they had come, to Nigel d'Aubigny, a person of nobility and an experienced knight, and someone of whom the king was very fond. This Nigel, I know, married Gundred, the daughter of Gerard of Gournay. In her he had an exceedingly noble and beautiful young lady, good and intelligent, and together she and Nigel, so I find, had Roger of Mowbray, a powerful knight of great influence who was to become their heir. (42742)

[30] *How King Rufus was killed.*

I have already explained to you how Duke Robert [Curthose] mortgaged Normandy in order to accompany those who went off to liberate the country where Jesus had chosen to live and where he had died, from the hands of God's mortal enemies, the Saracen heretics, ignorant and faithless people with a religion of evil. King Rufus was on the throne during this time, but because his attitude to God was one of hostility, he did not enjoy a long reign. How this came about you will now be able to hear for yourselves. (42756)

It is true, and a well-known fact, that there was mutual hatred between Rufus and [Gundulf,] the bishop of Rochester,* the chaplain – and rightfully so – of [Anselm,] the archbishop of Canterbury. The reason for the bishop's resentment against the king was that he had exiled Saint Anselm and driven him out of the country. The bishop had come to Winchester to see Rufus in order to ask for there to be peace between them, but was unable to get it. Moved by a pious compassion, this good man had spent a long time praying to our Lord to remember and turn his attention to this disagreeable situation. (42772)

Rufus had a sudden desire, which he shared with those around him, to go hunting with the bow in the New Forest at the first sign of light next morning. The night before, however, he spent feeling dejected and extremely anxious, and he was unable to fall asleep before dawn. When he could no longer stay awake, he had a frightening and violent dream, the likes of which had never before been heard or recorded.* He dreamt he entered a huge, splendid and beautiful church; even though he felt like praying, his mind kept turning to other things. He was seized with an unbelievable hunger, and so violent and all-consuming was it that he felt as if he was growing weak and about to faint, almost to the point where he would eat his own hands. And this he would have done, had there been no alternative. His gaze then fell on the altar where he saw – or so he thought – a huge stag that had been killed. In order to avoid the great act of apostasy he was about to commit on himself, he approached the animal with the intention of eating some of it, since his one and only desire was for food. At the very moment he was stretching out his hand, he suddenly realised – and it seemed to him to be absolutely certain – that it was in fact a man's body still bleeding from the wound that had killed him. He was seized with fear and revulsion at such a hideous sight. But so great was his hunger, and so strong was his craving for food, that he was unable, despite every effort he could possibly make, to prevent himself from being forced to eat some of it. He makes as if to pull off the man's hand, but the whole of the arm comes away from the body. This he immediately devours, and then, not being satisfied, wants to seize hold of the second hand also, since his hunger has not diminished in the least. Fearful and terror-stricken, he pulls it towards him, still attached to the arm, and eats it, but still his appetite is not satisfied. His hunger grew and grew but could not be sated. Biting savagely into the bone and flesh, he eats one of the feet, then the whole of the leg right up to the body. At this he feels twice as hungry as before, so without the slightest hesitation he imme-diately sets about devouring the second leg as well. This, however, is to no avail, for it has little or no effect on his hunger. At this moment, the man's face comes into view, and this also he feels an urge to eat. But the spectacle he beholds is a death-inducing one: an absolutely terrifying pair of eyes, so horrible and hideous and so excruciating to look at that all that remains is for him to die, and for his heart to cease beating in his breast. After Rufus had recovered from the faint he suffered, for a long time he could not tell whether he was dead or alive. After regaining consciousness, he was in a state of distress and felt tormented, and for a long time he stayed silent and lost in thought. He had no idea what he should do, or whom he should tell his dream to. His discomfort was all the greater because of his fear and the feeling he had of impending death. (42846)

After a long period of reflection he asked whether the bishop had already left. He was immediately sought out and brought before Rufus. He was on his own, so there were only the two of them. He gives the bishop an account of what happened, a task he finds bitterly unpleasant, for he is fully aware, beyond any doubt, of the extreme gravity of the meaning of his dream. The holy bishop lis-tens to the order of events, the actual words used, and the unfolding of the dream that had been so frightening and violent. (42860)

Gundulf then starts preaching him an authoritative sermon in which he points out that the church he entered represents Christianity, on which Holy Church is constructed and of which it is an apologist – the same Holy Church that Rufus has treated so contemptuously. His inability to carry out his intention of praying because of his obsessive and deadly hunger can only represent the dis-tractions, the vicissitudes, the ambitions and the evils of secular matters. These ensnare him so perniciously that he ignores God his Creator. Anyone whose life is not pleasing to God cannot expect God to be willing to do anything for him.

His being on the point of eating his own hands signifies his desire to destroy himself before all others, and to condemn himself to Hell with no possibility of redemption. The stag he believed he really saw on the altar and which he wanted to eat illustrates how every animal is all too ready to commit mortal sins, how his only ambition is to habitually and single-mindedly satisfy his own desires unreasonably, without any discrimination and without fear of God – all of which arouses God's anger against him. As for his believing and being convinced that the stag was actually a human being and his decision not to refrain from eating it, this is how the bishop wishes to interpret this part of the dream: anyone who is contemptuous of honest people and misleads and deceives them, and anyone who fails to show proper respect and loyalty to holy figures of great renown, and indeed to anyone in religious orders, such a person commits an offense against his heavenly Creator. The hands and arms that he ate without satisfying his hunger, these represent the acts of great evil that he committed against them, and which are still continuing: the seizures, the damage and the war that were being inflicted on them throughout his kingdom. This is what Saint Paul has to say: "Such people are members of Christ, and whosoever insults or oppresses them grows fat on living flesh." (42914)

"What I understand by the legs and feet and the whole length of the thighs right up to the body which you immediately proceeded to eat is that this is the result of one particular sin to which you are addicted,* which has its origin in that part of the body, and for which everyone fears that God will vent his anger on you and take the sort of vengeance that we have never heard of him taking on anyone before. Unless you repent, you are damned, destroyed and dead; you should rue the day that you were ever born. Here, finally, is what you can understand concerning the head that you wished immediately to attack, consume and devour, which seemed to you so alarming and forbidding, hideous, frightening, and more terrifying than anything could possibly be, which your eyes could not even bear to contemplate, such dread did they instil, and towards which you did not dare to stretch out your hand, even at the risk of losing your life: you should know that this is the gravest of all the wrongs you are committing, for it is God who is the head of all things, and you are attempting to perpetrate your crimes in him. This is something that he will not allow you to do. This has been an unattainable ambition of yours, and for this you have now, in your dream, stretched out your hand in submission.* (42942)

Steel yourself* and watch out that your power does not simply disappear from one moment to the next. God's vengefulness is something that you should be very much afraid of, as was the fierceness of his bearing and his face that you were incapable of even looking at in your dream. Nevertheless, were you to obey him, God, as well as being terrifying to those who break his law, is also compassionate and attractive to gaze upon to those who are dear to him, even if his limbs have been manhandled, eaten and devoured. What he is showing you by this – and this is how you can interpret your dream – is that he was simply willing to wait for you to make a sincere confession and thus have your sins forgiven. (42958)

Now, however, it is my opinion and understanding that you will no longer have any possibility of making contact with him or his head, for this is something that he refuses and denies you. You have no reason to feel secure; take urgent steps to mend your ways, and do not let your decision be postponed, for there is every need and necessity for you to take it soon. One piece of advice I wish to give you, one request I wish to make of you in the name of God, is that today you do not, please, go hunting in the woods or go fowling. You will do well to avoid doing so, and instead the proper thing for you to do is to confess your sins, without losing a moment, to someone who can give you instruction on what is the right course of action for you. And if you are able to come to love God, there will be no need for you to feel frightened by your dream." (42976)

The king listened with goodwill, composure and humility. He fully recognised the accuracy of the bishop's interpretation of his dream; with equanimity, and forgiving [Gundulf] the holy bishop for his animosity towards him, he firmly promised to mend his ways. Once he had the bishop's gracious agreement and his permission to leave, he did so cheerfully and in high spirits. While Rufus was still turning this episode over in his mind and recalling what had happened, a half dozen or so of his knights came riding up. Suitably dressed and equipped and ready to go, these young nobles already had their bows in their hands as they waited already mounted on their hunting horses, their hounds following along behind furiously barking. They are already blowing their horns as they wait outside for the king to join them. (42997)

Rufus's closest companions came in to fetch him and began urging him to come hunting in the forest. They took him severely to task for delaying so long: now was the time to be up and away. Each and every one of them ribbed him, saying they were scared that he was turning into a saint,* and they prayed God that he not include them in his prayers since they had so little trust in him. "Hold on there, my lords!" he says. "I'm actually a thoroughly bad person, a hundred times worse than you think! To cut a long story short, I'm giving up going hunting today: the last thing I want to do is go into the woods, and I never want to see the forest again." Everyone round him was convinced that he was joking, so they all began to put pressure on him. Each one of them speaks up, urging him to find some energy, be quick, and do what he really wants to do. So insistent are they that he ends up getting dressed and equipped and setting out with them straight to the forest. Now that he had found some measure of enjoyment after his agitation and was relishing the company of other people, he attached very little importance indeed to what he had previously been told. (43026)

I have no intention here of spinning out my story; suffice it to say that at least twenty times that day in different places they dismounted to shoot off their arrows. But as you are going to hear, something very grievous and distressing took place. The king – as has been reported to me – had ordered the hunters to gather round in a particular spot that he had come across, and they had taken up their positions behind the trees that surrounded it. When the quarry comes within range and the aim is the best possible, one particular knight is very quick off the mark and ready to shoot, and so the king instructs him to do so. The man, however, becomes apprehensive and takes fright because the king is standing very close to his line of fire. On at least two occasions, I think, he decides, with bow ready stretched, not to shoot. But King Rufus urges him to go ahead, so much so that he impulsively lets loose a barbed arrow which, with the Devil's connivance, strikes and glances off a sturdy branch, hitting the king close to his heart. Though quite incapable of speaking, Rufus nevertheless manages to say to the knight: "Run for it! Flee, don't lose a moment! You have killed me, and I only have myself to blame. God has taken vengeance on me here. I beg for mercy now and implore him, in his holy and precious compassion, to have pity on me this day, for I have sorely sinned against him." Whereupon he immediately died. The knight fled in such grief that he was able only to keep on repeating that he wished he were dead himself. (43060)

Those in the forest, meanwhile, having witnessed this distressing misfortune, broke out into howls, cries and loud laments, tearing their hair and beards, and repeatedly swooning and falling to the ground in their extreme anxiety and distress. Both because they were far from the city and because night was about to fall at any moment, they carried Rufus off without any further delay. It was late August but not yet September, and on the fourth day after he was killed, apparently, so I discover, he was buried at Winchester with great lamenting and many tears. This happened one thousand one hundred years – no more, no less – since the birth of Christ. He had reigned for not even thirteen years, as my Latin source recounts. (43078)

There can be absolutely no doubt about the fact that Saint Hugh, abbot of Cluny, knew the very moment that Rufus passed away, and I need to tell you exactly how this came about. Saint Anselm, archbishop of Canterbury, who was in exile, being a close friend of the abbot's, was with him at the time. They were sitting at table together, and it so happened that the abbot fell asleep. It was through divine revelation, so we read, that he came to know of Rufus's death, and he saw the shooting the very moment it happened. When he woke up, the first thing he did was to say to the archbishop: "My dear friend, go back to your own country; your stay here has come to an end." Saint Anselm felt both ashamed and alarmed, for he had no idea why the abbot was sending him away in this fashion. When Hugh saw Anselm's consternation, he proceeded to tell him the whole story of how Rufus was, beyond any shadow of doubt, dead and had passed away. (43108)

King William Rufus – this we know for certain – had a brother called Richard, a young man of most noble bearing. During the lifetime of his father, so I read, he was out hunting one day in the woods. I believe it was in the same place as Rufus was killed. He was hunting a stag at full gallop when he could not avoid striking a branch protruding from an enclosure he was crossing. Inevitably he had his eyes knocked out of their sockets, and he fell off his horse, landing on his back. He lay there for ages, pallid and blue in the face, unable to get up to save his life. His death was unavoidable. This is one way – amongst many others – that God makes his judgements known. (43126)

Immediately after the sorrowful burial that Count Henry arranged for his brother who had been killed, he came straight to London. Here, on the fourth day after his brother's death, he summoned all the most prominent men of the kingdom to come and join him at Westminster. Everyone, people of all descriptions, responded spontaneously by receiving him with great honour and accepting him as their lord and king. That very day they promptly placed the crown on his head. Unprecedented joy spread throughout the kingdom,* everyone being firmly convinced that God had provided them with someone who would be a compassionate and just father to the common people and to the country, who would rule over the kingdom, all people of goodwill and Holy Church, in peace, and would be very firm in maintaining justice. And thus it turned out: a king with such good qualities had never before been seen. No one, to our knowledge, had ever before done so much to support religious life, and no one had set his face more implacably against treason and crime. Towards wrong-doers he acted ruthlessly and mercilessly, while those who loved, served and obeyed him found themselves richly rewarded. He was never reluctant to maintain a sumptuous royal household, and no one cherished valorous knights more than he did. He was a steadfast king and a great lover of justice, and God demonstrated his favour by granting affluence and plenty to the people, their lands and the whole of the country over which Henry ruled during his lifetime. His reign was a fortunate and blessed one, and God caused him to prosper and greatly exalted him. (43168)

In his pursuit of a righteous and dutiful life, Henry lost no time in securing a companion and a wife in accordance with God's established custom. In the same year as he is crowned, he seeks out, marries and takes as his wife Matilda, a young lady of great beauty, daughter of King Malcolm of Scotland, and her mother was called Margaret. Many fine and memorable things have been written about Henry and Matilda. They were God-fearing people and devoted to God, and their way of life, we read, was devout. I find recorded in my source that Saint Anselm returned home in peace and in great godliness, and for the rest of his life King Henry acted as his lord and bosom friend. The Latin source informs me that Henry himself approved the arrangements for the marriage ceremony to take place at Westminster on Saint Martin's day, and Matilda, the lady of high degree and pious renown, was crowned queen on the same occasion and thus invested with great worldly eminence. (43194)

Not long afterwards Matilda had two children with her husband, one boy and the other a fine, upstanding and beautiful girl. The son, I know, was called William [Ætheling], and no finer boy than he was ever raised. The daughter, a noble girl of very attractive appearance, was also called Matilda.* There will be a great deal to say about her, for so plentiful is the material that everyone hearing even a fraction of what she achieved will declare that her like had never before existed, and that no one was more deserving of praise than she. She led her life with an eminence that distinguished her from all other women. No woman on earth had a more memorable life-story that could be written about her. The most valiant and superlatively virtuous Emperor Henry V, crowned at Rome and celebrated throughout the world, sought her hand in marriage. This worthy and intelligent young girl was only five years old, so my written source informs me, when ambassadors on behalf of her suitor came to good King Henry of England. These consisted of noble figures of great learning, wise and eloquent, bishops of great renown, counts, magnates and barons, and they were received with all due ceremony. After consulting his privy council, the king granted their petition, and when the formalities were completed, he sent his daughter off to Germany with a noble and lavish retinue and a wealth of precious objects that I will not itemise for you. Since the beginning of time and as long as the world survives, no king's daughter will, I think, have had a more sumptuous send-off. Preparations continued apace, and at Easter, so I find, the emperor married Matilda.* The ceremony, attended by many a mother's son of great nobility, was one of great splendour, unsurpassed in the whole of Germany. (43246)

As soon as summer arrived, she was crowned without further delay at Mainz on Saint James's day [25 July 1110] in front of a huge crowd of onlookers. The archbishop of Cologne officiated, and the archbishop of Trier, who was also the legate, supported her gently in his arms. As her husband, the emperor's wish is that his wife, as queen and empress, should be educated as befits a noble of her standing with no expense spared, and that she should learn German, together with those of the country's customs and laws that are necessary for an empress to be acquainted with, and that provision should be made for this until such time as she reaches adulthood. What we have mentioned so far is what is strictly necessary for you to know here concerning Matilda. But in time I shall have much more to write about such a widely celebrated figure, for it is my firm belief that there is nothing in the whole of my book that people would be happier to listen to, seeing that her impressive and highly regarded achievements are so much more extraordinary than those of any other person. (43272)

[31] *How King Henry's son [William Ætheling] drowned off Barfleur.*

My story, a very happy one so far, is now turning into a very sad one, bleak and gloomy, replete with misadventure. William, so named after Henry's younger brother, was a fine young man of great nobility whose valour and wisdom, so I read, were unequalled throughout the world. But just listen what a great and tragic loss was to come!* He set sail from Barfleur to cross the Channel to England [in November 1120]. Accompanying him were a large number of knights, noble young ladies and wives, not to mention helmsmen and sailors, handsome and clever young men, valuable objects and equipment. There was, however, a very strong wind, and the sea was exceedingly rough. It was a foul, moon-less night and, what is more, the sailors had been drinking heavily – foolishly so as they had become befuddled, heavy-headed and apathetic. They had been ready to leave as night fell at a time when the tide was still coming in. They headed straight for the Cateras [Quillebeuf] reef, in one of the most dangerous stretches of water between here and the Spanish frontier, and where a boat can easily get swamped and sink. They lost their sense of direction as they ploughed into these seas, and in less than no time, given the grave danger posed by the rocks and the height of the waves, their boat foundered, was smashed to pieces and sank to the bottom. Such cries of grief as could be heard there were the most desperate imaginable. The king's son drowned, as did all on board – to everyone's immense distress, subsequently, with people openly weeping at the news, grieving and mourning. The crew all perished, and there were no survivors. We find recorded that the master mariner could easily have made his escape, had he so wished, and might not have perished. But on seeing his lord drown, he gave up any idea of saving his own life and decided to join him in death. From the moment he saw himself coming to grief and in danger of dying on his own boat and through his own fault, he made absolutely no effort to escape. He was quite willing to drown and go down with the boat, and, as was widely reported at the time, this is exactly what he did. (43325)

There was utter consternation and anguish throughout Normandy when news of the accident spread, nor was there any question of reports of such an event being withheld in England. When King Henry got to hear of it, it is no wonder that he found every reason to loudly bewail his lot, having lost the son whom he had so excessively cherished and having no other heir but the empress of Germany. If Fortune had ever smiled upon him in the past, now it had turned against him in the most cruel and hard-hearted manner possible. There could be no better illustration of just how untrustworthy Fortune is, how happiness in this word in unknowable, deceptive, false and ever changeable, how unpredictable it is even to those whom it most favours. Let no one, therefore, rejoice or celebrate when they have no idea of what Fortune has in store for them! Often in the space of a single day someone who starts off with their mind full of happiness will end up care-ridden and depressed. Suffering and distress that carry with them no advantage serve no useful purpose. So everyone should behave with moderation, and in good times set a limit to their happiness and in bad times not complain, in the first case avoiding too much happiness, and in the second too much despair. This is exactly what happened with King Henry: he had never indulged in too much happiness, and in the terrible and deadly disaster that befell him he did not give way to excessive grief. Wise and high-minded as he was, he took what comfort he could right from the first moment he found out. My view is that it is not wise if someone, when faced with a grievous loss, should increase his stake threefold,* for is it not enough for him to lose his first stake without then going on to find himself completely ruined? I am firmly convinced that someone who makes two losses out of one is neither clever nor shrewd, and anyone who deprives himself of happiness and delight inflicts grave harm and injury on himself. Let everyone behave with moderation! Anyone beset by adversity should know that in the end both joy and sadness are fleeting things. It is extremely rare to see anyone whose grief, however great, does not eventually come to an end, and who does not succeed in regaining happiness. Ups and downs are part of everyone's life. May God, therefore, so keep and protect us that we remain free from adversity! (43386)

[32] *How Duke Robert [Curthose] returned from Jerusalem to seek the crown.*

After the holy conquest of Antioch in the East and the retaking of the Holy Sepulchre in which Jesus lay dead and from which he rose again, Duke Robert of Normandy returned home. This was a very unwise decision of his, for there was at that time no Christian in the whole world who was held in greater honour than he was. He was constantly begged to stay in the East, but he remained unmoved by people's entreaties. He could have occupied an extremely high position, but he had set his heart on coming back. And this, in short, is what he did [in September 1100], extremely wealthy and laden with gold. He was very eager to return because of the death of his brother. Although Robert had mortgaged Normandy, there was no question of his claim to it being contested, and in any case he had at his disposal all the money he needed to pay back the loan. No one, however, asked him for it, and indeed no one ever even raised the matter with him. When he learnt how his brother had treated him by getting himself crowned king, his anger was almost uncontrollable. Nothing he had ever heard in his life before had caused him to feel such contempt, and he hated Henry more than any man alive. He did everything in his power to intimidate him and remove him as king of England. He withdrew all support from him and defied him in every possible way. But this was a very reckless course of action for him to take. (43420)

    He organised a fleet and enlisted as many mounted and armed men as he could. At the earliest opportunity, as soon as the weather permitted, he set sail straight for the English ports with massed troops. King Henry, his brother, summoned as many allies and men as he possibly could, placing his trust in God his Lord to come to his assistance and rescue him. He would not have hesitated to put his own life at risk, for he would have preferred to die on the battlefield rather than let his brother take his life or take him prisoner or eject him from the kingdom. The upshot would have been that many a head would have been split open and many a soul snatched from its body unless some other solution were to be found. And this God saw to by establishing concord, harmony, love and peace between them. The agreement that the two brothers came to was that Henry should be king, and in return for an annual payment of 4,000 silver marks, Robert should cede full control of the entire kingdom to his brother without any further objection. According to my Latin source, Robert, unwilling to accept any of the money, handed the first payment over to good Queen Matilda. He did so out of kindness and in order to honour this most worthy of ladies. It was not, however, a wise step on his part to squander so much money that he had cause to regret it afterwards. Being so keen to give away what belonged to him inevitably involved depriving other people of it. This was bad practice and shows a measure of thoughtlessness. Good sense and moderation are much more preferable.* (43460)

Following the amicable agreement between the two lords, Duke Robert became extremely popular and much loved in England. He remained there, I find, for a considerable amount of time, so much so, in fact, that it grew to be very much to his liking, and he made every possible effort to stay. But then, with a modest retinue of followers, he returned to Normandy. If only at that moment he had been willing to turn his attention to acting as a good leader should, namely by being upright and just, avoiding corruption and dispensing justice, setting an example of valour and fulfilling the role of wise counsellor – let him fear and serve his Creator and protect the people entrusted to his care, so as to avoid failing God and his own subjects. If only the duke had been willing to behave in this way, he would have been able to see to it that the duchy of Normandy enjoyed uninterrupted peace for the remainder of his life. But none of this was of any concern to him. He failed to act as he should have done, and providing good, honest counsel was something he attached no importance to at all. On the contrary, he got into the habit of trusting common and disreputable individuals, malicious and vulgar people who left no stone unturned in their attempts to stir up enmity between him and his brother. This they found an easy task, as Robert had no defence against the bad, illegal, shameful, low-minded and misleading advice they gave him. They often talked him into taking distasteful actions designed to arouse the king's displeasure, and they made a regular habit of doing so. Their support of the duke and their attachment to him were, however, short-lived and soon turned to hatred. If the king lost patience with his brother, he had many reasons to do so, for repeatedly Duke Robert, naïvely and imprudently, gave away and endowed extremely disreputable people with the fiefs and honours that he had inherited from his ancestors, together with the finest and best-situated of his towns and castles, his woods and the properties from which he earned income. He carelessly and without consideration disposed of lands that his ancestors had fought hard to obtain and which had formed parts of their estates. The only property of his own that he was left with was the city of Rouen, and even this he would have given away time and time again if he had been able to do so. The townspeople, however – fine, noble people that they were – were never willing to give their agreement. (43523)

These unheard-of acts of devilry were more than King Henry could tolerate, and he was unwilling to let him damage his heirs in this way and bring his family into disrepute. He crossed the Channel [in July 1106] with a countless number of heavily armed troops. He came to Bayeux with the intention of capturing the town, but the inhabitants would not surrender. So he laid siege to it and finally took it, burning and pitilessly destroying it. Almost immediately afterwards, so I discover, he captured Caen, and from there, I know for certain, he set out to besiege Tinchebray. This belonged to [William,] the count of Mortain, who had no love lost for Henry, being a misguided supporter of the duke, his rightful lord. He was the sort who would never baulk at or turn down any clever move, any underhand trick, even if it risked being to his own disadvantage. The king was no friend of his, which explains why Henry besieged his castle. It resisted all assaults, however, and there was every expectation that it could hold out, since the siege had already lasted a considerable number of days. Meanwhile Duke Robert came to join Count William, who had mustered a huge number of well-armed troops, barons from the surrounding region, castellans and their most reliable and closest allies. They will, they claimed, get the upper hand over Henry and they will not put up with him anymore. If they fight with determination, the king will lose his crown. (43560)

Fully armed on their prize horses, grasping their weapons decorated with coloured devices, their tall, gold-studded standards unfurled, the companies into which the élite knights have been divided vie with each other as they gallop at the enemy who they fear might already turn and run. All that remains is for the battle to be engaged and the hand-to-hand fighting to start. King Henry had taken part of his army and devised a plan whereby they would stay carefully hidden in ambush in a place unknown to the enemy. He issued his orders, telling them exactly what he wanted them to do. The rest of the army he formed into units, companies and battalions to confront the enemy forces. There was a great forest of lances when the troops clashed and came to blows, and a thousand of them ended up in splinters. Never had there been such a bruising encounter or such an extraordinary clash, so fierce and so brutal that nowhere was shelter or safety to be found. Had the battle lasted for any length of time, losses would have been extremely high, a thousand heads would have been severed, a thousand trunks headless, if God had not intervened. Just listen to what happened with those of the king's men that were hidden in ambush! They all came rushing out together and fell on Duke Robert who had become separated from the rest of his men, and on Count William who was in close proximity. They were supporting the companies and battalions who were engaged in hand-to-hand fighting. Out of necessity and somewhat rashly they had fewer than two hundred knights with them. The king's men made their challenge and then struck. As was inevitable, a large number of the enemy were unhorsed and killed. Even the bravest of them would have preferred not to have been there. The end was not long in coming. The duke was unable to make his escape; he and the count were immediately taken prisoner. Not a single one of the others got away without either being struck down dead or captured on the spot and taken prisoner. (43610)

Without any further delay the great battle came to an end. As soon as those occupying the castle learnt of their defeat, there was not a single arrow shot, nor was there any way for them to extricate themselves: all of their most prominent figures were taken prisoner. God clearly brought an end to these dreadful, hateful and deadly hostilities, for as I read and know for certain, King Henry did not lose a single knight or person of rank that day. And on the other side there were, by all accounts, no more than fifty mortalities. In this way peace was re-established in Normandy, a country that had almost sunk into shame, and had known such destruction and been so ravaged that right and justice no longer existed, and where the enmity had been unparalleled. Henceforth peace was to reign there, and harmony was restored for as long as King Henry lived. It became a pleasant land to live in again, a place of honour, merriment and plenty. For as long as the good king reigned after winning this battle, it was a truly blessed land. As I read in my source, this happened in the year 1106, and the battle – I can be quite certain – actually took place in the month of October [= 28 September]. (43642)

King Henry then organised the land as he saw fit, appointing noble citizens and prosperous officials to guard its towers and accepting their oaths of fealty. Control of the lands that belonged to the count of Mortain was handed over to him and, without any opposition, he took personal possession of them. This had been his first concern, and there had been absolutely no question of William of Mortain being pardoned or released. When the king had settled all his business in such a way that he would encounter no more opposition, his wish was to cross the Channel taking Robert and William back with him, as well as a large number of other prisoners whose names I omit. He had these rich and powerful Normans put into enormously heavy iron shackles and thrown into prison where the only comfortable bed they were given was the hard ground. This is how things turned out for Duke Robert, whose treatment was to be kept a prisoner for the rest of his life, to be shown no mercy and not to have any possibility of being ransomed.* He had been duke for all of nineteen years, in addition to the time he had spent abroad during his stay in Jerusalem, as I explained to you earlier. No one returning from the Holy Land ever failed to say that Robert was the very best of the best, the paragon of all crusaders. He contrived, nonetheless, through great naïvety, dilatoriness and errors of judgement, to lose his land, his honour, his entire reputation. This caused considerable harm and was a matter of great regret. He will not be the only person to whom such things happen. (43684)

On his return from his journey overseas Duke Robert had taken as his wife the intelligent and courtly Sybilla, sister of Duke William of Conversano. This lady had one son with him, his only heir, I believe. He was known as William [Clito], and from a very early age he was someone of high reputation and military prowess. His mother, I can tell you, was one of the most beautiful women in the whole world, virtuous, wise and greatly loved. She was of a cheerful disposition in all circumstances, and was the most widely honoured of ladies. Whenever the duke was absent, thanks to her, things were invariably a hundred times better than when he was there in person. She was a person of great merit, and intelligent as well. Her life in Normandy was short, as prominent women grew jealous of her and brought about her death, so my Latin source informs me. Much later her son William Clito held the powerful position of count of Flanders, having been unable to remain in Normandy after his father's capture. His banishment to France led to his enjoying immense popularity. Then came the assassination of Charles [the Good] who was cut down in church at Bruges [in 1127], a terrible and deeply sinful crime. Fair Queen [Adelaide], the wife of King Louis [VI], intervened and, in conformity with the wishes of her husband, arranged for her sister [Jeanne of Montferrat] to be married to William Clito. This is how he came to be count of Flanders, and a good and worthy count he was. He did not live long, however. We find recorded that he was wounded by people defending a castle that he was attempting to capture, and because no help was at hand, he died of the wound [in 1128]. His death was a tragedy, and my source records that he was buried in the church of Saint-Bertin [at Saint-Omer]. The next count was Thierry of Alsace, a noble and courtly knight whose generosity was unparalleled and who then governed Flanders with great success. King Henry, I believe, gave him a beautiful and noble wife [in Sibyl of Anjou], the second sister of Count Geoffrey [Martel]. Theirs was a splendid marriage: they were a well-matched couple and they lived an extravagant life. (43742)

During this time Robert Curthose, still a prisoner – though he was able to lead an agreeable life of luxury and ease – died in Bristol [= Cardiff]. In charge of his incarceration was Robert, earl of Gloucester, a highly intelligent and courtly nobleman who had been entrusted with the task by King Henry. If what our source tells us is true, Duke Robert had spent twenty-eight years in prison. He left this world on 9 February [= 3 February 1134]. His body lies buried in Saint Peter's at Gloucester. It is our fervent wish that God grant him true forgiveness. The history records that Philippe [I], king of France, had died [in 1108] and was buried at Saint-Denis,* and his son Louis [VI] reigned after him. William [I Bonne-Âme], archbishop of Rouen, a most holy man, died [in 1111] and passed over to where we are all destined to go. Geoffrey [Brito], that fine cleric and dean of Le Mans – and by no means an old man – occupied the archbishop's throne after him, so I find recorded. (43770)

[33] *How [Waleran,] the count of Meulan, endured a long imprisonment by King Henry.*

For more than thirty years there had been widespread dissention and enmity between the barons of Normandy, and this was the cause of many reckless acts being committed. The barons inflicted great damage on one another, and many close friends and allies were lost as a result. There was much carnage and a great number of fatal confrontations. One such case was that of Waleran of Meulan who, one fine day, gathered together an army consisting of close relatives and allies who, with their Poitevin helmets firmly in place, marched to do battle against Roger [III] de Tosny. This led to much wailing and gnashing of teeth, as I understand from the written record. The struggle between them was a very destructive one: brains were spilled and entrails burst from bodies. But Ralph [IV de Tosny]* had a large contingent of the king's troops on his side, for Waleran had for a long time been acting against the interests of the king. There was much clanging of swords and exhausting combat, and finally Waleran was taken prisoner, and the majority of his troops killed. The most prominent of them, and those that had the greatest ransom value, were taken prisoner. Several of these, however, were improperly supervised, and with the collusion of their friends were allowed to escape. Count Amaury of Evreux and William Louvel of Ivry, whom Ralph de Tosny had taken captive and who had been held prisoner, were let go. What I read, if I understand correctly, is that this battle took place at Bourg-théroulde [in March 1124]. It was a hotly contested battle, and many a combatant in it landed up on a bier. (43812)

Several years were to pass before Waleran regained his liberty. He was a prisoner of King Henry's, together with those who had been captured at the same time. Henry razed the castle keep at Vatteville, destroying its walls and earthworks. He besieged Brionne where he encountered resistance, but he did not leave until he had gained possession of it by force and punished the official responsible for its defence by having both his eyes put out, as my source informs me. Those in charge of the castle at Beaumont saw how things were going. Terrified at the prospect of being tortured if captured, with great reluctance they hand their castle and its keep over to Henry. Thus peace and harmony were restored after such widespread and violent disturbances that had lasted for years on end, all these disputes and quarrels leading to countless children being made orphans, all this terrible slaughter. None of this would have been brought to a peaceful conclusion if good King Henry had not undertaken to do so. His voice had previously gone unheard despite the instructions he issued and the pleas he made, but now his enemies had been captured and brought low, and no more would the country resound to the voices of dissent, and no more towns would be burnt to the ground. What had formerly been endless tears of pity at the harm done to the country were now turned to tears of joy. (43846)

King Henry had, then, taken the lands and properties of his enemies under his personal control, and Waleran and his associates languished for several years in his prisons with no hope of pardon or release. Subsequently, however, the king took pity on Waleran and reinstated him in all his lands. Waleran, who thought the day of his release would never come and there would be no end to his suffering, finally saw his heavy shackles removed. His lands were returned to him without any of their fortresses, which the king kept under his own control in order that he could feel more secure. Of the other unfortunate and miserable wretches who had been captured at the same time as Waleran, some were never pardoned and were never released from prison for the next ten years. For the rest of the king's life, there was no further war or uprising or disorder either in Normandy or in England – only peace. We will, however, tell you of one exception. As our Latin source explains, Duke Robert's son, William Clito, who was lord and count of Flanders, felt very bitter towards King Henry for never having pardoned his father and for allowing him to languish in prison until he died. This is the reason why he undertook ventures intended to cause him considerable harm. What he liked doing most of all was making incursions over the border into Normandy, causing trouble and great destruction, and this he did frequently and unrelentingly. King Henry could not tolerate the land being violated in this way. Thanks to his considerable financial resources, he maintained knights and well-endowed and highly respected retinues all over the country whose task it was to defend Normandy from its mortal enemies if ever the territory were encroached upon. They had had no cause or opportunity, however, to do so, though in the case of those people most determined to provoke them, there had been bloodshed on many occasions. The king would be certain to ensure the security of the land, because he was very skilled in protecting it. (43898)

I need to remind you, if you would be king enough to listen, how wisely noble King Henry had acted in the war I have been describing to you – that extensive war he fought against Count Waleran and which had lasted the best part of a year, during which he had retained a large contingent of knights and distributed a great deal of wealth. When Henry was still in Normandy after the end of this war, a large amount of counterfeit silver coinage consisting largely of pewter was being minted in England. Without any warning or alert being given, some of this was brought over to Normandy in order to pay the king's knights. When they actually came to receive their wages, the fraud came to light. No one, be they knights or men-at-arms, found they had even enough money to place a bet with, or pledge a security or pay off a debt. This was something they could not keep hidden, so they informed the king of what had happened. Henry found the news highly distressing and was upset on behalf of his knights, to whom it would never have occurred to think that the king had done this on purpose. Henry grimly informed his justices, whom he had appointed all over England, of this shameful deception that made him extremely angry and unhappy, and gave orders that all those of the minters responsible for these coins and found guilty of issuing them should, at the very least, lose their right hands as well as being castrated.* This is how he dealt with the matter. I would add, and want you to know, that had he wished to seek financial reparations, the very minimum he would have got was 10,000 marks. He was, however, anxious not to be accused of corruptly profiteering and of ignoring justice for financial advantage. No sovereign, I find, ever incurred less blame for what he did than Henry. (43944)

[34] *How the Empress [Matilda] came back from Germany and how she married [Geoffrey,] the count of Anjou.*

I find in the written history that the Emperor Henry [V] died at not too advanced an age in the year of our Lord 1125. The empress, so I read, was overwhelmed with grief. She had had no child and heir with him, and because of this she had no reason to stay in Germany. There was not a single nobleman from Germany to Rome whose most cherished wish was not to become her proud husband. King Henry sent some of his most highly renowned and experienced barons to her, and she was brought back to England with even more honour and glory than she had originally gone with. Accompanying her from the Empire over which Rome is sovereign came the most prominent and the most influential people who had witnessed first-hand how illustrious she was and recognised just how wise and knowledgeable she was. So much so, in fact, that they would have been quite willing for her to take the place of their lord, and it was for this reason, to attempt to keep her, that they accompanied her to England. They made urgent requests and entreaties to King Henry, but his wishes lay in a quite different direction: he had sent for her in order for her to become heir to the whole of his kingdom without his having to transfer the title elsewhere.* He had no other children from his wife, and he wished everything he had to be made over to Matilda after his death. And to prevent her from being in any way wronged or dispossessed, he summoned all of his bishops and magnates, and in their presence he formally grants her everything pertaining to the crown. Then, in conformity with his instructions, all those present swore fealty to her on widely acclaimed holy relics: however things might turn out, and irrespective of how powerful they might be, and at the risk of their persons and their fortunes, they should act with loyalty and love towards her, and faithfully help her maintain the whole kingdom and its honour from all comers. This is the oath they took, but how far they kept their word and how things subsequently turned out we shall tell you later. All will be revealed and recorded on parchment before this work comes to an end. (44000)

There had been long-standing feelings of resentment, animosity, even hatred, and protracted hostilities between all the lords of Anjou – brave and valiant warriors as they were – and those of Normandy. In the course of these, many a lance was shattered, many a castle burnt down and destroyed, much productive countryside laid waste. Henry, the good king of England, wished to put an end to all this warring, restore peace, reconcile the people so troubled by enmity, and re-establish tranquillity in the country. (44016)

The celebrated Count Fulk [V of Anjou], who had been crowned king in the East at Jerusalem [in 1131], was the powerful ruler of this country. He had a son, Geoffrey Martel, a fine, strong knight of great renown, brave, wise and successful in war. No prince was more admirable than he; his reputation knew no bounds, and he had no equal or rival in good qualities in the whole of France this side of the Alps. He was lord of Anjou and Maine as well as of Touraine. This is the person to whom King Henry wished to see his daughter and heir – the wise and worthy empress – married. Geoffrey had made numerous requests to this effect, behaving most judiciously and with great discernment. The marriage settlement he had to offer was a splendid one. So many influential people intervened on his behalf and pleaded his cause that Henry finally decided to grant him his daughter's hand and to marry her to him. No married lady enjoyed a higher reputation. Theirs was a blessed match,* and together they made a magnificent couple – one the likes of which, in my view, you are never likely to see again. For as long as the world lasts, it will not be easy to find a lady and a knight with such outstanding qualities. This is all I am able to say about them at the moment, for I still have ahead of me a great deal of material to tell and recount to you. (44052)

The Empress Matilda, within a short space of time, had three fine children with her husband: Henry, Geoffrey and William. Henceforth the kingdom of England was not without its proper, legitimate, valid and appropriate heir. In this way the much celebrated empress was able to strengthen her lineage, for thanks to the fine heirs that she produced, the whole world is in a better position and will remain so until the end. More parchment is now needed in order to enable me to continue recounting the noble deeds and great accomplishments which, from now on, begin to take place – such major events and such unexpected developments, the likes of which no cleric will find written in any book. (44070)

[35] *How kings of France are descended by birth from the lords of Anjou.*

To any of those listening to our history who may think or maintain that the marriage of a high-ranking, consecrated empress to a count was not appropriate, proper or becoming, we intend to show that, on the contrary, it was something to be unreservedly approved of.* The powerful Roman emperor was, of course, of a higher rank than Count Geoffrey of Anjou, but might I remind you of the fact that, in times not too far removed from ours, the kings of France could claim descent from Geoffrey's close ancestors. This I shall prove to you, and I can easily demonstrate how, from one generation to the next, the line of descent comes right down to the present king. Listen to how this comes about! (44090)

After the death of Charles [II] the Bald [in 877], as the written source explains and as you can discover and read for yourselves, his son Louis [II the Stammerer] came to inherit the empire. Charles [III] the Simple followed him and held the kingdom in his turn. At the death of his father, however, he was still a small boy. Then came Robert [the Strong], count of Angers, an excellent knight of real Saxon extraction, as I read in my source. He had two sons, Odo and Robert [I], fine, brave and outstanding knights, with no equal in the whole of France in valour. Odo was prince and steward, and knew no equal or rival. It was to him that Charles the Simple, Louis' son, as I have said, was entrusted. So strong and successful was his rule that all of the kingdom of France, Burgundians as well as Poitevins, demanded nothing less than that he be anointed king. A strong king was, in fact, needed because during this time the Vikings were ravaging the country. He put up a brave defence against them, and his reign was a most illustrious one. A noble, honourable, powerful and wise leader, he was crowned king of France, I find, [in 888] and reigned for thirteen years and two months before Charles the Simple succeeded. Odo's brother Robert, a noble and wise man of great renown, was prince and duke of Paris during this period. He held a position of considerable power in France, and there was no one to rival him. He sought to emulate his brother's position before he had been king, but Charles grew very hostile towards him; the two fell into disagreement, and there was bad feeling between them. Robert did, however, become king of France and he reigned for a full year [in 922]. He took as his wife [Beatrice of Vermandois,] the noble daughter of [Herbert I,] the count of Péronne, and they had a son, Hugh the Great. His father Robert was killed at Soissons, so we read, and Robert's only son Hugh, a strong, powerful, wise, well informed and subtle man, was prince and duke of France. Our Latin source also tells us that Herbert, count of Péronne, had Charles the Simple forcibly captured, and he died his prisoner. Hugh the Great married [Hedwige,] the daughter [= sister] of the Emperor Otto [I], and Hugh Capet was their son. Hugh Capet was, as I have already told you, the first in the dynasty of all the kings who have reigned ever since in France; they all trace their ancestry back to him, and those in the know understand, therefore, that such kings are the heirs of Anjou. It has been one of their glories that they have always climbed and risen in status. This is why it was quite right and just that the latest in the line, Count Geoffrey, should have married into such a high rank, for this caused no disparagement to the empress. There was no woman anywhere who would not have been honoured by marrying him. (44170)

After the sad death [in 1118] of the noble Queen Matilda, mother of the empress – there was no more discerning lady in the whole world, in my opinion, and it was a great shame that she died at a relatively young age and in the prime of life – King Henry remarried: a young lady of excellent character who was the daughter of Count Godfrey [VII] of Louvain; her name was Adeliza. My source informs me that she and Henry failed to produce any heir, girl or boy. With various mistresses the king had seven daughters, noble and extremely worthy young ladies who lived good and honourable lives.* (44188)

During this time Archbishop Geoffrey [Brito] died at Rouen [in 1128]. The archbishopric was granted to Hugh [of Amiens], abbot of Reading – he was the first ever abbot there – an upright man of great renown who was duly anointed and consecrated. Then, before the end of the summer, at the start of June [1131], pope Innocent [II] came to Rouen at King Henry's invitation. Henry received him with great honour and agreed to all his wishes and requests. They discussed also more urgent matters and came to an agreement that they then ratified in formal council. Pope Calixtus [II], so my source informs me, had done the same thing some years earlier, and shortly before his death [in 1124] had come to Gisors to discuss Church business, questions of canon law and justice. On the present occasion Henry received Innocent with great ceremony and made him numerous gifts of considerable value; in the whole of his life the pope had never been so honoured as he was in Rouen. (44214)

Good King Henry constructed a number of strong, well provided for and well-situated castles with high walls and keeps. This is something he did consistently and without interruption throughout his lifetime. He had them built in several different places, and he renewed and improved the work that his ancestors had undertaken. He constructed Driencourt,* Châteauneuf-sur-Epte, around which the river flows, as well as Bonsmoulins and Verneuil, no ally of defiance, Nonancourt, [Châtillon-sur-Colmont]* and, towards Brittany, Pontorson. There were others, in addition, which he had renovated and whose names I had better not list. He maintained peace better than any man alive, not only within his own kingdom but in lands distant from his own, just as if they were his own personal property, for people between here and far-off India were able to reap the advantage of his skill and his experience in secular matters.* Everywhere people submitted to him. He got the better of the Welsh, who have always hated the English, and he subdued them, keeping them under strict control by having those of his men whose lands bordered theirs construct fortresses everywhere. After he came to the throne, people never made aggressive moves towards one another in his kingdom, as he had made himself greatly feared and much respected. (44246)

There was, however, one criticism that was levelled at him.* When he captured castles from those who opposed him in his own territory, he took great pains to have the walls properly repaired, renovated and reinforced as if the castles were permanently to remain his own property and that of his heirs. People did not always know what his real intention was in sometimes acting in this way and sometimes not, but I can tell you that they attributed unworthy motives to him. (44258)

Henry was also a very generous and beneficent king, open-handed towards people of religion, be they bishops, abbots, monks, nuns, solitary hermits or anyone else in holy orders. From here as far as the slopes of Montjoie [in Rome] people received generous gifts from him, as is recorded in his charters and pious endowments. In this way he was a father to all the people, and once every year he would distribute his gifts and remittances (44270).

His many achievements in England will be remembered for always. He founded Reading Abbey, well situated on the River Thames, a beautiful house extremely well endowed and with extensive income, and here he installed an abbot and monks. He constructed another church for canons, the abbey of Saint John at Cirencester, a most pleasant place for those who follow the rule of Saint Augustine to spend the rest of their days. In Rouen in Normandy he built Notre-Dame-du-Pré cathedral as well as the houses in Le Pré where there is a very well-endowed priory, a dependency of Le Bec, in a beautiful and attractive setting. It was Henry's mother who had begun the work there, but it advanced very little in comparison to what powerful King Henry subsequently had done there, the appointments and donations that he made, the sumptuous decoration that he introduced, and the fine, valuable and handsome vestments. (44296).

I also find in my source that he gave great support to the church at Cluny, and over several years constructed the [Cluniac] priory of Saint-Martin-des-Champs [in Paris]. The monks of Marmoutier [Tours]* also benefitted from the considerable amount of money he donated for the extensive works they undertook there and the expenses they incurred. We are told that he had them build a well-appointed dormitory which he paid for himself. At Chartres he expended a great deal of wealth for the construction of a lepers' hospital. The extent of his works can still be seen there today. He did much to benefit and advance the Templars as well; he was very supportive of them, giving them all sorts of financial help and other advantages. He did the same for the Hospitallers also, on many occasions. It is on record that the cathedral at Evreux was fired and burnt to the ground with evil intent by Henry himself in the course of his war and struggle against Count Amaury [in 1119]. He had it magnificently reconstructed, enlarging and embellishing it. He provided it with income and other buildings, in addition to numerous fine objects of great value which are still preserved there, and will be into the future for as long as Holy Church is allowed to flourish in peace. (44328)

[36] *Concerning the daughters of King William [the Conqueror].*

There is no reason for me to pass over in silence what my source has to say about King Henry's sisters, the female offspring of King William, conqueror of the kingdom of England. They were exceptionally worthy ladies, much honoured in secular society, held in high esteem and widely acclaimed. The eldest was, I know, called Cecilia; she was consecrated a nun at Caen and held the position of abbess for a long time before making a most pious death [in 1127]. The next was Constance, whose facial features, bearing and behaviour were the admiration of all. She was extremely knowledgeable, refined, generous and wise. She was given in marriage to Count Alan [IV] Fergant, lord of Brittany. She would have made an excellent companion for him if she had not gone to an early death [in 1090]. She left no heir, girl or boy, and because of her fine qualities her death was bitterly mourned by everyone. Alan then married a truly beautiful and highly esteemed young lady who belonged to the noble family of the counts of Anjou, namely [Ermengarde,] the daughter of Count Fulk [IV] the Surly. Their child was Conan [III], and as their son he duly inherited the land. When that fine, wise and handsome knight Geoffrey Martel [II], Count Fulk's eldest son, was treacherously and wickedly killed [in 1106], his second son inherited. This was the valiant and worthy Fulk [V] whose mother was Bertrade [de Montfort], a second wife and a most admirable lady who was, I know for certain, the sister of Count Amaury of Evreux. Fulk of Anjou subsequently made a most advantageous marriage which brought him Le Mans and the whole of Maine as a personal holding free of obligation. Fulk's wife was [Ermengarde,] the daughter of Count Hélie [I of

Maine], a lady of outstanding merit. She had two fine children with her husband, the elder was Geoffrey [V of Anjou] and the younger Hélie [II]. They also had two daughters, both worthy, beautiful and attractive. So well-bred and wise were they, so highly esteemed, that, up until then, there had been no one to equal them in merit in the whole world. It was impossible to choose between the two of them. One of them married the count of Saint-Gilles,* the other good Count Thierry [of Alsace], count of Flanders. (44390)

King William's third daughter, Adeliza, a young lady of outstanding merit, married King Harold [II Godwineson] but died a virgin.* The fourth daughter, the worthy and wise Adela, was married to Count Stephen [II Henry] of Blois, one of the most illustrious men among the French. In terms of appearance, merit and devotion to God, no lady superior to her entered the kingdom of France at that time. She had four sons in rapid succession: William, [count of Sully,] Thibaud [IV, count of Blois/Champagne], Henry [of Blois] and [King] Stephen who had a particularly privileged upbringing. Afterwards, I believe, she also had a daughter who married Count [Henry] of Eu,* though I understand that they were very closely related. Theobald [IV of Blois], one of the four brothers, was a rich, powerful and very influential person, illustrious and much praised, a supporter, defender and friend of the Church, who did much to advance people of good faith. He became count of Blois in succession to his father, something that his mother wanted and sought to achieve. Through skill and benevolence, so I find, he later purchased, from his uncle Count Hugh [of Troyes], the whole of the county and the city of Troyes. He remained in possession of Troyes, Chartres and Blois until he reached a ripe old age. He had a particularly noble wife in [Matilda,] the daughter of Count [Engelbert II, duke of Carinthia],* and their household was one much admired in secular courts. Another of the brothers I am talking about, Henry, became a monk of Cluny, but King Henry called him away from there to become an abbot in England, and then, as rapidly as he could, he made him bishop of Winchester. He was a clever, highly powerful and influential man. He certainly made his presence felt within his family. (44436)

Stephen, the last of the brothers, was an outstandingly good knight, a man of great determination and militant in the extreme. He was count of Mortain. My Latin source records that he married a beautiful, clever and attractive lady, Matilda, daughter of Eustace [III], count of Boulogne, a refined lady of outstanding merit and great skill. She and her husband quickly had children, though I do not know exactly how many. When King Henry's great capacities declined and he died, the bishop of Winchester, who had made himself a dominant power in the land, immediately sent for his brother, whom he had primed and prepared beforehand. He had him made king by foul and duplicitous means and under false pretences,* since the Empress Matilda was the true heir, and everyone had sworn an oath to this effect. But people ignored the agreement they had all come to, their oaths and the pledges they had made. The worthy empress, who at that time was with her small sons – such beautiful, noble, little children – and her husband in Anjou, had actually been with her father in the time leading up to his death. She had last seen the valiant, wise and courtly king in Normandy some time before his death, and had left him in a somewhat bad-tempered mood. She had taken him in her arms and begged him insistently, for love of her, to forgive William Talvas to whom he had taken a grave dislike. The king, however, was unwilling to do so, not out of any spitefulness or to be antagonistic towards William, but as a warning to him not to repeat his stupid behaviour and not to get into the habit of doing things that might make Henry unhappy. (44480)

This William Talvas was the son of Robert of Bellême who had always acted with arrogance and disloyalty towards the king, and had treated his neighbours like the lowest of the low and the worst sort of infidels. Because of his perfidious and criminal character, the king had thrown him into prison where he subsequently died without clemency, as he deserved. Henry took possession of the stronghold at Bellême, a fine and well-situated castle which he then gave to Count Rotrou of Perche. It is certain that William the Conqueror had purchased the lordship of it from King Philippe of France. It is common knowledge that, at the time when this purchase had taken place, control of this particular fief had maintained peace throughout the kingdom of France. (44500)

It would take a long time to translate,* recount and relate, in the order in which they happened, the events in which King Henry was involved. There are so many that one would rapidly lose one's bearings. It is for this reason that it is necessary now to bring this work to a close. No one, no cleric or author, and no book could possibly give an account of King Henry's eminence and virtues, however well written it might be, without it needing yet more material to be added and even greater deeds. And I for my part am definitely the sort of person who would be very anxious to avoid boring or annoying anyone. After a reign of many years, then, and a long life, the wise and valiant King Henry died. As the Latin history records, and as we can read there, his death occurred right at the start of the first week of December* at Lyons-la-Forêt [in Normandy]. He had been king of England for precisely thirty-five years and four months, and previous to that he had, according to the Latin Life, been duke of Normandy for exactly twenty-eight years and four months. On the day of his death, according to our source, no more than 1135 years had passed since the birth of Christ. No king made a more pious death. I know of no ruler who ever lived whose death was so lamented and who was so poignantly mourned throughout the world. He was taken to England and buried with the highest honours, appropriately dressed and with a fine embroidered shroud. His wish had been to be laid to rest in Reading, and it was here that he was buried and placed in a richly decorated tomb. His soul, pure and shining bright, waits in the presence of God to be crowned in glory together with those who will reign with him for ever and ever, *cum angelis in eternum per secula seculorum. Amen.* (44544)

Notes

33469 The Conqueror's mother Herleva, whom the French refer to as Arlette, is traditionally believed to come from a modest family of tanners or furriers (see Elisabeth M. C. van Houts, "The Origins of Herleva, Mother of William the Conqueror," *English Historical Review* 101 (1986): 389–404; David Douglas, *William the Conqueror* (Berkeley, 1967), pp. 379–82). Orderic Vitalis, however, makes her father into a ducal chamberlain, which could better explain how, in reality, she came into contact with the duke (*GND* 2: 96–7). Robert later has Herleva married off to a certain Herluin de Conteville, with whom she then has two sons (and therefore half-brothers to William), Odo, later bishop of Bayeux, and Robert, count of Mortain. Wace's version of the Conqueror's birth (*Rou* III: 2823–66) is similar to, but far less developed than, Benoît's. Both are independent of *GND*, which finds no room for what is obviously a fictional interpolation, and which must presumably have its origin in popular romance literature. Herleva's prophetic dream, also absent from *GND*, is taken by Benoît from Orderic Vitalis, but in a much-amplified form. Some elements of the portent of William's greatness reappear in William of Malmesbury (*GRA*, p. 426).

33507 The worldliness and pragmatism of the hermit brother, presumably imported wholesale from Benoît's unknown source, is somewhat reminiscent of the hermit Ogrin in Beroul's *Tristan* romance (1367 ff.), who turns out, contrary to expectation, to be the lovers' ally.

33545 Women are seldom at the centre of Benoît's history, and his portrait of Herleva/Arlette, heavily influenced by romance topoi, is unique. An untypically feisty heroine, she shows a level of self-assertiveness that befits a conqueror's mother but which belies what we are told of her origins. Her concern with her social status, however, is somewhat more realistic. One critic has seen her as a Madonna figure. Part of her role, of course, is to neutralise, as far as possible, the accusations of illegitimacy that will inevitably dog William in later life. As Orderic put it in *GND*, "as a bastard William was despised by the native nobility and especially by the descendants of both Dukes Richard" (2: 97).

33595 Never one to stint on the rhetorical superlatives, Benoît compares the newly born Conqueror to three of what were to become, in the fourteenth century, the Nine Worthies. Arthur reappears below at 41287.

33601–12 Benoît's special pleading attempts, somewhat disingenuously, to forestall the raising of any moral eyebrows at Robert's illicit liaison with Herleva.

33734 Premonitory dreams are a literary commonplace at the births of heroes. Thomas Becket's mother, for example, dreams that her son's bed sheet spreads out over the whole of England. Wace (*Rou* III: 2853–64) also has a version of Herleva's sprouting-tree dream. Cf. Herman Braet, "Le Songe de l'arbre chez Wace, Benoît et Aimon de Varennes," *Romania* 91 (1970): 255–67.

33796 William's precocious behaviour leading to the midwife's prediction of his all-conquering future first appears in the early twelfth-century Battle Abbey *Brevis Relatio*. It is recycled also by Wace (*Rou* III: 2869–86) and by William of Malmesbury (*GRA*, p. 426).

33944 Benoît seems pointedly to be declining here to copy from Wace, whose long and detailed passage on the duke's pilgrimage (*Rou* III: 2987–3240) could possibly have originated, according to van Houts' hypothesis, in family tradition (see *The History of the Norman People: Wace's* Roman de Rou, trans. Glyn S. Burgess (Woodbridge, 2004), p. xxxvi).

33972 Duke Robert set out on his fatal pilgrimage to Jerusalem in 1035 and died the same year. The familiar Norman spectre of death by poisoning – a convenient way of explaining any unexpected death – is also raised by Wace (*Rou* III: 3211–14) and William of Malmesbury (*GRA*, p. 309). Cf. note to 39173 below.

34120 Gilbert, described by Benoît as *quens d'Uismes*, is called *comes Ocensis* "of Eu" in *GND*, which Benoît seems to have confused with *Oximensis* (Hugo Andresen, "Über die von Benoît in seiner normannischen Chronik benutzen Quellen, insbesondere über sein Verhältnis zu Dudo, Wilhelm von Jumièges und Wace," *Romanische Forschungen* 2 (1886): 526). Gilbert is better known as Gilbert of Brionne.

34154 Gunnor was the long-term concubine and then wife of Duke Richard I. According to Wace she was of noble Danish extraction, well-educated and very courtly (*Rou* III: 235–72, 611–54). She bore Richard five sons and three daughters, of whom Emma was the eldest. Robert de Torigni recounts her first meeting with Richard, and Wace tells what we would today call a feminist anecdote concerning her marriage night. Cf. *GND* 2: 266–74.

34172 The disorder of which the episodes involving Vauquelin de Ferrières, Count Gilbert, the tutor Turold and Osbern the steward are illustrative, can be dated to between 1040 and 1042, and it is at the end of this period that William is thought to have reached majority and begun his ducal reign. He was born, we recall, in 1027 or 1028.

34208 More "shaming" even than William's illegitimacy was the lack of social status of his mother. The stigma of her non-nobility (*ignobilitas*) was sufficient to earn her son the scorn not only of some of his immediate entourage but of the common man also. See note to 36735 below, and cf. David Crouch, *The Image of the Aristocracy in Britain, 1000–1300* (London, 1992), pp. 4–19.

34295 According to Orderic Vitalis it was Roger's father Honfroi who founded Préaux (*The Ecclesiastical History of Orderic Vitalis*. Ed. and trans. Marjorie Chibnall. 6 vols. (Oxford, 1969–80), 2: 12).

34396 The castle of Tillières had been built by Duke Richard II on the French side of the river Avre, and so was in disputed territory. It was eventually handed back to William by Henri as a gesture of reconciliation in or around 1058 (see note to 38206 below).

34548 William is thought to have been knighted – by the king of France, according to William of Malmesbury (*GRA*, p. 427) – in or around 1042 when he was fifteen or so years old. William himself was to knight his own son Henry when the boy was 17 or 18, though knighting on coming of age at 21 seems, if Glanville is to be believed, to have been the norm in the twelfth century.

34689 Benoît is simply following the error of *GND* in placing the revolt of William d'Arques before 1047 and the Battle of Val-ès-Dunes; it actually took place in 1052–53 (Douglas, *William the Conqueror*, p. 390). Wace (*Rou* III: 3399 ff.) also places the revolt before Val-ès-Dunes (*Rou* III: 3818 ff.).

34803 Described by Benoît as count of Boulogne, Enguerrand is in fact count of Ponthieu, as both *GND* and Wace confirm.

34932–35332 The assassination plot at Valognes and the role of the court fool Golés reappear in Wace (*Rou* III: 3641–3760) whence Benoît is assumed to have borrowed them. Guy of Burgundy, known also as the count of Brionne, was the son of Adeliza, daughter of Duke Richard II, and one Rainald. He was William's cousin and childhood companion, and the duke treated him as his brother, but Guy's secret ambition was to become duke himself. William besieged him for three years in his castle at Brionne before he was finally captured and exiled (36108).

35026 Non-aristocratic figures are rare in Benoît's poem, and when they appear, as here in the shape of Golés, it is in order to fulfil some pre-ordained literary function. One of the stock outsider figures of courtly literature, the fool has the role of negating his madness by being a bearer of the truth. He is endowed with unusual powers and a curious impunity. A shaved head and a club (here at 35036; 3652 in Wace) are his traditional accoutrements. Tristan disguises himself as a fool in order to gain access to the otherwise inaccessible Iseut. See Jean-Marie Fritz, *Le Discours du fou au moyen âge: XIIe-XIIIe siècles. Étude comparée des discours littéraire, médical, juridique et théologique de la folie* (Paris, 1992).

35143 The *vile champestre* is named by Wace (*Rou* III: 3685) as *Rie*, which leads Andresen to suggest that Benoît's *Parmi une vile champestre* originally read *Par Rie, une vile champestre*. Ryes-en-Bessin is a few kilometres north-east of Bayeux.

35145–332 The episode in which Hubert de Ryes plays a prominent part seems very much to be cast in a romance mould, featuring a heroic protagonist engaged on an ultimately successful quest facilitated by a wise and loyal adjuvant. The same narrative structure characterises Wace's version (*Rou* III: 3685–3760) in which dialogue also plays a striking role. Hubert's ultimate reward for his loyalty to the duke was reaped by his son Eudo the steward (*dapifer*) who became sheriff of Essex and an important landowner in England (Douglas, *William the Conqueror*, p. 291).

35252 Behind the first meaning of Foupendant, "weeping beech tree" (from *fagum pendentem*), lies, by word-play, the sense "hanging madman." According to Paul Fichet, in *Benoît: Vie de Guillaume le Conquérant. Chronique des ducs de Normandie* (Bayeux, 1976), p. 135, there is today a hamlet called Foupendant near Espins south of Caen (but it is not a ford).

35376 William's father had provided crucial support after Queen Constance, third wife of King Robert II, had attempted to disinherit Henri in favour of his brother Robert in 1027. Vassalic reciprocity required that such *auxilium* be now acknowledged.

35497 On the battle of Val-ès-Dunes, described as "a decisive event in the development of Normandy," see Douglas, *William the Conqueror*, pp. 48–54; cf. David Bates, *William the Conqueror* (New Haven, 2016), pp. 81–85.

35528 Some names of individuals are not only common to Wace and Benoît but appear also to be exclusive to them in their particular narrative contexts. Thus, here, Ralph Taisson is attributed a pivotal role in the battle of Val-ès-Dunes in both Benoît (35528) and Wace (*Rou* III: 3849), and the loyal Hubert de Ryes figures prominently in both poets' accounts of William's flight from the Guy of Burgundy conspiracy (Benoît 35146; Wace, *Rou* III: 3687). The fool named Golés appears in both Wace (*Rou* III: 3652) and Benoît (35026). Other examples include Grimoult du Plessis (Benoît 34974; Wace, *Rou* III: 3621), Serlo of Lingèvres (Wace, *Rou* III: 4211; Benoît 36128), as well as obscure place-names such as the river Laison (Benoît 35431; Wace, *Rou* III: 3794), the fords at Béranger (Benoît 35514; Wace, *Rou* III: 3825) and Foupendant (Benoît 35252; Wace, *Rou* III: 3712). There is also near-identity in the battle-cries itemised by Wace (*Rou* III: 3935–44) and Benoît (35746–74) at Val-ès-Dunes. See also note to 36128 below.

35746 In the *Song of Roland*, "Munjoie" is Charlemagne's personal battle-cry, subsequently adopted by the whole of the French army. On battle-cries in general, see Robert W. Jones, *Bloodied Banners: Martial Display on the Medieval Battlefield* (Woodbridge, 2010), pp. 75–78.

35824 Wace reports the view that the king's assailant could have been Haimo Dentatus (*Rou* III: 4045–50), and William of Malmesbury presents this as a certainty (*GRA*, p. 428). As lord of Creully (Calvados), Haimo could, at a pinch, be described as a native of the Cotentin, as the rhyme of 35842–44 demands.

35904 The detail of the assault on Duke William's shield by Hardré does not figure in Wace's account of the battle where only William's ferocious counter-attack is described (*Rou* III: 4059–74).

36128 The case of the obscure Serlo of Lingèvres is cited by van Houts (*The History of the Norman People*, p. xxxix) as evidence that Wace consulted documentary as well as oral material in writing his *Rou*. That the name should re-emerge in Benoît is a strong indication that he must have copied it from Wace. Cf. note to 35528. For further parallels with Wace, see notes to 33944, 34932, 35145, 35528, 37648.

36142 This conflicts with Wace who explains that Grimoult's land was shared out between the church at Bayeux and the abbey at Caen (*Rou* III: 4221–26). But cf. van Houts, in *The History of the Norman People*, p. xxxviii.

36155 The fact that Emma was a Norman and the sister of Duke Richard II is curiously

ignored here. Nor is Edward the Confessor's half-Norman identity ever acknowledged. Cf. note to 38733 below.

36243 Repeated references to the Saracens as a term of abuse – it is even used of the
English at 40487 and 40925 – show the continuing influence on Benoît of epic discourse. Cf. Penny Eley, "Epic Elements in the *Chronique des ducs de Normandie*," in
Aspects de l'épopée romane: Mentalités, idéologies, intertextualités, ed. Hans Van Dijk
and Willen Noomen (Groningen, 1995), pp. 345–51, and note to 39120 below.

36318 According to the *Anglo-Saxon Chronicle* and Henry of Huntingdon, the murder
of Alfred Ætheling was the responsibility of Earl Godwine, but both William of
Poitiers and *GND* attribute the actual killing to Harold. See *The Anglo-Saxon Chronicles*, ed. and trans. Michael Swanton, 2nd ed. (London, 2000). The decimation
scene at Guildford also appears in Wace (*Rou* III: 4701–12), as well as Henry of
Huntingdon (p. 373), whence it passes into Gaimar's *Estoire des Engleis* (4807–42).
William of Malmesbury places the whole episode in the category of "tales told by
rumour-mongers" (*GRA*, p. 336).

36351–80 Compared to both *GND* and Wace, Benoît gives an exceptionally favourable
portrait of Harthacnut. William of Poitiers remarks that, having inherited his (Norman) mother's good nature, he was able to rule without the cruelty that had char-
acterised the reigns of his father and his brother (Guillaume de Poitiers, *Histoire de
Guillaume le Conquérant*, ed. and trans. Raymonde Foreville (Paris, 1952), p. 13).

36402 Called Gonnille by Benoît (to secure a rhyme), Godwine's daughter, who was
also Harold's sister, is better known as Eadgyth/Edith. She lacked personal beauty,
so William of Malmesbury tells us, but not intellectual humility; indeed, "in her
bosom there was a school of all the liberal arts" (*GRA*, p. 353). William of Poitiers
would have us believe that she resolutely opposed Harold's decision to fight at Hastings (Benoît 41059–88).

36429 The reference is presumably to Edward the Confessor's deathbed prophecy of
the green tree chopped in half but eventually reunited and able to bear fruit. The
vision was generally interpreted as foretelling the punishment of the English people
– a symbolic warning of the Norman Conquest and its consequences. See Frank
Barlow, *The Life of King Edward Who Lies at Westminster*, 2nd ed. (Oxford, 1992),
p. 118.

36472–78 Much of what Benoît has to say here about Geoffrey Martel, and also at
37869–37910 below, is taken from William of Poitiers (ed. Foreville, pp. 32–34, 86–
88). However, to avoid displeasing his patron by criticising his ancestor, Benoît here
ignores William's description of Geoffrey as "a ferocious tyrant," and instead heaps
praise on him. Wace, on the other hand, consistently paints him in a bad light (*Rou*
III: 4227–76, 4372–4492, 4995–5062). William of Jumièges also categorises Martel as "deceitful in every respect" (*GND* 1: 122), and William of Malmesbury calls
him "exceptionally arrogant" (*GRA*, p. 430).

36538 Could Benoît possibly be voicing here a residual resentment in Touraine against
Angevin expansionism?

36621 Benoît seems to be implying that the duke was acting rashly and taking an unnecessary risk.

36735 The pelterer deals in pelts, skins and furs. The meanings "tailor" or even "undertaker" have also been suggested for the Latin *pollinctor*. The possibility that Benoît's *reins* "lower backs" is a mistranslation of Latin *renones* "pelts," as suggested by Andresen and repeated by van Houts ("The Origins of Herleva"), seems remote given his mastery of Latin elsewhere in his history. The ferocity of William's reaction (36783) shows how sensitive he was to the common man's taunts regarding his mother's lack of social status and his bastardy. Cf. Alice Curteis and Chris Given-Wilson, *The Royal Bastards of Medieval England* (London, 1995), and more recently, Sara McDougall, *Royal Bastards: The Birth of Illegitimacy, 800–1230* (Oxford, 2016), pp. 117–19.

36948 The arms of Geoffrey le Bel, visible on his tombal effigy at Le Mans, were gold lions on a blue background. This is thought to be the origin of the royal coat of arms of England, namely gules, three lions passant guardant in pale or. See Adrian Ailes, *The Origins of the Royal Arms of England* (Reading, 1982); cf. Michel Pastoureau, *Figures de l'héraldique* (Paris, 1996).

36988 One man's guilty flight is another man's innocent retreat, especially if the man in question is your patron's ancestor.

37171 The Conqueror's second half-brother was Robert, son of Herleva and Herluin de Conteville (Bates, *William the Conqueror*, p. 155). There was a third sibling, Muriel, who married Eudo, viscount of the Cotentin.

37277 Benoît rectifies this error later in his narrative when he specifies that the abbess of Caen was called Cecilia (44337–40). On the Conqueror's daughters see 44329–44500 below and Douglas, *William the Conqueror*, pp. 393–95.

37301 Archbishop Malger (Mauger) of Rouen, son of Duke Richard II, is described by William of Poitiers as "a most rapacious plunderer" (ed. Foreville, p. 131–33) He had not only opposed the Conqueror's marriage on the grounds of consanguinity, but was in addition suspected of conspiring against the duke, who was also his nephew. He was deposed in 1054. Wace has some entertaining stories of his exile on the Channel Islands (*Rou* III: 4561–4618).

37335 Matthew 7:12, Luke 6:31; cf. Mark 12:31.

37355–65 Without actually naming Becket, Benoît is clearly referring to Henry II's great antagonist whose political opposition grew progressively more acute and public as from 1163. The writing of this passage obviously predates Becket's death in December 1170. Benoît can be seen elsewhere to have used the first, unrevised version of Wace's *Rou*, written after the crowning of the Young King in June 1170 (cf. III: 178–79, also 11431). The two poets were apparently, therefore, writing simultaneously rather than successively, as is usually assumed from Wace's somewhat peevish epilogue. Although all the textual evidence seems to point to Benoît having copied a number of passages from Wace, borrowing in the other direction cannot, at least in theory, be ruled out. While both mention, for example, the reinterment of Richards

I and II at Fécamp in March 1162, Wace makes the additional claim of having himself been present at the ceremony (*Rou* III: 2242; cf. in our text 32054–61).

37480 The identification of *Valie* as Beaufort-sur-Vallée is that of Holden, *Le Roman de Rou de Wace*, 3: 305. *Valie* reappears in Wace (II: 3926) as the battle-cry of the Angevins.

37609 This sentence gives the appearance of having been added by Benoît in order to explain the surprising lack of vigilance on the part of the French army.

37648 Whatever his written source, Benoît is unlikely here to have been translating either *GND* or Orderic, whose narratives of the battle of Mortemer are shorter and far less dramatic. Wace also has a detailed version (*Rou* III: 4867–4924), though Benoît's is significantly more amplified still. The positive gloss that Benoît places on the reverses suffered by Odo and Guy of Ponthieu contrasts with Wace's very matter-of-fact treatment of the same episode (*Rou* III: 4901–8). Both, incidentally, misname Guy's brother Enguerrand (II) as Waleran.

37733 Benoît dramatises an already dramatic scene by making Ralph de Tosny, William's herald, shout out the news of the Norman victory from the top of an overhanging cliff in the middle of the night, and by relaying Ralph's triumphalist proclamation in direct speech. Wace who does not name the herald ("a young lad or squire, I know not"), follows William of Poitiers in having him climb to the top of a tree to deliver his message (*Rou* III: 4934).

37816 *GND* has *Rogerius Contumax*. He was subsequently earl of Hereford, and one of the ringleaders of the Revolt of the Three Earls in 1075–76.

38025 The implausible German connection derives from William of Poitiers. Foreville suggests a possible Breton link via Conan II, Margaret's mother's son by her first marriage (Guillaume de Poitiers, *Histoire de Guillaume le Conquérant*, p. 93 note). Cf. p. 62 n2 in the Davis and Chibnall edition of William of Poitiers.

38219 As Fichet points out in *Vie de Guillaume le Conquérant*, p. 141, the error here derives from *GND*. It was Henri's third wife, Anne, daughter of Yaroslav, prince of Kiev, who was the mother of the king's four children.

38409–13 Could the name of Guaimar (IV), prince of Salerno (d. 1052) lurk behind *GND*'s *Walmarchus* here? *GND* continues: "The first leader of the Normans in Apulia ... was Thurstan called Scitel" (2: 157), and *Scisteiaus/Scistel* perhaps evokes Asclettin, a Norman mercenary under Guaimar. Like the Tostain of our text (38492), Asclettin was the first count of Aversa.

38519 Benoît's *Wase* corresponds to *GND*'s *Wazo* and Orderic's *Waszo*, count of Naples.

38548 Honfroi's hyperbolic revenge would seem to be an addition by Benoît to his source.

38550 Benoît does not always follow the *GND* narrative slavishly, but can be found abbreviating it, sometimes quite extensively. In book VII, for example, the whole of chapters 9 to 18, describing *inter alia* the exploits of William Talvas, are simply omitted, as are chapters 22, 23 and 26 of the same book. Occasionally also, as here, Benoît alters the narrative order so as to better integrate the events he is describing. Having given a detailed account of the Normans in Italy and Sicily from *GND*'s chapter 30 (38287–550), he then jumps forward directly to chapter 43 in order to tell the story of Robert Guiscard (38550–38724), thereby ensuring the continuity of his subject matter. He then returns to pursue the *GND*'s narrative with chapter 31 (38733 ff.). Benoît curtails the end of his history by displacing chapter 33 of book VIII and proceeding to omit chapter 34 and the whole of chapters 36 to 42.

38594 *GND* tells us that Guaimar's daughter was called Sichelgaita: *filiam Gaumarii principis Salerni nomine Sichelgaitam*, a sentence Benoît, or his source manuscript, appears to have misconstrued.

38623 Among Robert Guiscard's victories Benoît mentions one against *Alexis Gregoire*, for which *GND* reads *Alexium Graecorum*, presumably misread as *Gregorem*.

38686 The praise is presumably directed not so much at the prince of Antioch himself than at Eleanor's illustrious ancestry.

38733 Noteworthy by its absence is any reference to Edward's sanctity despite his canonisation in 1161. This ignorance (or is it indifference?) is shared by Wace.

38743 According to *GND* 2: 157, the archbishop, whom Benoît does not name here, was Robert of Jumièges whose embassy to Normandy was said to have taken place as early as 1051. Cf. 36451 above.

38801 *Mestraire le merel* is a dicing term meaning "to have bad luck in gambling"; see Adolf Tobler and Erhard Lommatzsch, *Altfranzösisches Wörterbuch*, 12 vols. (Berlin, 1925–2008), 5: 1515. *Ja erent li merel mestreit* in the Anglo-Norman *Vie de saint Gilles* (1598) means "things will turn out badly."

38831–32 According to Wace (*Rou* III: 5685–98), less of a prisoner of Norman orthodoxy than Benoît, William concealed a whole battery of holy relics under the reliquary on which the unsuspecting Harold swore his oath. For Benoît, the wording of the oath was Harold's own, whereas for Wace it was prescribed for him.

38864 Of ultimately Biblical origin (Luke 7:45, John 13:5), the kissing of feet is a symbolic act of vassalic subjugation with which Benoît here embroiders his source. Wace famously tells how Rollo, refusing to bend to kiss the king of France's foot, instead lifted the king's foot up to his lips and sent him tumbling over backwards (*Rou* II: 1152–56).

38898 Presumably Benoît considers Archbishop Stigand unqualified to officiate at Harold's coronation and to perform the rituals necessary to confer legitimacy. On the possibility that the ceremony was actually performed by Archbishop Ealdred of York, see Bates, *William the Conqueror*, p. 216.

38996 Gruffudd ap Llewelyn, king of Gwynedd, was killed in Ireland in 1063 and his head presented to King Edward by Harold. Harold then married Gruffudd's widow Ealdgyth, sister of Edwin, earl of Mercia (Bates, *William the Conqueror*, pp. 191–92).

39006 Benoît here embroiders his source in order to emphasise Harold's uncouth and uncourtly behaviour.

39009 Halley's comet was visible in England between 24 and 30 April 1066. The *Anglo-Saxon Chronicle* affirms that it shone for a week; Orderic writes that it was almost fifteen days. On the comet's return in 1145, see Simon Keynes, "The Comet in the Eadwine Psalter," in *The Eadwine Psalter*, ed. Margaret Gibson et al. (London and University Park, PA, 1992), pp. 157–64.

39042   The papal banner, "a token of kingship" according to William of Malmesbury (*GRA*, p. 449), is illustrated in the contemporary Ramsey Benedictional (MS Paris, BnF, lat. 987, f. 111r). It reappears in the Bayeux Tapestry in the hands of Eustace of Boulogne, and, more speculatively, in the elaborate ensign flying from the mast-head of William's flagship, the Mora. According to Wace (*Rou* III: 6311–14), the pope also sent a ring inset with a tooth of St Peter. In the *Song of Roland*, Geoffrey of Anjou, Charlemagne's standard bearer, carries the golden *oriflamme*, called Romaine in honour of St Peter (3093–95). It had supposedly been presented to Charlemagne by Pope Leo III in 795.

39080   Benoît confuses Harald Hárfagri with Harold Hardrada, a notorious error shared by Orderic Vitalis (*Ecclesiastical History*, 2: 142) and the *Anglo-Saxon Chronicle* (D) s.a. 1066. Gaimar (*Estoire des Engleis* 5197) follows suit.

39109   The manuscript reads *Alains, cil de Bretaigne*. There are further examples of the confusion, in the surviving manuscript tradition, between the names of Conan and Alan at 39117 and 39175 below. Conan II was the son and heir of Alan III of Brittany, who was the son of Duke Robert I's sister Hawise (Bates, *William the Conqueror*, p. 59).

39120   The adjective *vieneis/vïaneis* is a stock epithet in French epic texts for steel or swords (e.g. *Song of Roland* 997). It is generally assumed that the town of Viana in Navarre is meant rather than Vienne in the French Dauphiné or Vienna.

39173   The poisoning of Conan of Brittany, if Orderic is to be believed (*GND*, 2: 162–64), was carried out at the instigation of Duke William himself in December 1066. Conan, of course, had earlier declared himself to be the rightful ruler of Normandy (39124–34) and so was, in some sense, a rival of William's. Benoît's addition of a passage (39214–18) describing William's regret at the death could be seen as an effort to disculpate him. The implausible nature of the detail of how the poison was supposedly administered, however, is sufficient to discredit the whole story. See Douglas, *William the Conqueror*, pp. 408–15 ("On poisoning as a method of political action ...").

39251   The identification of Hugh is made in *GND*.

39285–334 Burgess is wrong to claim that the story of the baron is unique to Wace (*The History of the Norman People*, p. 166). This Norman informant resident in England has his origins in William of Poitiers, who names him as *Rodbertus filius Guimarae* (ed. Foreville, p. 171). In Wace's version (*Rou* III: 6711–40) he tells William that he has insufficient troops for the invasion and advises him to call it off. On the other hand, Benoît, who turns the narrative into dialogue, gives him the role of informing the duke of the movements of Harold's army, and of simply counselling caution.

39354   Benoît's general approach to the Conquest is to religiously toe the Norman party line, something which Wace seems to have deliberately avoided doing. Benoît's precise sources for his account of the battle of Hastings are unknown. Compared to

Wace's neo-epic treatment of the episode (*Rou* III: 6465–8972), which seems to serve as the climax to his entire narrative and dramatises William's military role as conqueror, Benoît's version is relatively low-key; its modest 300 lines portray William as simply enforcing his legitimate right to the throne denied him by a perjurous and treacherous Harold. William's superiority is moral rather than military. See Penny Eley and Philip E. Bennett, "The Battle of Hastings According to Gaimar, Wace and Benoît: Rhetoric and Politics," *Nottingham Medieval Studies* 43 (1999): 47–78; cf. also Elisabeth M. C. van Houts, "The Memory of 1066 in Written and Oral Traditions," *Anglo-Norman Studies* 19 (1997): 167–80. Notably absent from Benoît's version is the singing of the *Song of Roland*, which impressed even William of Malmesbury (*GRA*, p. 455).

39473–88 William's address to his troops, in grandiloquent terms borrowed from William of Poitiers, is in free indirect discourse, a not uncommon Medieval French stylistic device. See Sophie Marnette, "Réflexions sur le discours indirect libre en français médiéval," *Romania* 114 (1996): 1–49. For this and for other aspects of Benoît's rhetoric, see Françoise Laurent, *Pour Dieu et pour le roi: rhétorique et idéologie dans* l'Histoire des ducs de Normandie *de Benoît de Sainte-Maure* (Paris: 2010).

39481 Literally: "There is no call here for any playful scrap/minor skirmish" – a sort of litotes. On *hobleïz* see Tobler-Lommatzsch 4: 1115.

39686 These details of Harold's wounds do not appear in any of Benoît's known sources. Thirteen wounds are specified later at 39826. Wace mentions Harold's wound in the eye (as had Amatus of Montecassino and Baudri de Bourgueil before him), but adds that he knows no authoritative evidence as to who killed him or with what weapon (*Rou* III: 8807–10, 8851–55).

39732 On the popular and ubiquitous character Taillefer, the heroic commoner who seems to belong more to literature than to history, see William Sayers, "The Jongleur Taillefer at Hastings," *Viator* 14 (1983): 77–88. "Histrio quem cor audax nobilitabat" is how he is described in the sixteen verses that the *Carmen de Hastingae Proelio* devotes to him. It looks likely that Benoît borrowed the figure from sources other than Wace (*Rou* III: 8013–40).

39801 Benoît dates the battle of Hastings to 1 instead of 14 October, no doubt, according to Andresen, as a result of a misreading of *GND*'s *pridie Idus Octobris* as *primo die Octobris*.

39811–24 The tears of pity that William is moved to shed after Hastings have their origin in William of Poitiers' *Gesta Guillelmi* (ed. Foreville, p. 205). Orderic wrote that the scene of destruction was so terrible that it would have moved to pity anyone who saw it (*Ecclesiastical History*, 2: 178).

39875 It is tempting to see the reference to Agamemnon and Troy as being an addition from the pen of the *Roman de Troie* poet himself, but it actually figures in what is Benoît's source here, namely William of Poitiers' *Gesta Guillelmi* (ed. Foreville, p. 209).

39887 Alternatively: "without him being awarded [the crown] in council."

39965 Portrayed in the Bayeux Tapestry brandishing a maniple (or a token pallium?),

Stigant was, in the words of William of Poitiers, the most powerful, influential and high-ranking of all Englishmen (ed. Foreville, p. 215). For William of Malmesbury, on the contrary, he was a prelate with a bad reputation for ambition who solicited promotion beyond his due (*GRA*, p. 360–3). Consecrated archbishop of Canterbury in 1043, he was excommunicated and deposed in 1070.

39978 William of Poitiers describes Edgar as an adolescent member of King Edward's family. According to the *Anglo-Saxon Chronicle, s.a.* 1066, the kingship of Edgar, who was only 13 years old at the time, would have been "his natural right." William of Malmesbury tells us that, even though Edgar was "nearest to the throne by birth," he was elected by only a very small minority of people (*GRA*, pp. 416, 445). There is, in fact, no evidence that he was ever actually crowned.

40076 The fire which, according to both William of Poitiers (ed. Foreville, p. 221) and Orderic Vitalis (*Ecclesiastical History*, 2: 184), disturbed the coronation ceremony and caused general confusion and panic, fails to find its way into Benoît's resolutely positive narrative.

40115 Sometimes known as the Fighting Man, the richly decorated banner that had belonged personally to Harold is also described by William of Poitiers (ed. Foreville, p. 225), William of Malmesbury (*GRA*, p. 454) and Wace (*Rou* III: 7838–44). It is to be distinguished from the wyvern or winged-dragon standard illustrated in the Bayeux Tapestry.

40343 The identification of *Werre* as Vièvre belongs to Fichet, *Vie de Guillaume le Conquérant*, p. 144.

40384 The reading *ganz* is from the London manuscript. The glove is the most common of a wide range of symbolic objects of conveyance whose function was to physically preserve the memory of a particularly significant act or event. They have been described as "props in the theatre of memory" (Michael Clanchy, *From Memory to Written Record: England 1066–1307*, 2nd ed. (Oxford, 1993), p. 38; also 254–60). Cf. the modern survival of "to throw down the gauntlet."

40409 The term *life* used in a historiographic context is also encountered at 42007 and 44520. It does not necessarily refer to a separate written source.

40422 As we learned previously (40220), these two viceroys were Odo and William fitz Osbern. Cf. William of Poitiers (ed. Foreville, pp. 238–42).

40450 Orderic Vitalis tells us that Eustace II of Boulogne undertook his unsuccessful attempt to capture Dover castle in 1067 at the invitation of some Kentish locals "goaded to rebellion by Norman oppression" (*Eccesiastical History* 2: 204). *GND* 2: 177, on the other hand, explains that Eustace was "corrupted by the wickedness of some Englishmen from Kent." Eustace had been a companion of the Conqueror at Hastings, where he was wounded, and the Bayeux Tapestry portrays him carrying the papal banner. His other claim to fame, apart from his descent from Charlemagne (via his wife), was that he was the father of the celebrated crusader Godfrey of Bouillon, who was to become the first ruler of the Kingdom of Jerusalem in 1099.

40578 The Tours manuscript reads *Pevenesel*, to which the London manuscript's *Wincenesel* is, as Orderic (*Ecclesiastical History* 2: 209) confirms, preferable.

40637 Edgar Ætheling is introduced here, following *GND* 2: 181, as if he were a new character, even though he has been mentioned previously in the narrative on at least five occasions as from 39978. For his role in this revolt, see Bates, *William the Conqueror*, p. 303.

40895–909 For the assault on Durham Benoît is using Orderic Vitalis (*Ecclesiastical History*, 2: 220–22) as his source. Newly created earl of Northumbria, the Fleming Robert de Commines was ambushed together with all his men in January 1069.

41018 Benoît seems to speak approvingly of William fitz Osbern's castrating and blinding of his enemy prisoner. Orderic (*Ecclesiastical History*, 2: 230–32), on the other hand, criticises the Conqueror's suppression of the York rebellion as brutal (*feralis*). Cf. John Gillingham, "William the Bastard at War," in *Anglo-Norman Warfare*, ed. Matthew Strickland (Woodbridge, 1992), pp. 143–60.

41025 *Tenir grant lieu* means "to deputise for, represent" (Tobler-Lommatzsch 5: 427). The expression survives in *lieutenant*. Orderic Vitalis was outspoken with regard to the achievements of Willam fiz Osbern, the steward of Normandy, the Conqueror's sometime regent, his cousin and one of his closest counsellors. He was "a warlike military leader and the first and greatest oppressor of the English ... But he received the retribution he deserved, for having killed many by the sword, he himself perished by the sword in unexpected circumstances" (*Ecclesiastical History*, 2: 318–20). For William of Poitiers, fitz Osbern was "the darling of the Normans but the scourge of the English" (ed. Foreville, p. 241).

41147 While William of Malmesbury considered Waltheof a martyr (*Gesta pontificum Anglorum*, ed. and trans. Michael Winterbottom and Rodney M. Thomson, 2 vols. (Oxford, 2007), 1: 486), in *GND* Waltheof's only role is to be a rebel, and his death does not even merit a mention.

41169 Elnoc, an otherwise unknown rebel, appears in Orderic Vitalis (*Ecclesiastical History*, 2: 228). On the revolt, see Ann Williams, *The English and the Norman Conquest* (Woodbridge, 1995), pp. 29–32.

41221 Montacute Castle in Somerset, newly constructed by Robert of Mortain in 1066, was attacked by what Orderic refers to as the West Saxons of Dorset and Somerset (*Ecclesiastical History*, 2: 228). These were either part of the multi-national army raised by Swein Estrithson, king of Denmark, in 1069, or, more likely, people from Wessex which Gaimar twice (*Estoire des Engleis*, 921 and 2023) refers to as *Sesoigne*, the usual word for Saxony. The figure of more than seven thousand troops is, of course, fantasy; what is meant is a large number, just like Orderic's figure of 50,000 knights (*Ecclesiastical History*, 2: 168) said to be in William's invading force.

41267 The adjective *inde* in Medieval French designates the colour indigo (Tobler-Lommatzsch 4: 1370–73). Benoît's attaching the epithet *vermeille* to India here looks like a play on words. Cf. also 40754, 44235.

41287 The mention of Cornwall here, independent of any of Benoît's known sources, seems entirely gratuitous. Arthur's links with Cornwall, especially with Tintagel where he was conceived, were established by Geoffrey of Monmouth in the 1130s.

41297 The palaeographic difference between *Estanfort* "Stamford" and *Estafort* "Stafford" (mentioned by Orderic, *Ecclesiastical History*, 2: 228) is minimal, and the two could easily be confused.

41316 As John Gillingham points out, the king had not in fact left England at this time, according to Orderic (*Ecclesiastical History*, 2: 230) whom Benoît is using as his source for this episode.

41361 The mysterious word *braholes*, apparently unattested elsewhere, could possibly be an alternative form of *bruieroi(e)* "heath," as found, for example, in Wace (*Rou* II: 3040), coined to rhyme with *goles*. Cf. Tobler-Lommatzsch 1: 1171.

41454 Benoît abruptly curtails his account of English history at precisely the point where Orderic Vitalis interrupts his own narrative in order to indicate where William of Poitiers' surviving text, that he has been following, comes to an end (*Ecclesiastical History*, 2: 258).

41533 William's last illness was the subject of conflicting diagnoses: either heat stroke exacerbated by obesity, abdominal injury from the pommel of his saddle, or intestinal inflammation, i.e. peritonitis. Whatever it was, it sufficiently alarmed his physicians at Rouen for them to immediately declare him a lost cause (*GRA*, p. 510).

41595 The love of which William speaks here reflects a widespread chivalric notion which celebrates a bond between knights that is rooted in mutual respect and an ethos of obligatory reciprocity. This sense of vassalic solidarity is integral, in tandem with fealty, to the homage formula as embodied, for example, in the *Song of Roland*: "I will become his man *par amur e par feid*" (86). On Benoît's use of the term *amur*, see H. B. Teunis, "Benoît de Sainte-Maure and William the Conqueror's *amor*," *Anglo-Norman Studies* 12 (1990): 199–209, and Stephanie Mooers Chriselow, "The Royal Love in Anglo-Norman England: Fiscal or Courtly Concept?," *Haskins Society Journal* 8 (1996): 27–42.

41699 Compare the tone of William's confession in Wace: "I conquered England wrongfully, and many a man was wrongfully killed. Their heirs I killed wrongfully and I seized the kingdom [of England] wrongfully" (*Rou* III: 9141–44).

41741–44 Henry's eminently practical words to his dying father are from the pen of Orderic Vitalis (*Ecclesastical History*, 4: 94–95).

41858 It is tempting to see this unusually violent diatribe against William's half-brother as illustrating contemporary attitudes to family disloyalty and betrayal. It also serves to validate the proposition that "the prime influence on William as a ruler was the demand for loyalty" (Bates, *William the Conqueror*, p. 525).

41933 Benoît's eloquent lament is borrowed directly from Orderic Vitalis (*Ecclesastical History*, 4: 102–3), but he passes over in silence the criticisms of him that Orderic also voices. Cf. Bates, *William the Conqueror*, pp. 524–27.

41991 According to Orderic Vitalis, Benoît's source here, the unnamed abbot accompanying William's body was Giselbert, abbot of Saint-Etienne at Caen.

42049–54 As Charity Urbanski (*Writing History for the King: Henry II and the Politics of Vernacular Historiography* (Ithaca, 2013), pp. 191–92) points out, by avoiding any mention here of Curthose or Rufus, Benoît is promoting Henry over his two elder brothers in order to anticipate his political ascendancy. For him Henry I is the only true heir of the Conqueror, and in his turn the only true ancestor of Henry II.

42062–68 Benoît celebrates the skill of the poet as craftsman, as fresco painter and decorator of words. The simile of the plasterer, reminiscent of the tropes of *Deus artifex* and *Deus pictor*, seems to be Benoît's own elaboration of a passage in *GND* (2: 202) in which Henry I is said to outshine his two brothers in the same way as the colour red is enhanced by painters setting it against an iron-rust background. The historian William of Poitiers had an altogether different perspective on poetry: "Parturire suo pectore bella quae calamo ederentur poetis licebat, atque amplificare utcumque cognita per campos figmentorum divagando" ("Poets are allowed to create wars in their imaginations so that they can reproduce them in writing, and amplify what is known by meandering, whenever they wish, through the fields of fiction") (ed. Foreville, p. 44; ed. Davis and Chibnall, p. 28). Cf. also Introduction above p. 10.

42071 On *deça* "on this side" used in the sense of "on this side of death," see the gloss "in this world" to *Lumere as leis* (12812) in the *Anglo-Norman Dictionary*, 2nd ed., A-E, ed. William Rothwell et al. (London, 2005).

42085 My translation relies on correcting the incomprehensible reading, in both manuscripts, *lesut* to *leust*, the preterite tense of the impersonal verb *leisir* "to be permitted."

42110–26 With his negative portrayal of Rufus here and, in more grisly detail, at 42743–43078, Benoît is merely following the fashion of character assassination current among ecclesiastical historians of his day. See John Gillingham, *William II the Red King* (London, 2015), pp. 97–100.

42127 Orderic Vitalis (*Ecclesiastical History*, 2: 356) describes Duke Robert using portrait topoi dating back to Suetonius: "He was talkative and excessively generous, audacious and highly courageous in battle, a strong-armed and accurate archer. He had a loud voice and a fluent tongue, and was plain-spoken. His face was round, and his figure squat; he was short in height and was nicknamed, in the vernacular, Fat-Legs or Curt-Hose." William of Malmesbury adds that he had a potbelly, and that his father mockingly called him Robin Curt-Hose (*GRA*, p. 700–3).

42220–21 The syntax is unusual in that the pluperfect indicative replaces the expected imperfect subjunctive; see Sven Sandqvist, *Études syntaxiques sur la* Chronique des ducs de Normandie *par Benoît* (Lund, 1976), pp. 122–23.

42250 I read Benoît's obscure *de puis* as *de pis* "worse"; cf. Tobler-Lommatzsch 7: 975.

42323–25 As John Gillingham points out in a personal communication, Benoît seems to have misconstrued the pronoun *ille* of *GND* (2: 206–7) which shows Rufus, not Robert, as occupying Fécamp.

42420 The detail *de Beuvron* is an addition by Benoît to *quod Sancti Jacobi appellatum est* of *GND*. The castle in question is near Pontorson.

42694 The ambush and killing of Malcolm III, king of Scots, took place near Alnwick in November 1093. Mowbray spent the last thirty years of his life in prison. See Henry of Huntingdon, pp. 418–21, and Gaimar, *Estoire des Engleis*, 6111–78.

42759   The London manuscript reading *Rovecestre* "Rochester" is preferable to that of the Tours manuscript which has *Wirecestre* "Worcester." Bishop Gundulf worked intimately with both Lanfranc and Anselm; see Marylon Ruud, "Monks in the World: The Case of Gundulf of Rochester," *Anglo-Norman Studies* 11 (1989): 245–60; Martin Brett, "Gundulf and the Cathedral Communities of Canterbury and Rochester," in *Canterbury and the Norman Conquest*, ed. Richard Eales and Richard Sharpe (London, 1995), pp. 15–25. The source of this passage is unclear.

42782   Some elements of this vivid, not to say gruesome nightmare, which is quite independent of *GND*, reappear in William of Malmesbury (*GRA*, p. 572), while Orderic reports on portents dreamt remotely by various third parties (*Ecclesiastical History*, 5: 284–89). Benoît's dream has a literary afterlife in Langtoft and the Prose Brut. *GND*, it should be noted, devotes no more than two lines to the death of Rufus. Benoît's source here is also unknown but must have been similar to Wace's. Wace's account (*Rou* III: 10036–116), which makes no mention of any dreams, is relatively neutral compared to the hostility and vengefulness of Benoît's. Benoît fails to mention Walter Tirel, Rufus's assumed Norman assassin, whose role is emphasised in Gaimar, Wace, Walter Map and others; see Emma Mason, *William II Rufus, the Red King* (Stroud, 2005), pp. 219–31.

42918   Jean Blacker takes this reference to a particular but unspecified sin, as well as the earlier mention of sins to which every animal is prone, to be indirect allusions to Rufus's alleged homosexuality (*The Faces of Time: Portrayal of the Past in Old French and Latin Historical Narrative of the Anglo-Norman* Regnum (Austin, 1994), p. 129).

42942   For stretching out the hand as a gesture of submission, see Tobler-Lommatzsch 5: 820 ("sich ergeben").

42943   The verb used is *escremir* "to fence," the secondary meaning of which is "defend" or "protect oneself"; Tobler-Lommatzsch 3: 995–96.

43004   Fahlin's (and Michel's) reading *saitisse* is meaningless and needs correction to *sai[n]tisse*.

43141   Henry's accession was, according to Benoît, sanctioned by God and greeted with universal joy. For Wace, on the other hand, Henry simply installed himself in the kingdom in the absence of Curthose "whom no one waited for" (*Rou* III: 10298–99). For C. Warren Hollister, Henry's title to the crown was "debatable" rather than "fraudulent" (*Henry I*, ed. Amanda Clark Frost (New Haven, 2001), pp. 105–6).

43201   Matilda is, of course, a prefiguration of her son, and her glory anticipates his. Robert de Torigni was a great admirer of Matilda and a defender of her legitimacy as queen of England, and his support for her is well and faithfully reflected in Benoît's text. On Matilda see Marjorie Chibnall, *The Empress Matilda: Queen Consort, Queen Mother and Lady of the English* (Oxford, 1991). Cf. note to 43952–44000 below.

43244–64   Details concerning Matilda's wedding ceremony are thought to have been given to Robert de Torigni by Matilda herself (Chibnall, *The Empress Matilda*, p. 25).

43282   The White Ship disaster, an alcohol-fuelled accident in which the crew were as drunk as the passengers, finds the historians at their most poetic: the oarsmen were "flooded to overflowing with wine"; the nobles' sons who "flocked aboard as though for a youthful frolic" were not only "young hotheads" but "reputedly bore the stain of sodomy"; "the boat sped swifter than a feathered arrow," but soon "hidden rocks smashed into its bottom and the victorious sea crept through the last plank"; the passengers ended up "food for the fishes," "buried in their bellies at the bottom of the ocean" (Orderic, *Ecclesiastical History*, 6: 294–301; *GRA*, pp. 758–62). Cf. Wace, who adds that the sole survivor was one Beroul, a butcher from Rouen (*Rou III*: 10173–204) – a detail corroborated by Orderic (*Ecclesiastical History*, 6: 298). The future king was drowned, and another future king, Count Stephen of Blois, could well have joined him. He, however, had been feeling unwell and disembarked just before the boat set out. As Hollister memorably put it, "Stephen's diarrhoea probably determined the history of England ... between 1135 and 1154" (*Henry I*, p. 277).

43369–70 The London manuscript reads *traz e tanz* for *treis itanz* in Tours. I conjecture that the image could be taken from gambling. Cf. note to 38801 above.

43460 Benoît's addition emphasises Robert's misplaced generosity and lack of political foresight, both character failings to which Orderic Vitalis also draws attention: "He diminished his inheritance daily by his foolish prodigality ... as he impoverished himself, he strengthened the hand of others against him" (*Ecclesastical History*, 4: 114–15).

43667 For Hollister Henry's life-long incarceration of his brother was a "prudent act" (*Henry I*, p. 206). John Gillingham, on the other hand, shows that it was part of a series of "dishonourable actions" committed by Henry (*The English in the Twelfth Century*, pp. 212–13). Whereas William of Malmesbury thought that Curthose was lucky to get away with his life (*GRA*, p. 706), Henry of Huntingdon used his fate to illustrate the saying "Royal business is wickedness" (p. 604). Cf. note to 44247.

43761 According to Abbot Suger, Philip I was buried at the abbey of Saint-Benoît-sur-Loire, having declined, out of humility, to be buried at Saint-Denis (*Suger: Vie de Louis VI le Gros*, ed. and trans. Henri Waquet (Paris, 1929), p. 85).

43791 Ralph IV de Tosny (d. 1126) was the father of Roger III de Tosny (d. 1157). Wace (*Rou III*: 1473; 1569–71) also links them in his account of the battle. Cf. Lucien Musset, "Aux Origines d'une classe dirigeante: les Tosny." *Francia* 5 (1977): 45–80.

43933–35 Henry's mutilation of the English counterfeiters met not only with Robert de Torigni's warm approval, but also that of the *Anglo-Saxon Chronicle* which declared (*s.a.* 1124) that the moneyers got exactly what they deserved. Henry of Huntingdon also condones what he describes as Henry's "severity towards evil-doers" (p. 474). In the impassive words of the *Dialogue of the Exchequer*, people punished by mutilation are "a pitiable spectacle for the people and discourage similar crimes by their frightening example." Cf. note to 41014 above.

43952–44000 Benoît's insistence on Henry I's designation of Matilda as his successor is to be read in conjunction with his laborious justification of her marriage to Geoffrey of Anjou (44071–170): Henry II's legitimacy is the logical extension of his mother's. As her epitaph put it, Matilda was "Ortu magna, viro major, sed maxima partu"

("Great by birth, greater still by marriage, but greatest of all in her offspring"). For Benoît (but not for Robert de Torigni) Stephen was little better than a usurper, and he was made king "par seduction" (44455).

44043 The "blessed match" of a couple comprising a widow in her mid-twenties and a 14-year-old boy was in reality less euphoric than Benoît describes; see Chibnall, *The Empress Matilda*, p. 55. *GND* mentions Matilda's reluctance, which Benoît conveniently overlooks. According to the *Anglo-Saxon Chronicle* (*s.a.* 1127), the marriage "offended all the French and English."

44071–170 The first of two related genealogies, this passage is designed to demonstrate that the ex-empress Matilda was not disparaged (though she clearly was) when she became the wife of Count Geoffrey of Anjou. The supposed links between the counts of Angers and the twelfth-century kings of France are tenuous in the extreme. The second genealogy, at 44329–500, will provide a legitimate link between William and the house of Anjou in the persons of William's daughter Constance and Alan Fergant, whose second marriage was to the daughter of Fulk the Surly.

44188 Henry is reputed to have sired as many as twenty-four illegitimate children in all. William of Malmesbury believed (or pretended to) that the king's promiscuity was politically inspired: "He was the master of his libido, not its servant" (Hollister, *Henry I*, pp. 41–45).

44223 Benoît's syntax mistakenly conflates *Driencort* and *Chastel nof*, which in *GND* are two separate localities: *Driemcurtis, Novum-castrum*, meaning the castles of Driencourt and Châteauneuf-sur-Epte.

44227 Benoît's text has Couesnon, which looks suspiciously like a deformation of *GND*'s *Colmiae Mons*, that is Châtillon-sur-Colmont. Wace, however, states "He fortified a castle on the river Couesnon, some say at Pontorson, others at Carues" (*Rou* III: 2605–7), by which is meant Cherrueix. Cf. Benoît's earlier statement that "What was first called Charrues is now called Pontorson" (33027–30).

44235–37 Literally: "His skill and strength ... were of great utility in secular matters and carried weight." Henry's foreign influence might conceivably have stretched as far as Flemish Brabant and even Germany, but this is still some way short of India.

44247 This one criticism levelled at Henry, Robert de Torigni's rather than Benoît's, is a rare instance of a baronial voice being raised, albeit discreetly. According to Hollister, Henry's policy on disseisin was actually well intentioned (*Henry I*, p. 330–34). As for the king's supposed ruthlessness, brutality and cruelty (Southern, it will be recalled, spoke of Henry's "Byzantine ferocity"), such charges are dismissed by Hollister as misunderstandings (*Henry I*, pp. 484–93). See now Judith Green, *Henry I: King of England and Duke of Normandy* (Cambridge, 2006), pp. 314–16.

44301 The mention of Marmoutier, to which monastery Benoît is thought to have been attached, seems to be the result of a misreading (perhaps deliberate?) of *GND*'s *monachorum Tironis* "Tiron" (i.e. Thiron-Gardais) as *Turonis* "Tours."

44388 The count of Saint-Gilles mentioned here is a ghost character who owes his existence to a textual muddle. Benoît is said (by Andresen "Über die Quellen," 2, 1886: 537–38) to have confused "Willelmo filio Henrici regis Anglorum" of *GND* with

the William who appears later in the same chapter as the count who "honorem Soreii regendum a patre suscepit," and the assumption is that *Soreii* [= Sully] was then
somehow misinterpreted as *Sancti Egidii*.

44393 More accurately, as Orderic makes clear, there was only a promise of marriage,
namely a betrothal (Bates, *William the Conqueror*, pp. 198, 266).

44409 Benoît is wrong in stating that the daughter of Stephen-Henry and Adela married Henry of Eu; she in fact married Richard d'Avranches, earl of Chester. Henry
of Eu married the daughter of William, count of Sully. This is the third error that
Benoît commits within the last 300 or so lines of his history (cf. notes to 44223 and
44388 above). These are attributed by Andresen to authorial carelessness. But given
the abrupt ending of the narrative, and the wholesale omission of chapters 34 and 36
to 42 of *GND*, one could conjecture that the usually careful Benoît, in his haste to
finish, was distracted by illness, perhaps, or even approaching death.

44426 Benoît's *Behaigne* designates Bohemia. Carinthia is in today's southern Bavaria.
Engelbert's daughter Matilda was the mother of Adèle of Champagne, third wife of
Louis VII.

44455 Benoît's outspoken denunciation of Stephen's succession in 1135, which he
regards as illegitimate, is independent of *GND*, 2: 274, which states baldly that "with
the support of his brother Henry, bishop of Winchester, he obtained (*adeptus est*)
the crown of the kingdom." Benoît's judgement of the Bellêmes, incidentally, is
equally forthright. Henry of Huntingdon reports the pope's opinion that Stephen
had broken his oath by seizing the crown (p. 759).

44502 In the twelfth century, *translater* connotes an interpretative vernacular adaptation of a Latin source rather than a purely linguistic transfer from one language into
another; see Peter Damian-Grint, *The New Historians of the Twelfth-Century Renaissance: Inventing Vernacular Authority* (Woodbridge, 1999), pp. 22–31, 228–33.

44516 Henry I died not on 8 December, as Benoît writes, but in the night of 1–2 December 1135. *GND* reads .*iv. nonas Decembris*, by which is meant 2 December
(Andresen, "Über die Quellen," 2 (1886): 535). Benoît stops with Henry's death,
though Robert de Torigni's narrative continues up until 1137.

Bibliography

An up-to-date online bibliography is available at
http://www.arlima.net/ad/benoit_de_sainte-maure.html.

Manuscripts

London, British Library, Harley 1717, ff. 1r–250r (Anglo-Norman, first quarter, thirteenth century)
> There is a nineteenth-century copy of the Harley text in Madrid, Biblioteca Nacional, MS 17773, ff. 1–333.

Tours, Bibliothèque municipale, 903, ff. 1r–222v (Touraine, last quarter, twelfth century)

Note: According to Charity Urbanski, *Writing History for the King: Henry II and the Politics of Vernacular Historiography* (Ithaca, NY, 2013), p. 21 n44, a fifteenth-century prose version of Benoît's history is preserved in Los Angeles, J. Paul Getty Museum, MS Ludwig XIII 4.

Editions

Chronique des ducs de Normandie par Benoît, trouvère anglo-normand du XIIe siècle, publiée pour la première fois d'après un manuscrit du Musée britannique. Ed. Francisque Michel. 3 vols. Paris: Imprimerie nationale, 1836–44.
Chronique des ducs de Normandie par Benoît, publiée d'après le manuscrit de Tours avec les variantes du manuscrit de Londres. Vols. 1 and 2: *Texte,* ed. Carin Fahlin; vol. 3: *Glossaire,* by Östen Södergård; vol. 4: *Notes,* by Sven Sandqvist. 4 vols. Uppsala: Almqvist and Wiksell, 1951–79.

Other Primary Sources

The Anglo-Saxon Chronicles. Ed. and trans. Michael Swanton. London: Phoenix, 2000.
[Benoît de Sainte-Maure.] *Le Roman de Troie par Benoît de Sainte-Maure.* Ed. Léopold Constans. 6 vols. Paris: SATF, 1904–12.

—. *The* Roman de Troie *by Benoît de Sainte-Maure*. Trans. Glyn S. Burgess and Douglas Kelly. Cambridge: D.S. Brewer, 2017.

Geffrei Gaimar. *Estoire des Engleis / History of the English*. Ed. and trans. Ian Short. Oxford: Oxford University Press, 2009.

The Gesta Normannorum Ducum *of William of Jumièges, Orderic Vitalis and Robert of Torigni*. Ed. Elisabeth M.C. van Houts. 2 vols. Oxford Medieval Texts. Oxford: Clarendon Press, 1992–95.

Giraldi Cambrensis Opera. Ed. J.S. Brewer. 8 vols. Rolls Series. London: Longman, 1861–91.

Guernes de Pont-Sainte-Maxence. *La Vie de saint Thomas Becket*. Ed. Emmanuel Walberg. Paris: Champion, 1936; repr. 1964.

—. *La Vie de saint Thomas de Canterbury*. Ed. and trans. Jacques T.E. Thomas. 2 vols. Louvain: Peeters, 2002.

—. *A Life of Thomas Becket in Verse: La Vie de saint Thomas Becket by Guernes de Pont-Sainte-Maxence*. Trans. Ian Short. Mediaeval Sources in Translation 56. Toronto: Pontifical Institute of Mediaeval Studies, 2013.

Guillaume de Poitiers. *Histoire de Guillaume le Conquérant*. Ed. and trans. Raymonde Foreville. Paris: Belles Lettres, 1952.

—. *The* Gesta Guillelmi *of William of Poitiers*. Ed. and trans. R.H.C. Davis and Marjorie Chibnall. Oxford Medieval Texts. Oxford: Clarendon Press, 1998.

Henry, Archdeacon of Huntingdon. *Historia Anglorum / The History of the English People*. Ed. and trans. Diana Greenway. Oxford Medieval Texts. Oxford: Clarendon Press, 1996.

[Jordan Fantosme.] *Jordan Fantosme's Chronicle*. Ed. and trans. R.C. Johnston. Oxford: Clarendon Press, 1981.

[Ordericus Vitalis.] *The Ecclesiastical History of Orderic Vitalis*. Ed. and trans. with introduction and notes by Marjorie Chibnall. 6 vols. Oxford Medieval Texts. Oxford: Clarendon Press, 1969–80.

Suger: Vie de Louis VI le Gros. Ed. and trans. Henri Waquet. Paris: Champion, 1929.

[Wace.] *Le Roman de Brut de Wace*. Ed. Ivor Arnold. 2 vols. Paris: SATF, 1938–40.

—. *Le Roman de Rou de Wace*. Ed. A.J. Holden. 3 vols. Paris: SATF, 1970–73.

—. *The History of the Norman People: Wace's* "Roman de Rou." Trans. Glyn S. Burgess, with notes by Glyn S. Burgess and Elisabeth van Houts. Woodbridge: Boydell, 2004. A first version, published by the Société Jersiaise in 2002, reproduces Holden's French text.

William of Malmesbury. *Gesta pontificum Anglorum*. Ed. and trans. Michael Winterbottom and Rodney M. Thomson. 2 vols. Oxford: Clarendon Press, 2007.

—. *Gesta Regum Anglorum / The History of the English Kings*. Ed. and trans. R.A.B. Mynors, completed by R.M. Thomson and Michael Winterbottom. 2 vols. Oxford Medieval Texts. Oxford: Clarendon Press, 1998–99.

Studies

Ailes, Adrian. *The Origins of the Royal Arms of England*. Reading: Reading University Press, 1982.

Albu, Emily. *The Normans in Their Histories: Propaganda, Myth and Subversion*. Woodbridge: Brewer, 2001.

Andresen, Hugo. "Über die von Benoit in seiner normannischen Chronik benutzen Quellen, insbesondere über sein Verhältnis zu Dudo, Wilhelm von Jumièges und Wace." *Romanische Forschungen* 1 (1883): 327–412; 2 (1886): 477–538.

—. "Zu Benoit's *Chronique des ducs de Normandie*." *Zeitschrift für romanische Philologie* 11 (1888): 231–40, 345–70.

Anglo-Norman Dictionary. 2nd ed., A–E. Ed. William Rothwell et al. London: Modern Humanities Research Association, 2005. Electronic edition available at: http://www.anglo-norman.net.

Ashe, Laura. *Fiction and History in England, 1066–1200*. Cambridge: Cambridge University Press, 2007.

Barlow, Frank. *The Life of King Edward Who Lies at Westminster*. 2nd ed. Oxford: Clarendon Press, 1992.

Bassnett, Susan. *Translation Studies*. 4th ed. London and New York: Routledge, 2014.

Bates, David. *William the Conqueror*. New Haven: Yale University Press, 2016.

Baumgartner, Emmanuèle. "Ecrire et penser l'histoire selon *l'Histoire des ducs de Normandie* de Benoît de Sainte-Maure." In *Le Travail sur le modèle*, ed. Danielle Buschinger, pp. 41–49. Amiens: Presses de l'Université de Picardie, 2002.

—. "Vocabulaire de la technique littéraire dans le *Roman de Troie* de Benoît de Sainte-Maure." *Cahiers de lexicologie* 51 (1987): 39–48.

Beckmann, Gustav. *Trojaroman und Normannenchronik: Die Identität der beiden Benoît und die Chronologie ihrer Werke*. Munich: Hueber, 1965.

Bennett, Matthew. "Poetry as History? The *Roman de Rou* of Wace as a Source for the Norman Conquest." *Anglo-Norman Studies* 5 (1983): 19–39.

Bennett, Philip. "La *Chronique* de Jordan Fantosme: Épique et public lettré au XIIe siècle." *Cahiers de civilisation médiévale* 40 (1997): 37–56.

Bezzola, Reto R. *Les Origines et la formation de la littérature courtoise en Occident, 500–1200*. 3 vols. in 5. Paris: Champion, 1960–63.

Blacker, Jean. *The Faces of Time: Portrayal of the Past in Old French and Latin Historical Narrative of the Anglo-Norman "Regnum."* Austin, TX: University of Texas Press, 1994.

—. *Wace: A Critical Bibliography*. St Helier: Société Jersiaise, 2008.

Braet, Herman. "Le Songe de l'arbre chez Wace, Benoît et Aimon de Varennes." *Romania* 91 (1970): 255–67.

Brett, Martin. "Gundulf and the Cathedral Communities of Canterbury and Rochester." In *Canterbury and the Norman Conquest: Churches, Saints and Scholars, 1066–1109*, ed. Richard Eales and Richard Sharpe, pp. 15–25. London: Hambledon, 1995.

Broadhurst, Karen. "Henry II of England and Eleanor of Aquitaine: Patrons of Literature in French?" *Viator* 27 (1996): 53–84.

Careri, Maria, Christine Ruby, and Ian Short. *Livres et écritures en français et en occitan au XIIe siècle: Catalogue illustré.* Rome: Viella, 2011.

Chibnall, Marjorie. *The Empress Matilda: Queen Consort, Queen Mother and Lady of the English.* Oxford: Blackwell, 1991.

Chriselow, Stephanie Mooers. "The Royal Love in Anglo-Norman England: Fiscal or Courtly Concept?" *Haskins Society Journal* 8 (1996): 27–42.

Clanchy, Michael. *From Memory to Written Record: England 1066–1307.* 2nd ed. Oxford: Blackwell, 1993.

Courroux, Pierre. *L'Écriture de l'histoire dans les chroniques françaises (XIIe – XVe siècle).* Paris: Garnier, 2016.

Crouch, David. *The Image of the Aristocracy in Britain, 1000–1300.* London: Routledge, 1992.

Curteis, Alice and Chris Given-Wilson. *The Royal Bastards of Medieval England.* London: Barnes and Noble, 1995.

Damian-Grint, Peter. "*En nul leu nel truis escrit*: Research and Invention in Benoît de Sainte-Maure's *Chronique des ducs de Normandie*." *Anglo-Norman Studies* 21 (1999): 11–30.

—. "Learning and Authority in Benoît de Sainte-Maure's Cosmography." *Reading Medieval Studies* 24 (1998): 25–52.

—. *The New Historians of the Twelfth-Century Renaissance: Inventing Vernacular Authority.* Woodbridge: Brewer, 1999.

Dictionnaire des lettres françaises: Le Moyen Âge. Ed. Geneviève Hasenohr and Michel Zink. Paris: Fayard, 1992.

Douglas, David. *William the Conqueror.* Berkeley: University of California Press, 1967.

Eley, Penny. "Epic Elements in the *Chronique des ducs de Normandie*." In *Aspects de l'épopée romane: Mentalités, idéologies, intertextualités*, ed. Hans Van Dijk and Willen Noomen, pp. 345–51. Groningen: E. Forsten, 1995.

—. "History and Romance in the *Chronique des ducs de Normandie*." *Medium Ævum* 68 (1999): 81–95.

Eley, Penny and Philip E. Bennett. "The Battle of Hastings According to Gaimar, Wace and Benoît: Rhetoric and Politics." *Nottingham Medieval Studies* 43 (1999): 47–78.

Fahlin, Carin. *Étude sur le manuscrit de Tours de la* Chronique des ducs de Normandie *par Benoît.* Uppsala: Almqvist and Wiksell, 1937.

Fichet, Paul. *Benoît: Vie de Guillaume le Conquérant. Chronique des ducs de Normandie.* Bayeux: Heimdal, 1976.

Field, Rosalind, "Romance as History, History as Romance." In *Romance in Medieval England*, ed. Maldwyn Mills et al., pp. 164–73. Cambridge: Cambridge University Press, 1991.

Fritz, Jean-Marie. *Le Discours du fou au moyen âge: XIIe–XIIIe siècles. Étude comparée des discours littéraire, médical, juridique et théologique de la folie.* Paris: Presses Universitaires de France, 1992.

Gillingham, John. "The Cultivation of History, Legend and Courtesy at the Court of

Henry II." In *Writers of the Reign of Henry II: Twelve Essays*, ed. Ruth Kennedy and Simon Meecham-Jones, pp. 25–52. New York: Palgrave, 2006.

—. *The English in the Twelfth Century: Imperialism, National Identity and Political Values.* Woodbridge: Boydell, 2000.

—. *William II the Red King.* London: Penguin, 2015.

—. "William the Bastard at War." In *Anglo-Norman Warfare*, ed. Matthew Strickland, pp. 143–60. Woodbridge: Brewer, 1992.

Gouttebroze, Jean-Guy. "Pourquoi congédier un historiographe: Henri II Plantagenêt et Wace." *Romania* 112 (1991): 289–311.

Green, Judith. *Henry I: King of England and Duke of Normandy.* Cambridge: Cambridge University Press, 2006.

Hollister, C. Warren. *Henry I.* Ed. Amanda Clark Frost. New Haven: Yale University Press, 2001.

Jones, Robert W. *Bloodied Banners: Martial Display on the Medieval Battlefield.* Woodbridge: Boydell, 2010.

Jung, Marc-René. *La Légende de Troie en France au Moyen Age: Analyse des versions françaises et bibliographie raisonnée des manuscrits.* Basel: Francke, 1996.

—. "La *Translatio* chez Benoît de Sainte-Maure: De l'*estoire* au livre." *Perspectives Médiévales* 26 (2001): 155–76.

Kelly, Douglas. *The Art of Medieval French Romance.* Madison: University of Wisconsin Press, 1992.

Keynes, Simon. "The Comet in the Eadwine Psalter." In *The Eadwine Psalter: Text, Image, and Monastic Culture in Twelfth-Century Canterbury*, ed. Margaret Gibson et al., pp. 157–64. London and University Park, PA: The Modern Humanities Research Association, 1992.

Labory, Gillette. "Essai d'une histoire nationale au XIIIe siècle." *Bibliothèque de l'Ecole des Chartes* 148 (1990): 301–54.

Laurent, Françoise. *Pour Dieu et pour le roi: Rhétorique et idéologie dans l'*Histoire des ducs de Normandie *de Benoît de Sainte-Maure.* Paris: Champion, 2010.

Legge, M. Dominica. *Anglo-Norman Literature and its Background.* Oxford: Clarendon Press, 1963.

Le Saux, Françoise H. M. *A Companion to Wace.* Cambridge: Brewer, 2005.

Marnette, Sophie. "Réflexions sur le discours indirect libre en français médiéval." *Romania* 114 (1996): 1–49.

Mason, Emma. *William II Rufus, the Red King.* Stroud: Tempus, 2005.

Mathey-Maille, Laurence. *Écritures du passé: Histoires des ducs de Normandie.* Paris: Champion, 2007.

McDougall, Sara. *Royal Bastards: The Birth of Illegitimacy, 800–1230.* Oxford: Oxford University Press, 2016.

Musset, Lucien. "Aux Origines d'une classe dirigeante: les Tosny." *Francia* 5 (1977): 45–80.

Otter, Monika. *Inventiones: Fiction and Referentiality in Twelfth-Century English Historical Writing.* Chapel Hill: University of North Carolina Press, 1996.

The Oxford Handbook of Translation Studies. Ed. Kirsten Malmkjær and Kevin Windle. Oxford: Oxford University Press, 2011.

Paradisi, Gioia. "Enrico II Plantageneto, i Capetingi e il 'peso della storia': sul successo della *Geste des Normanz* di Wace e della *Chronique des ducs de Normandie* di Benoît." *Critica del testo* 7.1 (2004): 127–62.

—. *Le Passioni della storia: Scrittura e memoria nell'opera di Wace.* Rome: Bagatto, 2002.

Pastoureau, Michel. *Figures de l'héraldique.* Paris: Gallimard, 1996.

Rector, Geoff. "*Faites le mien desir*: Studious Persuasion and Baronial Desire in Jordan Fantosme's *Chronicle.*" *Journal of Medieval History* 34 (2008): 311–46.

Ruud, Marylon. "Monks in the World: The Case of Gundulf of Rochester." *Anglo-Norman Studies* 11 (1989): 245–60.

Sandqvist, Sven. *Études syntaxiques sur la* Chronique des ducs de Normandie *par Benoît.* Lund: Gleerup, 1976.

Sayers, William. "The Jongleur Taillefer at Hastings." *Viator* 14 (1983): 77–88.

Short, Ian. "Tam Angli quam Franci: Self-Definition in Anglo-Norman England." *Anglo-Norman Studies* 18 (1995): 153–75.

Southern, R.W. "England in the Twelfth-Century Renaissance." *History* 45 (1960): 201–16.

Spiegel, Gabrielle M. *Romancing the Past: The Rise of Vernacular Prose History in Thirteenth-Century France.* Berkeley: University of California Press, 1993.

Teunis, H.B. "Benoît de Sainte-Maure and William the Conqueror's *amor.*" *Anglo-Norman Studies* 12 (1990): 199–209.

Thomas, Hugh M. *The English and the Normans: Ethnic Hostility, Assimilation, and Identity 1066–c. 1220.* Oxford: Oxford University Press, 2003.

Tillmann-Bartylla, Dagmar. "Höfische Welt und Geschichtsbedürfnis: Die anglonormannischen Verschroniken des XII. Jahrhunderts." In *La Littérature historiographique des origines à 1500*, ed. Hans Ulrich Gumbrecht et al., pp. 313–50. Grundriss der romanischen Literaturen des Mittelalters 11.1. Heidelberg: Winter, 1986.

Tobler, Adolf and Erhard Lommatzsch. *Altfranzösisches Wörterbuch.* 12 vols. Berlin: Weidmann and Wiesbaden: Steiner, 1925–2008.

Urbanski, Charity. *Writing History for the King: Henry II and the Politics of Vernacular Historiography.* Ithaca, NY: Cornell University Press, 2013.

van Houts, Elisabeth M.C. "The Adaptation of the *Gesta Normannorum ducum* by Wace and Benoît." In *Non nova, sed nove: Mélanges de civilisation médiévale dédiés à Willem Noomen*, ed. Martin Gosman and Jaap van Os, pp. 115–124. Groningen: Benjamins, 1984.

—. "The Memory of 1066 in Written and Oral Traditions." *Anglo-Norman Studies* 19 (1997): 167–80.

—. "The Origins of Herleva, Mother of William the Conqueror." *English Historical Review* 101 (1986): 389–404.

—. "Le Roi et son historien: Henri II Plantagenêt et Robert de Torigni." *Cahiers de civilisation médiévale* 37 (1994): 115–18.

——. "Wace as Historian." In *The History of the Norman People: Wace's* "Roman de Rou." Trans. Glyn S. Burgess, with notes by Glyn S. Burgess and Elisabeth van Houts, pp. xxxv–lxii. Woodbridge: Boydell, 2004.

Vielliard, Françoise. "De la première rédaction de la partie octosyllabique longue du *Roman de Rou* à la seconde: Étude des procédés d'amplification." In *Le Texte dans le texte: L'interpolation médiévale*, ed. Annie Combes and Michelle Skilnik, pp. 41–61. Paris: Garnier, 2013.

——. "Les deux versions de la partie octosyllabique du *Roman de Rou.*" *Medioevo Romanzo* 35 (2011): 35–57.

Ward, H.L.D and J.A. Herbert. *Catalogue of Romances in the Department of Manuscripts in the British Museum.* 3 vols. London: British Museum, 1883–1910.

Weiss, Judith. "*History* in Anglo-Norman Romance." In *The Long Twelfth-Century View of the Anglo-Saxon Past*, ed. Martin Brett and David Woodman, pp. 275–87. Farmham: Ashgate, 2015.

Williams, Ann. *The English and the Norman Conquest.* Woodbridge: Boydell, 1995.

Index

All references in this index are to line numbers in the translation. The index is organized alphabetically; however, individual names are ordered first by chronological royal title (emperor, empress; king, queen) and then alphabetically by family relation, cognomen, or location.